M000165264

Inseparable across Lifetimes

Inseparable across Lifetimes

The Lives and Love Letters of the Tibetan Visionaries Namtrul Rinpoche and Khandro Tāre Lhamo

Holly Gayley

SNOW LION
BOULDER
2019

Snow Lion
An imprint of Shambhala Publications, Inc.
4720 Walnut Street
Boulder, Colorado 80301
www.shambhala.com

9 8 7 6 5 4 3 2 1

First edition
Printed in the United States of America

⊗This edition is printed on acid-free paper that meets the American National Standards Institute Z39.48 Standard.
♻This book is printed on 30% postconsumer recycled paper.
For more information please visit www.shambhala.com.

Snow Lion is distributed worldwide by
Penguin Random House, Inc., and its subsidiaries.

Library of Congress Cataloging-in-Publication Data
Names: Gayley, Holly, translator, editor. | O-rgyan-'jigs-med-nam-mkha'-gling-pa, Rin-po-che, 1944–2011. Correspondence. Selections. English. | Tā-re Bde-chen-lha-mo, Mkha'-'gro Rin-po-che. Correspondence. Selections. English. Title: Inseparable across lifetimes: the lives and love letters of the Tibetan visionaries Namtrul Rinpoche and Khandro Tāre Lhamo / Namtrul Jigme Phuntsok, Khandro Tāre Lhamo; [translated by] Holly Gayley.
Description: First edition. | Boulder, Colorado: Snow Lion, 2019. | Includes bibliographical references. Identifiers: LCCN 2018013700 | ISBN 9781559394642 (paperback)
Subjects: LCSH: O-rgyan-'jigs-med-nam-mkha'-gling-pa, Rin-po-che, 1944–2011—Correspondence. | Tā-re Bde-chen-lha-mo, Mkha'-'gro Rin-po-che—Correspondence. | Buddhists—Tibet Region—Correspondence. | Rnying-ma-pa (Sect)—Tibet Region. | BISAC: RELIGION / Buddhism / Tibetan. | BIOGRAPHY & AUTOBIOGRAPHY / Religious. | HISTORY / Asia / General.
Classification: LCC BQ976.R47 A4 2018 | DDC 294.3/9230922 [B]—dc23
LC record available at https://lccn.loc.gov/2018013700

In the cool domain of Tibet, the Land of Snow,
We came together across seven lifetimes.
We practiced the profound path of secret mantra,
Engaging in the four joys, the means to bliss-emptiness.

—Namtrul Rinpoche, Letter 11

You, sublime son of good family and pure origin,
And I the mantra-born woman, Devī, the two of us,
In order to rescue beings from strife in degenerate times,
We have been appointed by Orgyan Padmasambhava.
Awakening together past deeds, aspirations, and the
entrustment,
It is our promise to guide all mother beings.

—Khandro Tāre Lhamo, Letter 17

Contents

Foreword

Tulku Thondup

Since 1984, I returned to my homeland of Golok a number of times. Every time, I visited Khandro Tāre Lhamo and Namtrul Rinpoche at their residence in Nyenlung Monastery, where my late father was also a parishioner. I had the great fortune of performing the "ḍākinī feast" ceremonies of Yumka Dechen Gyalmo with them on a number of occasions.[1]

Khandro Tāre Lhamo (1938–2002) was well respected as an emanation and one of the well-known teachers and revealers of many esoteric teachings as treasures in our age.[2] During the political struggles culminating in the Cultural Revolution, she survived by caring for domestic animals for many years, although her first husband along with all of her three tulku brothers perished. She then married Namtrul Jigme Phuntsok (1944–2011),[3] also a revealer of treasures. In the 1980s, Namtrul Rinpoche and Tāre Lhamo rebuilt the monasteries at Nyenlung in the Do valley and Tsimda in the Mar valley.[4] They revealed many treasure teachings, together and individually, and bestowed transmissions of esoteric teachings to numerous Tibetan and Chinese devotees. Since Tāre Lhamo and Namtrul Rinpoche passed away, his son Tulku Laksam Namdak has become the propagator of their dharma lineage and legacy.

Inseparable across Lifetimes reveals Khandro Tāre Lhamo's innate wisdom, undiluted love, and mystical stories in partnership with Namtrul Rinpoche—strung together into a garland of enchanting poetry. I am sure that this book will inspire many by learning of this couple's nectar-like dharma qualities. I am grateful to Holly Gayley for bringing their inspiring stories and poetic letters from the highlands of Golok to share as a dharma feast for Western readers.

Preface

In 2004, I ventured to the grasslands of Golok in eastern Tibet for the first time, two years after Khandro Tāre Lhamo passed away. Having read her biography in Tibetan, I hoped to meet her husband Namtrul Rinpoche and request a copy of their complete corpus of writings and revelations. This aspiration took me to Nyenlung Monastery, the couple's teaching seat in a bucolic valley amid rolling hills outside Serta in Sichuan province. In our initial meeting, Namtrul Rinpoche seemed pleased that I wanted to do research on Tāre Lhamo and translate their biographies. Without hesitation, he gave his blessings to the project.

On that occasion, Namtrul Rinpoche offered me a copy of their corpus in twelve volumes and a separate volume containing their letters, exchanged between 1978 and 1980, which had recently been published as a facsimile edition. Soon thereafter, I realized the significance of their correspondence, which chronicles the evolution of a Buddhist tantric partnership in contemporary times and illuminates a key historical transition as Tibetans in China emerged from the devastation of the Cultural Revolution. With the help of Tibetan interlocutors, I began to explore the various poetic and folk song styles contained in the letters, composed almost entirely in verse, and to appreciate the rich set of resources from Buddhist tantra and Tibetan lore that this couple drew on to imagine their future together.

As the correspondence unfolds, it has a surprisingly playful and direct quality, showing the human side of a tantric partnership. While geared toward the revelation of esoteric teachings and practices, the courtship between Tāre Lhamo and Namtrul Rinpoche was also full of affection. Without sources like these, we might think that Buddhist masters are somehow above ordinary longings and emotions, that enlightenment magically lifts them out of the mire of their historical circumstances, or that teachings on the ultimate nature of reality diminish the importance of personal relationships and connections that turn out to be at the very heart of Buddhist communities. The lives and letters of Tāre Lhamo and Namtrul Rinpoche provide a poignant example of how the visionary and human aspects of Tibetan Buddhism are interwoven. In this case, their partnership was integral to their overall mission to heal the damage of the Maoist period following the Chinese Communist takeover of Tibetan areas and to restore Buddhist institutions, teachings, and practices in the region of Golok.

Rarely do we hear about love in a tantric partnership and especially about an older female Buddhist master initiating a consort relationship with a younger male lama. I found it so refreshing to read, in their own words, about the mutuality of affection and enduring bond between Tāre Lhamo and Namtrul Rinpoche. This was no casual liaison, but a committed relationship in which the two traveled and taught, side by side on elevated thrones, during the 1980s and 1990s. This is what has inspired me for more than a decade to continue with researching, writing on, and translating materials by and about this visionary Buddhist couple. Now, more than ever, it feels important to explore an example of a consort relationship in which both partners were respected and indeed revered.

In preparing this translation, I grappled with how to make this unique source material accessible to a wide audience. Some of the letters, especially the love songs, are universal in appeal, expressing fondness through folksy metaphors and heartfelt language. Yet others contain references to advanced Buddhist practices and feature Tibetan literary conventions that may not be familiar to English readers. Their biographies present an even greater challenge, given the episodic nature of the narrative, the miracle tales that permeate it, and the array of names for local people and places. All this requires some background and historical context to fully appreciate. In the end, I decided the best way to maintain the integrity of their life stories and letters, while making them accessible, would be to divide the translation into sections and add explanatory remarks to present the relevant background. In this way, I endeavor to maintain the foreign flavor of Tibetan lived worlds, letter writing, and styles of storytelling, while opening a window into that world beyond specialists in Tibet or Buddhism.

I am indebted to many who helped with this project: to Namtrul Rinpoche and his son Tulku Laksam Namdak for their permission to craft these translations; to Tulku Thondup, Ringu Tulku, and Lama Chönam for help with difficult passages in the correspondence; to Khenpo Rigdzin Dargye for sharing an early version of his new biography of Tāre Lhamo with me; to Pema Ösal Thaye for clarifying questions related to the biographies of the couple that he composed; to Ju Kalzang, Drukmo Kyi, Nyingpo Tsering, and Jamyang Lodrö for their invaluable assistance in understanding Tibetan poetic and song styles; to Jean-François Buliard, whose French translation of Pemal Ösal Thaye's work provided several alternate readings; and to many other friends and colleagues who served as traveling companions, sounding boards, and conversation partners over the years. In addition, I would like to express my appreciation to Nikko Odiseos, Casey Kemp, Liz Shaw, and others at Shambhala Publications for their dedication to this project and editorial acumen at every stage of the process. Finally, thanks to my partner, Rick Merrill, whose patience, humor, and love have been a great support along the way.

Inseparable across Lifetimes

Introduction

A Visionary Buddhist Couple

In 1978, at the age of forty, the female Tibetan visionary Khandro Tāre Lhamo sent a prophecy to a reincarnate lama six years her junior, known as Namtrul Rinpoche,[1] about the Buddhist teachings they were destined to reveal together. He responded joyfully, imagining himself as a peacock dancing with delight at the thunder of her news, a classic image from Indian literature related to the monsoon and season of love. In his reply, he added a personal touch:

> Please bear in mind that I have great affection
> For my inseparable companion across many lifetimes.

As their courtship progressed in an extended correspondence, the future couple expressed a range of emotions—from joy at rediscovering their companionship across lifetimes to sorrow at their separation across province borders at a time when travel was highly restricted. As Namtrul Rinpoche states in his Letter 6,

> Our connection from previous lives dawns in mind.
> Happy and sad, tears fall as a steady stream of rain.

In her Letter 7, Tāre Lhamo echoes this sentiment:

> The sketch of past lives becomes clearer;
> Mind yearning, my fondness increases.

Their courtship took place across fifty-six letters,[2] exchanged over more than a year, sharing visionary recollections of their past lives together and effusive expressions of affection.

Writing in the wake of the Cultural Revolution (1966–1976), when most visible signs of Tibetan culture were destroyed and religious practice forbidden, Namtrul Rinpoche and Tāre Lhamo prepared to harness their visionary talents toward restoring Buddhism in the region of Golok in eastern Tibet. They envisioned collaborating on the revelation of *terma*, or "treasures," ancient relics and esoteric teachings traced to Tibet's imperial period in the seventh to ninth centuries when Buddhism first spread on the plateau.[3] It was socially recognized that their own past lives included Namkhai Nyingpo and Yeshe Tsogyal, who were among the twenty-five disciples of the Indian master Padmasambhava, a central figure in the lore of that period.[4] Based on the shared vision and personal bond developed through their correspondence, in 1980 Tāre Lhamo left her homeland in Padma County of Qinghai Province to join Namtrul Rinpoche in neighboring Serta in Sichuan Province. During the 1980s and 1990s, the couple taught side by side to large assemblies throughout Golok and beyond, playing a significant role in the restoration of Buddhist teachings, practices, and institutions in the post-Mao era.

Despite the prevalence in Tibetan art of tantric deities in ecstatic embrace,[5] we find few living or historical examples of Buddhist visionary couples in which both partners are publicly visible and acknowledged in the lineage transmission. Within the Nyingma tradition, it is common for male lamas to marry and have children, routinely passing lineages of esoteric teachings through the family. Yet, rarely does the tantric consort play a significant role in public teachings and rituals,[6] and often she fades from view when the religious activities of a great master are recorded for posterity.[7] So far, only a few cases of eminent couples who publicly gave teachings together have come to light in Tibetan literature. In the nineteenth-century, the Bön couple Dechen Chökyi Wangmo and Sangngak Lingpa traveled and taught together,[8] and in the early twentieth-century the Nyingma visionary Sera Khandro chronicled the few years she spent living, practicing, and revealing treasures with her destined consort and teacher Drime Özer before his untimely death.[9] Namtrul Rinpoche and Tāre Lhamo were fortunate to spend more than twenty years together, discovering and disseminating their treasures widely, and this is documented at length in his life story where they serve as joint protagonists.[10]

The lives and letters of Namtrul Rinpoche and Tāre Lhamo provide a unique window into a tantric partnership in contemporary times. The narrative of their life together shows them on annual teaching tours to reestablish Buddhist teachings and practices, while their letters provide an intimate account of love and sexuality in Buddhist tantra. The tantric rite of sexual union plays an integral role in the process of treasure revelation,[11] and the two anticipate this practice in suggestive ways in their correspondence. For example, their letters contain recurring references to "performing the secret path of means, bliss-emptiness" and "enjoying the glory of the four joys."[12] References of this kind are suggestive of ritual methods involving sexuality to manipulate the elements of the subtle body and access meditative states of nondual bliss and wisdom, known in tantric literature as the "four joys." These joys provide access to the depths of mind, the very site where Padmasambhava is said to have deposited treasures, to be revealed in subsequent lifetimes by his appointed emissaries.[13]

In reply to her initial message containing a prophecy, in his Letter 1, Namtrul Rinpoche refers to Tāre Lhamo as:

> . . . the lady of bliss-emptiness,
> Who is skilled in guiding to the wisdom expanse of the four joys,
> With the iron hook that conjures the sport of attraction.[14]

This sets the tone for playful exchanges that include flirtatious quips and erotic innuendos as well as heartfelt expressions of affection and assurances of their steadfast commitment. For this reason, I refer to the collection of their correspondence as "love letters," the first collection of its kind between tantric partners to come to light in Tibetan literature. Adding to their literary merit, the letters were composed almost entirely in verse, employing a range of Tibetan oral and literary styles. Within their letters, I identify a Buddhist articulation of a "love without attachment," whereby affection and passion are valorized outside of an ego-centered framework.[15] Instead, their partnership is oriented toward the greater mission to restore Buddhist teachings in Golok and beyond through treasure revelation. Seamlessly, Namtrul Rinpoche and Tāre Lhamo synthesize their prophetic calling with the personal intimacies of an extended courtship and long-term partnership. Their life stories and selected letters, translated into English for the first time in this book, have much to convey about the creative potential of a tantric partnership in Buddhism and the resilience of Tibetans under the vagaries of Chinese rule.

Golok Treasure Scene

Tāre Lhamo and Namtrul Rinpoche were raised in the esoteric milieu of the Nyingma tradition in Golok and northern Kham. Bordered by two sacred mountain ranges, Amnye Machen to the northwest and Nyenpo Yutse to the southeast, Golok is a nomadic region with rolling high-alpine grasslands suitable for nomadic pastoralism. These mountain ranges are tied to the origin myths for the clans of Golok, which have historically been fiercely independent.[16] Nonetheless, the area was integrated into regional networks of Buddhist monasteries, especially influential Nyingma ones in Kham such as Katok, Palyul, and Dzokchen. Perhaps for this reason, there has been a Nyingma predominance in Golok, particularly Padma County and neighboring Serta,[17] making the region a hub for treasure revelation. A number of the great *tertöns*, or "revealers of treasures," of the nineteenth and early twentieth centuries lived and operated in Golok and adjoining areas in northern Kham, including Dudjom Lingpa, Do Khyentse Yeshe Dorje, Lerab Lingpa, Sera Khandro, and Apang Terchen, who was Tāre Lhamo's father. This legacy has continued into the present, playing an important role in restoring Buddhism in the region in the wake of the Cultural Revolution.[18]

In 1938, Tāre Lhamo was born into her vocation as a tertön. She was the daughter of Apang Terchen,[19] a Nyingma master of local import, and Damtsik Drolma, the daughter of a local chieftain. As an infant, she was recognized as an emanation of Yeshe Tsogyal and Sera Khandro by the revered master Dudjom Rinpoche,[20] who became the head of the Nyingma lineage among Tibetans in exile. As the daughter of religious elite, Tāre Lhamo was steeped in esoteric teachings in her youth but received little formal education. Although her father died when she was only nine,[21] he had by then transmitted the entirety of his treasure corpus to her, and thereafter she traveled with her mother to study with the great masters of her day, including the Rigdzin Jalu Dorje, the fourth in the prominent line of Dodrupchen incarnations.[22] In addition, her root teacher, Dzongter Kunzang Nyima, was the grandson and speech emanation of Dudjom Lingpa, a towering figure in the Golok treasure scene. At the age of twenty, she married his son, Mingyur Dorje,[23] and they joined his father's inner circle at his encampment at Rizab.[24] Due to historical circumstances, their marriage was short-lived, and their only child died at a young age.[25] Dzongter Kunzang Nyima transmitted his own treasure cycle to Tāre Lhamo and appointed her as the trustee for his liturgical cycle dedicated to Yeshe Tsogyal, the preeminent lady of treasure lore and consort to Padmasambhava.

Born in 1944, Namtrul Rinpoche was recognized as the fourth emanation of Namkhai Nyingpo in youth and enthroned at Zhuchen Monastery in Serta, a branch of Katok Monastery. He received a monastic education, including systematic study of the traditional domains of knowledge, such as grammar, composition, logic, poetics, and Buddhist philosophy.[26] There, he studied the sūtras and tantras, performed the preliminaries for tantric practice, and received the transmission for the treasure collections of Rigdzin Dudul Dorje and Rigdzin Longsal Nyingpo, part of the Katok liturgical system. At thirteen, he took monastic ordination, though he later reverted to lay status and briefly married in accordance with the times.[27] His son, Laksam Namdak, was recognized as the reincarnation of his own teacher Zhuchen Kunzang Nyima and now serves as the main lineage holder for the treasure teachings of Namtrul Rinpoche and Tāre Lhamo.

Though their partnership began later in life, the lives of Namtrul Rinpoche and Tāre Lhamo are intertwined in their *namthars*, or stories of "complete liberation."[28] These are no ordinary biographies; rather, the genre itself suggests the spiritual realization of its protagonists.[29] In their namthars, Namtrul Rinpoche and Tāre Lhamo are presented as the emanation of tantric deities and past masters, and prophecies anticipate their birth. For Tāre Lhamo, the figure of the *ḍākinī*, a class of female deities, plays a special role given her identification with the tantric deity Vajravārāhī and her title, Khandro, which translates the Sanskrit term.[30] Both are presented as enlightened from birth, though we catch a few glimpses of their spiritual practice along the way: her dedication to the practice of Tārā (her namesake) in youth, his surreptitious retreats during the Cultural Revolution, and the unfolding of their visionary experiences in the midst of ritual activities during the post-Mao era.

The namthars *Jewel Garland: The Liberation of Namtrul Jigme Phuntsok* and *Spiraling Vine of Faith: The Liberation of Khandro Tāre Lhamo*,[31] translated here, were written by Pema Ösal Thaye, a cleric-scholar, devoted disciple, and local historian. These could be considered their official biographies since the couple commissioned their publication and contributed to their content. As namthars narrated in the third person, *Jewel Garland* and *Spiraling Vine of Faith* present idealized accounts of their lives, including miraculous interventions to benefit their local communities during the years leading up to and including the Cultural Revolution.[32] Nonetheless, these works offer compelling portraits of their early training in Nyingma circles in youth, their heroism and resilience coming of age during the Maoist period, and their remarkable partnership later in life, traveling and teaching together during the 1980s and 1990s.

Resilience amid Devastation

In the late 1950s, the socialist transformation of Tibetan areas changed everything. The next two decades witnessed the wholesale destruction of Tibetan culture including the demolition of most Buddhist temples and monasteries, the looting of valuable statues, the burning of sacred texts, and the imprisonment of Buddhist teachers. During this period, Tāre Lhamo lost her first husband, Mingyur Dorje; her three brothers, all reincarnate lamas who died in prison; and her two main teachers.[33] Despite the devastation of this period, their namthars emphasize how Namtrul Rinpoche and Tāre Lhamo never lost sight of Buddhist principles and stayed true to their vow as *bodhisattvas*, or "awakened beings," working for the benefit of others. Their steadfastness and compassionate orientation served as important factors in their resilience alongside their continued practice in secret. The miracle tales contained in their namthars show how each cared for their own community and continued to be viewed by locals as enlightened masters, despite the Chinese Communist State's attempt to turn religious figures into class enemies.

A handful of Buddhist masters survived under exceptional circumstances. Among prominent tertöns in Golok, Khenpo Jigme Phuntsok escaped imprisonment by manifesting a horrible deformity when the authorities came to arrest him, and Kusum Lingpa withstood harsh treatment in prison while maintaining a buoyant countenance.[34] Another Nyingma lama, Aku Chöying, told me that he survived the period living as a wild animal in the mountains.[35] For her part, Tāre Lhamo was spared imprisonment, likely due to her gender, yet she was subjected to manual labor through much of her 20s and 30s and endured harsh treatment during struggle sessions.[36] Meanwhile, Namtrul Rinpoche was only a teenager during the socialist transformation of Tibetan areas, so he and other religious figures his age were initially not viewed as a threat. Instead, his literary skills were put to use as the secretary for his work unit. That said, none were spared deprivation, given the onset of famine during the Great Leap Forward (1958–61) and the mayhem of the Cultural Revolution.

Despite these hardships, *Spiraling Vine of Faith* suggests that Tāre Lhamo was able to embrace misfortune with others at the forefront of her mind. One story illustrates her compassionate orientation well. During the Cultural Revolution, when a state policy in the region reportedly required Tibetans to kill rodents and dogs, Tāre Lhamo was resolute in her defiance. With fierce compassion, she declared, "I would rather die myself than kill those creatures." Such a statement illustrates her unwavering commitment to the Buddhist principles of nonviolence and compassion, even under duress. That night, the tantric protectress Dorje Rachigma (an alternative name for Ekajaṭī) came to her in a dream and told her, "It is not yet time to die! Since you must accomplish great benefit for the dharma and beings, you are not allowed to die."[37] Instead the protectress stamped her foot, producing an earthquake in the region. In the morning, a dog corpse (presumably fake) appeared on her doorstep for her to submit to the authorities in fulfillment of this policy. An equally dramatic account can be found in *Jewel Garland* when Namtrul Rinpoche spent two months in prison in the early 1970s. At that time, the prison warden commanded him to slaughter a *dzo* (yak and cow hybrid) and he refused, suffering a brutal beating as a result.

Another significant aspect of their resilience during this period was their continued tantric practice in secret. *Jewel Garland* depicts Namtrul Rinpoche receiving further teachings from Lama Rigdzin Nyima and even sequestering himself for periods of retreat during this period. While *Spiraling Vine of Faith* remains silent on this topic, a more recent and unpublished version of Tāre Lhamo's life by Khenpo Rigdzin Dargye mentions her ongoing religious practice.[38] Tāre Lhamo is depicted reciting prayers while performing nomadic chores, performing monthly tantric feasts on the appropriate days in the liturgical calendar, and giving esoteric teachings to close disciples. From someone in her work unit, I also heard that secretly at night locals would come to Tāre Lhamo's tent to request prophecies about family members and rituals on behalf of the dead. Ongoing tantric practice is also an important theme in the namthars of Khenpo Jigme Phuntsok and Kusum Lingpa. Evading capture, the great Khenpo continued to practice and teach a small group of disciples while hidden in the mountains. Despite his imprisonment, Kusum Lingpa performed healings, managed to practice and teach others secretly, and even revealed treasures during this period.[39]

Those tantric masters who survived the Maoist period became the natural leaders in the restoration of Buddhism in the region. With the death of Mao Zedong in 1976, revolutionary fervor gave way to liberalization in economic and cultural terms under Deng Xiaoping's leadership. This shift in state policy became palpable in Tibetan areas by the early 1980s and made possible efforts to revitalize Tibetan culture, including Buddhist teachings and practices. *Spiraling Vine of Faith* provides a list of the most important surviving lamas and cleric-scholars in Golok, referring to them as "defenders of the teachings and beings."[40] Tāre Lhamo is shown to be on par with these figures by conducting a long-life empowerment on their behalf from a ritual text among her own treasure revelations.[41]

Love without Attachment

Tāre Lhamo's first letter arose out of her esoteric training in youth and the tragedy of her times. Having lost her first husband in the late 1950s and her only child at the onset of the Cultural Revolution, Tāre Lhamo could have become irrevocably lost in despair. A brief liaison with Doli Nyima, the grandson of Sera Khandro, may have provided some relief, but in the mid-1960s he too disappeared after she had reportedly secured his release from prison, never to be seen again.[42] These devastating losses make her opening letter to Namtrul Rinpoche all the more remarkable. With a prophecy about their future revelations, Tāre Lhamo proposes starting anew to restore Buddhist teachings through treasure revelation and join together with Namtrul Rinpoche in order to do so.

I refer to this as an *epistolary courtship* since their prophetic mission and personal bond developed primarily through their exchange of letters.[43] The correspondence started in late 1978, and Namtrul Rinpoche ventured to Markhok sometime in mid-1979 to visit her and meet her relatives. Then in early 1980, Tāre Lhamo left her homeland to live with him at Nyenlung, the monastery in Serta that they rebuilt together. The act of letter writing is referenced on a number of instances with respect to receiving or requesting news, admiring the designs of ink on paper, taking delight in each other's speech, and reflecting on the beloved's words as a source of inspiration and solace. Certain epistolary conventions, such as artful praises, are peppered throughout the correspondence as well as gestures of humility that are culturally dictated for the first-person voice in Tibetan.[44] On occasion, Tāre Lhamo refers to herself as a "gullible lady," and Namtrul Rinpoche refers to himself as "lowly" and a "madman," the latter being a reference to tantric antinomianism.[45]

I have selected forty-two letters out of the fifty-six total to translate into

English for the first time in this book.[46] This should give the reader a sense for the rich array of content and style—from ornate poetry to folk songs—employed as the couple awakened their visionary talents and mutual affection. Across a number of letters, Namtrul Rinpoche and Tāre Lhamo shared back and forth their recollections of past lives together in India, Nepal, and Tibet, as well as prophecies regarding the locations of treasures in the landscape. Each set of recollections brings joy and inspiration, fueling the visionary process. Less frequently, they gesture to the challenges they faced, including Namtrul Rinpoche's recurrent bouts of illness and the reluctance of Tāre Lhamo's relatives to see her depart. They also strike a heroic tone in passages in which they declare victory over barbaric and demonic forces, a way to tacitly reference the dark period of history from which they had just emerged and to assert their own role in ushering in a new era of flourishing for Buddhism and the Tibetan people. In more intimate moments, Tāre Lhamo articulates the ordinary longings of a woman, confessing to pine for her beloved a hundred (even a thousand) times a day and swearing her unwavering affection in this life and the next. For his part, Namtrul Rinpoche declares that Tāre Lhamo is dearer to him than his own eyes and heart, promising to honor her always and forever.

What sort of love is expressed in their epistolary courtship? I suggest that their letters illuminate a kind of love without attachment. This is not the universal love of Buddhist contemplation, nor an instrumental tantric liaison for the purpose of attaining realization or revealing treasures. Scholars have suggested that "love plays no part in the *Tantras*," since Indian tantric literature tends to portray the ideal partner for tantric sexual practices as the *parakīyā*, or "one who belongs to another."[47] Reinforcing this, the songs of the Indian *siddhas* ("accomplished ones") tend to portray illicit trysts with low-caste women in the role of consort.[48] However, this characterization does not pertain across the board, especially not in Tibetan contexts.[49] Today, the Tibetan term *sangyum*, or "secret consort," is most often used as an honorific for the long-term partner or wife of an esteemed tantric master.[50]

For Namtrul Rinpoche and Tāre Lhamo, a language of the heart permeates the correspondence as found in terms of endearment like "sweetheart," "jewel of the heart," "beloved companion," and "darling."[51] These epithets are complemented by an ongoing acknowledgment of their exalted religious status in more formal modes of address: for him, this is the great adept Namkhai Nyingpo, and for her, the goddess Sarasvatī, the tantric heroine Yeshe Tsogyal, and the female tertön Sera Khandro (referred to by her alias, Dewe Dorje, in the correspondence). As the letters progress, they create a growing sense of intimacy, using nicknames for each other, Tarpo and Tsebo (from his childhood name, Tsedzin), based on the local practice of taking the first syllable of names for religious figures and adding *lo*, *po*, or *bo*. As expressed, their bond is infused with affection and passion, while oriented toward a broader shared mission: the revelation of treasures that will serve to "heal the damage" of recent history. Within their letters, Namtrul Rinpoche and Tāre Lhamo clearly imagined a long-term domestic partnership, describing their aim to "converge in one household." For these reasons, their connection had as much to do with their prophetic vocation as tertöns as it did with personal expressions of mutual compatibility reminiscent of romantic love.[52]

In their letters, Tāre Lhamo and Namtrul Rinpoche articulated their unique compatibility for each other in a number of ways. They describe themselves as inseparable across lifetimes with a shared destiny due to deeds and aspirations performed together in previous lives. As part of their identities as tertöns, they trace their past lives to figures from Tibet's imperial period as well as the legendary reign of Gesar of Ling, which locals situate in Golok and northern Kham.[53] Moreover, they invoke the tantric vow of *samaya* as an oath of the past that binds the two together in their destiny to reveal treasures. This is an oath that they situate in a tantric initiation presided over by Padmasambhava in the eighth century, taken during their previous lives as his close disciples, Namkhai Nyingpo and Yeshe Tsogyal—though they mention other identifications for the same period, him as Atsara Sale and her as Shelkar Dorje Tso. The samaya vow sealed their shared destiny along with the prophetic entrustment of treasures bestowed upon the pair by Padmasambhava.

In a more folksy vein, toward the middle of the correspondence, Namtrul Rinpoche and Tāre Lhamo conveyed their mutual compatibility and assured each other of their steadfast commitment through a series of naturalistic images. The two depicted their destiny to be together by comparing themselves to a juniper branch and its berry, a snow lion and mountain peak, and a pair of black ravens traversing the sky in tandem. They are "inseparable companions" due to the "legacy of the past,"[54] whether this legacy is conceived in karmic terms based on their deeds and aspirations in previous lifetimes and in naturalistic terms as the pairing of animals and their habitats. The question that hangs over the correspondence is whether the *tendrel*, or "coincidence," for these causal factors will click into place so that they can join together as a couple.[55] Yet they never express doubt about their shared destiny or mutual compatibility.

Things get more complex once passion is added to the picture. Sarah Jacoby has noted a strict delineation between "spiritual love." or *tsewa*, and "carnal lust," or *döchak*, in the (auto)biographical writings of the female visionary Sera Khandro.[56] In her writings, the term *tsewa* is reserved for spiritual and hierarchical relationships, such as guru and disciple, in which love flows downward. This positive type of love is distinguished from lust, which appears in episodes where others taunt Sera Khandro about the possibility of having the wrong motivation for engaging in tantric sexual practices. Whereas Sera Khandro felt the need to defend her spiritual longings and role as a consort in order to address potential criticism, Namtrul Rinpoche and Tāre Lhamo do not seem so encumbered in their correspondence. While employing several of the same terms, they marshal them in a slightly different way.

As one difference, the language of love and affection in their letters is mutual without a discernable hierarchy at play. The term *tsewa* is most commonly used in the compound *tsedung*, a standard epithet for "beloved" in Tibetan, and it also describes their "loving affection" and "yearning fondness" for each other.[57] Namtrul Rinpoche and Tāre Lhamo expressed being mutually sustained, emboldened, and delighted by one another's words of affection.[58] In his Letter 15, as he journeyed to meet her in Markhok, Namtrul Rinpoche wrote,

> I hold in mind the tender words of your speech.
> Dear, my heart breaks with yearning and devotion,
> Hoping soon that we can meet face to face.[59]

In her Letter 18, in the midst of his visit, Tāre Lhamo recalled the "tender affection of the loving friend" and went so far as to say that her affection for him is "etched on my skull," a reference to destiny.[60]

As another key point of difference, the two valorized passion in their correspondence with little discernible concern for the possible taint of lust. Recall that in his first letter, Namtrul Rinpoche coined the term, "the sport of attraction," to characterize Tāre Lhamo's capacity to conjure passion.[61] The term I translate as "attraction" (the first half of *döchak*) also can mean "lust, desire, or passion," and here it is used in a positive sense to refer to the erotic play of courtship leading to consummation in the tantric rite of sexual union. In cultivating the "sport of attraction" in the correspondence itself, the two made ample use of erotic imagery drawn from Indian literature, like the bee circling the lotus in order to drink its nectar, the peacock dancing in the monsoon season to attract a mate, and the sidelong glances they flash back and forth, invoking a flirtatious language of the eyes.

In valorizing passion, Namtrul Rinpoche and Tāre Lhamo use tantalizing innuendos to gesture to the tantric rite of sexual union. As examples, they reference "liberation through touch" in his Letter 3, the ritual occasion to "sip the elixir together" in her Letter 8, "a pair of supreme adepts, male and female, / quivering in postures as partners in dance" in his Letter 22, anticipating "the delight of the ḍāki's body" in her Letter 24, and "inciting complete blissful joy through great passion" in his Letter 25.[62] Unlike the sense of caution evident in her antecedent's writings, Tāre Lhamo is unabashed in her active pursuit of Namtrul Rinpoche, depicting herself in her Letter 5 as a tigress (her birth year) circling a monkey (his birth year).[63] What's more, their use of erotic and affectionate language creates an amorous mood that unlocked their visionary potential through their courtship and correspondence in a way yet to be remarked in the scholarship on treasure revelation.[64]

An important distinction made in their letters sheds light on what I am referring to as love without attachment. At one point, in her Letter 13, Tāre Lhamo wonders about this "infatuated talk" and whether they will be able to fulfill their aims after all.[65] Then, in her Letter 15, after an initial encounter with Namtrul Rinpoche, she makes a strong statement of self-definition.[66] I hypothesize that she ventured out a ways to greet him, as is Tibetan custom, and that their initial encounter is referenced in this and his Letter 15. The first part of his Letter 15 recounts challenges along the journey to Markhok, then midway Namtrul Rinpoche playfully teases Tāre Lhamo for her reticence in their initial meeting. In her Letter 15, she replies by describing her own challenges in pursuing their aim, including state policy, local gossip, and the dissent of relatives. Perhaps as a justification in the face of these challenges, she gives a list of reasons why she *is* and *is not* pursuing a partnership with Namtrul Rinpoche. Notably, she rejects self-centered motivations, such as the need for material support, feelings of loneliness, attachment to worldly concerns and activities, or the confusion of negative emotions.

Projecting a sense of self-assurance, Tāre Lhamo proclaims instead that she is bound by the prophecy of Padmasambhava and the oath of ḍākinīs. As the second half of the term *döchak*, "attachment" appears in her concern over "infatuated talk" and in her denial of acting out of "attachment to worldly activities in saṃsāra." Thus, while passion and affection are valorized in their correspondence, these are distinguished—in this key moment of self-definition—from attachment, which in Buddhism has a negative association with ego-clinging. Her distinction resonates with a general view in Buddhist tantra. Rather than rejecting passion, as celibate monasticism prescribes, the tantric rite of sexual union harnesses it in pursuit of the "four joys," which are conducive to realization and also, for those duly appointed Tibetan visionaries, treasure revelation. In her statement, forms of self-gratification are rejected in favor of expedient tantric methods for liberation and an orientation toward the greater good. Nonetheless, their vision of a tantric partnership allows ample room for affection, intimacy, playfulness, passion, mutual support, humor, and commitment.

The culmination of their correspondence comes in his Letter 25 as Tāre Lhamo's arrival at Nyenlung was imminent.[67] Namtrul Rinpoche shared a celebratory "song of joyous tidings," playing off of the Tibetan custom of drinking liquor and singing songs at weddings. Only here the setting is portrayed as a tantric feast and, as the guest of honor, Tāre Lhamo is addressed as the goddess Sarasvatī. The liquor offered symbolizes their union as "method and wisdom" and offers a range of benefits: embodying the blessings of lineage gurus, accomplishing the aims of Padmasambhava, engaging profound and vast treasure teachings, clearing away adversity, and accomplishing whatever mind desires. Along the way, Namtrul Rinpoche details the movements of the subtle body in the tantric rite of sexual yoga, as the knots in the *nāḍīs*, or channels, are released at their various gathering points, the *cakras*. The resulting bliss allows the revelatory process to unfold, or in his words, "the treasure gate effortlessly opens within."[68] This represents the consummation of their union, and he gleefully exclaims:

> Hail to you, the beloved, sublime bliss-emptiness,
> And to me, the playful *vajra* engaged in intercourse.[69]

Note that in standard tantric code, the vajra represents the male sexual organ and the lotus, the female, making this the most explicit reference to sexual union found in the correspondence.

But the resulting joy and good fortune was not theirs alone. This moment heralded a historical reversal, given the healing powers they ascribe to treasure revelation. Namtrul Rinpoche concludes:

> Hoist the victory banner of dharma, the Buddha's teachings!
> The sun of happiness shines for mother beings,
> Pacifying strife, the damage of degenerate times!
> Coincidence converges in the joy of dharma!
> Now, each person sing a happy song!

Victory is declared. Images of darkness shift to light as the sun of Buddhist teachings was poised to rise once again in Tibetan areas.

Partners in Collaboration

To mark the occasion when Tāre Lhamo joined Namtrul Rinpoche at Nyenlung in 1980, *Jewel Garland* announces: "From then on, as defenders of the teachings and beings, the Eminent Couple converged in one residence and together awakened the deeds, aspiration, and coincidence to heal the extensive damage of degenerate times." This statement sets the stage for their prodigious activities in the 1980s and 1990s as part of a group of surviving Nyingma masters who spearheaded the revitalization of Buddhism in Golok and adjacent regions. For this period, *Jewel Garland* features the "eminent couple" as joint protagonists.[70] This means that Namtrul Rinpoche and Tāre Lhamo share center stage for much of its narration, acting in concert and sometimes even speaking in one voice. Together they traveled on pilgrimage, revealed treasures at sacred sites, performed rituals accompanied by their entourage, sponsored the construction of stūpas and temples, and gave teachings to large audiences of monastics and laity in the region. In this way, their efforts exemplify David Germano's characterization of contemporary treasure revelation as a vital strategy among the Nyingma in eastern Tibet to "reconstitute the cultural body of Tibet."[71]

Jewel Garland highlights their interactions with other surviving Buddhist teachers, situating them as part of a vibrant nexus of Nyingma masters coordinating their restoration efforts. Most significant were their interactions with Khenpo Jigme Phuntsok, a key figure who reinvigorated monastic scholasticism through founding an ecumenical institute, Larung Buddhist Academy (also known as Larung Gar) in Serta.[72] In 1980, he transmitted the treasures of Apang Terchen to the two as a couple, though

Tāre Lhamo had received it directly from her father as a child. In 1986, on the occasion of the Kālacakra empowerment at Larung, he pulled the couple aside to transmit the treasures of Lerab Lingpa and also authorize them as tertöns. After that, in 1990, Dola Chökyi Nyima transmitted the treasure corpus of his father, Dudjom Rinpoche, and authorized them to spread it widely. Although not mentioned in *Jewel Garland*, Tāre Lhamo garnered international attention the following year for recognizing one of the reincarnations of Dudjom Rinpoche, none other than Dola Chökyi Nyima's own son.[73]

Although their initial prominence derived from Tāre Lhamo's stature and family lineage in the region, over time their teachings and travels extended beyond Golok. Needless to say, their first large-scale teaching occurred in 1985 at Tsimda Monastery, founded by Tāre Lhamo's father, where they transmitted the treasures of Apang Terchen and their own to a large gathering. In 1987, they joined Khenpo Jigme Phuntsok on his historic pilgrimage to Wutai Shan—the abode of Mañjuśrī, bodhisattva of wisdom—in central China, revealing their own treasures at the site. On their way home, they stopped at sacred sites in northern Amdo and toured monasteries closer to home. From then on, they began to travel widely to discover and disseminate their treasures, including trips to the Nyingma enclave in Rebkong and pilgrimage to Central Tibet. Despite this broad terrain, their main sphere of influence and activity remained in Golok and adjacent areas.

Prophecies and miracles pepper the narrative, alongside auspicious signs that accompanied their activities at every turn, such as rainbows appearing, flowers blooming out of season, and unusual cloud formations. The miracles for this period are mainly attributed to Namtrul Rinpoche given that *Jewel Garland* is, after all, his namthar.[74] These are particularly prominent during their tour of sacred sites in Central Tibet where, for example, he reenacts the taming of gods and demons by Padmasambhava at Hepo Hill above Samye Temple and, in the process, rescues Tāre Lhamo from an attack by a malevolent spirit.[75] Namtrul Rinpoche is also credited with placing his footprint in rock, a stock miracle in siddha tales that signals the superhuman powers of a realized master.[76] Yet the "eminent couple" remain at the center of the action, surrounded by disciples likened to "constellations in the sky."[77] In a symbolic moment, *Jewel Garland* reports that during a feast at Samye, Tibet's earliest Buddhist temple, a visionary apparition of Padmasambhava appeared and crowned the couple with their tertön names,

Orgyan Jigme Namkha Lingpa and Ḍāki Tāre Dechen Gyalmo.[78] Shortly thereafter, while practicing a freshly revealed *sādhana*, or liturgical practice, of the horse-headed tantric deity Hayagrīva with their entourage, the deity is reported to have neighed, presumably in approval.[79]

Some facets of their life together are not covered in *Jewel Garland.* As a third-person account, the personal side of their partnership, so richly conveyed in their correspondence, is altogether absent, so too are more private types of activities. As one omission, the couple spent six months each year on retreat, while they dedicated the other six months to their public activities.[80] This seems noteworthy as it shows the balance they cultivated between inwardly and outwardly focused activities. Moreover, Pema Ösal Thaye seems more interested in chronicling the rituals they conducted and established at various monasteries throughout the region than their reconstruction projects. For this reason, their substantial achievements in rebuilding the two main monasteries under their supervision, Nyenlung in Serta and Tsimda in Padma, are not discussed in any detail, nor is their considerable financial and spiritual support to other monasteries in the region.[81] *Jewel Garland* does mention their contribution to revitalizing the Gesar tradition, referencing the Gesar temple they constructed at the foot of the Amnye Machen mountain range and the Gesar performance they established based on their revelations.[82]

Other aspects of their teaching career together are not found because they occurred after the narration of *Jewel Garland* ends in 1995. What stands out here is their annual dharma gathering at Nyenlung during the auspicious month of Sagadawa, which began in 1996 and still continues today under the auspices of Namtrul Rinpoche's son, Tulku Laksam Namdak. At their annual gathering at Nyenlung in 2006, which I attended, Namtrul Rinpoche announced that Tulku Laksam is none other than the reincarnation of Tāre Lhamo's own son who died during the Cultural Revolution. This identification amplifies his legitimacy as a lineage holder for the treasure corpus of Apang Terchen as well as for that of Namtrul Rinpoche and Tāre Lhamo. In a similar vein, later in life Namtrul Rinpoche appropriated certain aspects of Tāre Lhamo's identity by asserting a claim to be the reincarnation of her father, Apang Terchen, and her consort in a previous lifetime, Drime Özer.[83]

Needless to say, their final years together are beyond the narrative frame of *Jewel Garland*, not to mention the passing of Tāre Lhamo in 2002 and Namtrul Rinpoche in 2011, which I discuss elsewhere.[84] Suffice it to say that, after her passing, Namtrul Rinpoche continued to propagate their treasures, replicating their annual teaching tours and visiting many of the same monasteries that the couple had in their two decades of traveling and teaching together. In addition, he gathered a sizeable following of Han Chinese students, who came to Nyenlung for the annual dharma gathering.[85] Though Namtrul Rinpoche had another consort during those final years, she never occupied the places of honor that Tāre Lhamo had.[86] An empty throne remained beside Namtrul Rinpoche in the main assembly hall at Nyenlung, signifying both her absence and enduring presence through his activities.[87]

In her last testament, an unpublished document that narrates her final days, Tāre Lhamo swore to always remain at Namtrul Rinpoche's side: "Effortlessly, I will continue to be of general benefit to the teachings and beings by virtue of not being separated even for a moment from my constant, precious companion until attaining awakening. This is my aspiration and oath to the three roots, protectors, and Apang Terchen in whom I take refuge."[88] This is a potent statement of her lingering presence and ongoing benefit through him. Complementing this, on the anniversary of her passing, Namtrul Rinpoche wrote one final letter to his beloved, which is included in this book as his Letter 30. In the letter, he expressed grief in vivid terms and recounted a vision of Tāre Lhamo appearing in the sky to console him. Their final exchange is a moving testament to their inseparability as a couple, even transcending death.

Living Lineage

Due to the recent interest of Han Chinese followers of Tibetan Buddhism, Nyenlung now has practice groups and subsidiary monasteries in mainland China. Their lineage heir is Namtrul Rinpoche's son Tulku Laksam Namdak who, as mentioned above, was identified as the reincarnation of Tāre Lhamo's own son. Being fluent in both Tibetan and Chinese, Tulku Laksam teaches and travels in both Tibetan areas and Chinese cities, carrying on the significant legacy of this visionary couple. Given the tendency for esoteric teachings in the Nyingma tradition to pass through the family, it should come as no surprise that Namtrul Rinpoche's own reincarnation was recently identified as the youngest child and only son of Tulku Laksam, named Drime Wangchuk and born in 2014.

In a fascinating twist on family lineage, Tāre Lhamo's incarnation has been identified in the family of the 41st Sakya Trizin as his granddaughter, Jetsun Kunga Trinley Palter, born in 2007.[89] Note that the Sakya Trizin was the earliest recognized reincarnation of Tāre Lhamo's own father, Apang Terchen.[90] While it seems clear that Namtrul Rinpoche's reincarnation will be raised to carry on the family lineage, it is uncertain what role the Sakya Trizin's granddaughter might play. With its sphere of influence in Serta and Golok, a growing following across China, and new connections in exile, how far and wide the lineage of Namtrul Rinpoche and Tāre Lhamo will spread remains to be seen.

The Lives and Letters: Translations

1. Early Life of Tāre Lhamo

Enlightened Eons Ago

Khandro Tāre Lhamo's story began well before she was born. Her garland of past lives extends back to the time of the Buddha and beyond, anchoring her identity as an enlightened female master in key moments of Buddhist myth and history. As the woman Gaṅgādevī, she received a prediction of her future enlightenment from the Buddha himself. Before that, as the unnamed daughter of a merchant, she accompanied the "ever-weeping" bodhisattva Sadāprarudita to seek out the perfection of wisdom teachings. Both figures appear in the *Prajñāpāramitā* literature, where they miraculously change sex and take male form in anticipation of their liberation.[1] Departing from their Indian heritage on this point, Tibetans chose to affirm the potential for enlightenment in female form, and these figures serve as precursors to introduce and authorize Tāre Lhamo's own story.

In a timeless fashion, Tāre Lhamo is presented as enlightened from eons ago as none other than the primordial female buddha, Samantabhadrī. Known formally as Khandro Rinpoche Tāre Dechen Gyalmo, she is also considered a speech emanation of the tantric goddess, Vajravārāhī. After opening verses of praise, her story of liberation, *Spiraling Vine of Faith*, begins:

> The speech emanation of the noble queen Vajravārāhī, the Supreme Khandro Rinpoche Tāre Dechen Gyalmo, amassed an ocean of the two accumulations of merit and wisdom long ago in innumerable eons past. Having purified the two obscurations, cognitive and emotional, together with karmic residues, she reached buddhahood as the essence of blissful Samantabhadrī.
>
> As it is said:

Inconceivable is a blessed buddha;
In order to benefit sentient beings,
The eternal body of one thus gone
Displays myriad guises and forms.

And:

Though for many eons they've been fully enlightened,
Still again they show the way to enlightenment,
Being skilled at the marvel of taming disciples.
Do not regard this as a fault of redundancy.

With devotion, recollect wholeheartedly
The marvelous qualities of buddhas, inconceivable,
beyond estimation.
Supplicate and praise them as worthy of honor;
No doubt, the corresponding fruit will appear.

Accordingly, perfect buddhas who serve as guides—until saṃsāra is emptied—perform the benefit of beings through various guises, emanating into all the mundane realms. Likewise, Khandro Rinpoche has emanated into our world.

At the time of the noble Sadāprarudita, in the presence of the bodhisattva Dharmodgata, she made an irreversible aspiration and upon death immediately departed for the numerous pure realms. Later, in the presence of the blessed Buddha, she emanated as the Gaṅgādevī and functioned as a compiler of his teachings.[2] In particular, during the time of the mighty king Trisong Detsen, she took birth as the ḍākinī Yeshe Tsogyal.

Since the enlightened ones are said to emanate again and again in order to work for the benefit of beings, her garland of lives proceeds from there.

Emanation of Yeshe Tsogyal

With Yeshe Tsogyal, her garland of past lives lands squarely in Tibet. Yeshe Tsogyal is a central figure in the lore surrounding the advent of Buddhism in Tibet.[3] The seventh to ninth centuries was a time when the Tibetan empire commanded vast tracts of Central Asia, and Yeshe Tsogyal is remembered as queen of the emperor, Trisong Detsen. Through a twist of fate, she became the preeminent disciple and consort of Padmasambhava, the eighth-century Indian tantric master celebrated for taming the gods and demons of Tibet and thereby making the land hospitable to Buddhism.

Yeshe Tsogyal abandoned a life of privilege to undergo rigorous austerities in pursuit of enlightenment. In the best-known story of her life,[4] she endures starvation and other privations on retreat, converts thieves to the dharma through a song of realization, and even transforms the trauma of rape into a tantric initiation for her assailants. Her forthright character and resilience in adversity provides a model for Tāre Lhamo's heroism in the devastation leading up to and including the Cultural Revolution.

Spiraling Vine of Faith excerpts a set of verses from Taksham Nuden Dorje's revelation of Yeshe Tsogyal's life story.[5] The main events of her journey to enlightenment are recounted in summary fashion: her austerities and practice of "inner heat," or *tummo*, her miraculous resurrection of a dead boy in order to ransom the Nepali slave Atsara Sale to be her consort, her mastery of the winds and vital drops in the channels of the subtle body, and her attainment of *siddhi*, or "meditative accomplishment," through deity yoga practices. Other versions of her life tell a different story,[6] but this one is the most widely known. The subtle body practices mentioned in these verses remain central to advanced tantric practice in Tibetan Buddhism, and Tāre Lhamo herself was accomplished in them.

In Yeshe's Tsogyal's voice, as quoted in *Spiraling Vine of Faith*:

> At Tidro, encouraged by indications from the ḍākinīs,
> I engaged in eight austerities and signs of attainment arose.
>
> At Slate Mountain, I accomplished the heat of tummo
> And dispensed of the worldly garments of cyclic existence.
> At an assembly, acquiring the fourth initiation,
> I purified appearances as sacred outlook toward the guru.
>
> In Nepal, I raised the corpse of a dead boy
> And in this manner ransomed Atsara Sale.
>
> On the profound path, I attained the essential siddhi.
> Physically, I perfected the rainbow body of a sky dweller;
> Vocally, I possessed the melodious speech of Brahma;
> Mentally, I gained omniscience over the three times.

At Lion Fortress, I extracted medicinal elixirs
And encountered the assembly of medicine gods.
At Nering, I subdued a host of demonic forces
And attained siddhi at Longtsar Fortress.

Having visions of whatever deity I practiced,
Readily I obtained the corresponding siddhi.
At Paro Taksang, I practiced the profound path
With three companions, *herukas* of great bliss.

I obtained control over the channels, winds, and vital drops,
And I gained mastery over the five elements,
Transforming body, speech, and mind into their
enlightened forms.

From Amitāyus I obtained a prophecy
That I am inseparable from Vajravārāhī herself,
Anointed queen of all *maṇḍalas*.

At Ophu Taksang, when practicing Vajrakīla,
I was offered the life and heart of 3,000 gods and demons.
In a vision of the divine assembly of Amitāyus,
I attained the state of an immortal knowledge-holder.
Like a vajra, I became invincible and indestructible.

Throughout the whole land of Tibet
There are countless places where I practiced.
There is not a handful or bit of earth
That has not been blessed by me.

Successively, in the future, the signs of truth
Will be revealed, extracted one by one as treasures.
In an inconceivable number of little places,
Filled with my hand- and footprints in rock,
Are placed mantras, seed syllables, and statues,
Left behind as the basis for faith in the future
With aspirations to benefit those connected with me.

My accomplishments are detailed elsewhere:
The way I defeated demons and heretics,

> And how by penetrating the five elements,
> I filled the entire earth with treasures.
>
> Attaining the *dhāraṇī* of memory
> I collected the teachings of Padmasambhava.
> Discovering fearless confidence,
> I trained living beings according to prophecy.
> Becoming equal to all the buddhas,
> I completed acts of the buddhas of the three times.
> Thus I am adorned with accomplishment.
>
> In line with this statement, her emanation *body* was the equal to that of Padmasambhava, the second Buddha, having attained mastery over all apparent phenomena. Equal to his *speech*, she overflowed with dharma teachings on sūtra and tantra. Equal to his *mind*, she benefited beings through wisdom and method. Equal in discernable *qualities*, she accomplished great benefit for dharma and beings. Equal in performing *actions*, she spontaneously adhered to the actions of pacifying, enriching, magnetizing, and destroying.
>
> In thusness, Padmasambhava, the Lotus-Born One, and Yeshe Tsogyal, the Princess of Karchen, are identified with the primordial buddha in male and female form, called "the Lotus-Born Samantabhadra couple." Thereafter, through body, speech, mind, quality, and action emanations, she performed manifold benefit for the teachings and beings.

The verses above conclude by describing Yeshe Tsogyal's all-important role in recording and hiding teachings by Padmasambhava throughout the Tibetan and Himalayan landscape as treasures. For the Nyingma tradition, which traces its lineages back to Padmasambhava and other masters of the imperial period, treasures are hidden for posterity for periods of decline and strife when they are most needed. As an emanation of Yeshe Tsogyal, Tāre Lhamo was well established to play the role of a tertön, one who reveals such treasures when the time is right.

In the closing frame for this episode, Pema Ösal Thaye emphasizes Yeshe Tsogyal's achievement of the highest realization, on par with Padmasambhava in every way. This may be a tacit way to suggest Tāre Lhamo's own parity with her male partners.

Across the Generations to Golok

The garland of her past lives continues from Yeshe Tsogyal across the centuries, including both male and female figures.[7] The female ones are well known, such as the Indian princess Lakṣmīṇkarā, whose story appears in the tales of the eighty-four *mahāsiddhas* or "great accomplished ones" from India.[8] As recounted, Lakṣmīṇkarā was promised to a Lankan prince, but she refused to marry. Instead, she fled to a charnel ground and, practicing for a number of years, became an accomplished *yoginī*. Closer to home, Tāre Lhamo was linked in childhood to the legendary king Gesar of Ling through one of the prominent maidens of his kingdom, named Ne'u Chung. The Gesar epic spread far and wide across central Asia, but locals in Golok and northern Kham trace its events to their own land, and the epic remains central to their heritage and identity still today. Ne'u Chung is remembered alongside Drukmo, Gesar's wife, in statues at Gesar temples throughout Golok.

In the immediately preceding generation, Tāre Lhamo is considered the rebirth of two important figures from Golok, one male and one female: Tra Gelong (1866–1937),[9] a monastic teacher of regional renown, and Sera Khandro (1892–1940), a female tertön also considered an emanation of Yeshe Tsogyal. *Spiraling Vine of Faith* emphasizes her connection to Sera Khandro by including an extensive excerpt, almost verbatim, of her short autobiography in verse form (this is omitted here since the work has already been translated twice into English).[10] The short autobiography chronicles Sera Khandro's struggles to pursue the path of liberation, beginning with her desperate decision to flee an elite Lhasa upbringing and arranged marriage to venture into the rugged grasslands of Golok.

Once there, Sera Khandro encountered considerable hardships as an outsider of the tightly knit system of clans in the region. As she laments, initially she was not taken seriously as a spiritual practitioner, an unfortunate circumstance that she attributed to her female body.[11] Ḍākinīs appeared to her in visions to console her at various turning points, including the Great Mother, Yum Chenmo, who asserted the irrelevance of gender to attaining enlightenment and encouraged her to persevere despite an unhappy first marriage. At long last, she united with her destined consort Drime Özer to reveal treasures and, after his untimely death, became a formidable teacher in her own right. Sera Khandro appears in *Spiraling Vine of Faith* by different names, including Uza Khandro, the Ḍākinī from Central Tibet and Dewe Dorje, meaning Blissful Scepter and translating the Sanskrit, Sukhavajra.[12]

Spiraling Vine of Faith records exchanges between Tāre Lhamo's mother, Damtsik Drolma, and both of these figures prior to her birth. When meeting with Tra Gelong at a ritual occasion, he presented her with gifts and pronounced that he would soon be reborn in her home. Later, after he passed away, the smoke from his funeral pyre reportedly lingered over the encampment of Tāre Lhamo's family at the sacred mountain Drongri in Serta. Meanwhile, Sera Khandro gave Damtsik Drolma a knotted protection cord, tied it around her neck as a sign of their connection, and announced her imminent arrival in her home.

In the end, Sera Khandro passed away two years after Tāre Lhamo was born, but this did not prevent Buddhist masters in the region from correlating the two. *Spiraling Vine of Faith* includes prophecies to that effect by renowned masters, including her father, Apang Terchen, also known as Orgyan Trinley Lingpa, and Dudjom Rinpoche, the reincarnation of the great Golok tertön Dudjom Lingpa, who went on to become the head of the Nyingma lineage in exile. From a *Garand of Lives*:

> In a previous life, when the supreme Orgyan,[13]
> Heart son of the buddhas of the three times,
> Ventured to Tibet, the Land of Snow,
> She was renowned as the ḍākinī Lady of Karchen.[14]
>
> At the time of Gesar of Ling, as Ne'u Chung Drön,
> She was nurtured by the noble queen Tārā.
> Henceforth, in an Indian kingdom called Gaushö,[15]
> She was famed as the princess Lakṣmīṇkarā.
>
> To the north, in the valley of Yuyi Dabmin,
> She was known as the conch-bearer Vajradeva;
> In Dokham, at Gangchar in the Zalmo Range,
> She was famed as the holder of the three trainings, Sīla;
>
> At the base of Dabzang Dungri,
> She was renowned as one called Palkyi Lodrö;
> At the holy site of Dzumdenzhu,
> She was known as Shedrup Tenpe Nyima;

The beauty with a gloriously youthful body,
She was known by the name Sukha.
This limitless treasury and garland of lives
In actuality is one in the sphere of wisdom.

As indicated, immediately prior to this lifetime, she was Kunzang Dekyong Chönyi Wangmo, the ḍākinī Sukhavajra (Sera Khandro) who was Yeshe Tsogyal in person, transmitting the ocean of teachings from the oral lineage.[16]

Next is the account of how the Supreme Khandro took birth in this land of Do Kham. Her mother was Damtsik Drolma, the speech emanation of the ḍākinī Yeshe Tsogyal and a maiden of the Tongpön clan. Once Tra Gelong bestowed to her a sky-dweller transmission, presenting a ritual bell and so forth. With immeasurable compassion, he pronounced, "My reincarnation will take birth in your home." Later, while on the verge of death, he entrusted all of his possessions and implements, such as his liturgies and ḍākinī bell, to his attendant Alogowa, stating: "In the Male Earth Tiger Year (1938), go before Apang Terchen and tell him that I have been born there." Thereafter, the smoke from Tra Gelong's cremation circled around Drongri, the protector of Serta and place where the supreme lama, Apang Terchen, was residing. The smoke did not fade for a whole week.

In addition to that, Uza Khandro Dewe Dorje gave a red protection cord to the mother of the Supreme Khandro, saying: "Preserve this well and one day when the knot disappears, I will arrive in your home."

Her father, the eminent teacher Orgyan Trinley Lingpa, likewise uttered a prophecy: "To the pair of us, a great holy being will be born for the vast benefit of beings, far and wide. The child is a single emanation whose identity coalesces two figures: the ḍākinī Sukhavajra, who is Yeshe Tsogyal in person, and Tra Gelong Tsultrim Lodrö."

Furthermore, Dudjom Rinpoche Jigdral Yeshe Dorje from Kham prophesized:

Joint emanation of the noble queen Vārāhī and Tsogyal,
Bearing the name of Sukha, the ḍākinī from Do Kham,
Her reincarnation is the mantra-born Tāre,

> Whose activities will spread in India, Tibet, and China.
> Whoever encounters her will be guided to celestial realms.

From Pema Garwang Tsal:

> The emanation of the noble queen Vārāhī is named Tāre.
> For whoever encounters her, the door to birth in the lower realms is shut.

And from Do-ngak Tenpe Nyima:

> In this domain, the cool Snow Land of Tibet,
> The friend who causes the dharma lotus of the secret mantra to bloom,
> The lotus yoginī, the mother who gives birth to buddhas,
> These days, in this place, radiates the pleasing smile of magical display.

These prophecies identify Tāre Lhamo with significant figures of the past and forecast her prominence and salvific activities. From this illustrious garland of past lives, *Spiraling Vine of Faith* moves on to recount her own birth and the first part of her life.

No Ordinary Girl

Tāre Lhamo was born in the valley, Bökyi Yumolung, in eastern Tibet, not far from the monastery her father Apang Terchen founded. In Buddhist modes of storytelling, miracles accompany the birth of a great master, and Tāre Lhamo was no exception. Wondrous signs were reported, such as colored lights, perfume scents, and the sound of musical instruments. These signal the response of the phenomenal world to the fortunes of humans and hint at the cosmic significance of the event.

Her father Apang Terchen (1895–1945) was a tertön of regional renown. His own garland of past lives linked him to such distinguished figures as the Indian *mahāsiddha* Kṛṣṇācārya and the famed revealer of northern treasures, Rigdzin Gödem. After studying with Lerab Lingpa and other esteemed masters of his day, in 1925 he founded Tsimda Gompa, a monastery along the Mar River in Padma County, Golok. Tāre Lhamo was the fourth of five children and the only girl. All were recognized as reincarnations of past masters, though one died in childbirth.[17]

From an early age, Tāre Lhamo defied easy categorization. *Spiraling Vine of Faith* emphasizes that she was unlike other girls, being especially devout and possessing a mastery of mind well beyond her years. For example, from an early age, she had visions of Padmasambhava, also known as the Lotus-Born One, Guru Rinpoche, and the Great Orgyan. Due to her exceptional nature, it refers to her as the "Supreme Maiden" in youth and later the "Supreme Khandro" or "Khandro Rinpoche." The term "khandro" translates the Sanskrit *ḍākinī*, referring to a class of female tantric deities.[18] Tibetans use this term as a title for exceptional women, the wife of a high lama or a female Buddhist master in her own right.

Remarkably, as a child, her father deferred to her wishes when Alogowa arrived to fetch Tāre Lhamo who was the reincarnation of his former master, Tra Gelong. At first, Apang Terchen put him off by saying that she was too young. When Alogowa returned several years later, her father left the decision up to her. Did Tāre Lhamo want to become a nun and return to Tra Gelong's monastery to continue his legacy or did she want to remain a householder under the tutelage of her father? In choosing her vocation, Tāre Lhamo defied the usual options of nun or householder, stating: "I am determined to be both venerable (*jomo*) and a householder." Colloquially, the term "jomo" refers to "nuns" but it has the broader meaning of "venerable," an epithet for an esteemed religious practitioner. Tāre Lhamo thereby asserted her wish to be a householder dedicating her life to spiritual pursuits.

Tibet has an array of non-monastic religious specialists, full-time tantric practitioners who do not take a vow of celibacy. This type of vocation is especially common in the Nyingma tradition, where lineages of teachings are typically passed through the family. Tāre Lhamo received extensive teachings from her father Apang Terchen including the *Nyingtik Yabshi*, a key cycle of teachings in the Nyingma tradition, and the entirety of his own treasure corpus, which Tāre Lhamo would propagate far and wide later in life. Grief stricken when her father died before she turned ten, Tāre Lhamo showed her devotion and tenacity in the face of adversity by offering her own jewelry to decorate his reliquary.

> To the Lord of Secrets in person, Apang Terchen Pawo Chöying Dorje, alias Orgyan Trinley Lingpa, the great tertön and emanation of indisputable renown, and his wife, Damtsik Drolma, foremost among ḍākinīs and maiden of the Tongpön clan, was born

a daughter in the Male Earth Tiger Year (1938) in the sixteenth Tibetan sexagenary cycle at a place called Bökyi Yumolung. Her mother experienced no birth pains whatsoever. At that time, various musical instruments resounded, rainbows formed a dome in the sky, and a mist of perfume issued forth. Many wondrous signs appeared.

On that occasion, the attendant Alogowa arrived and conveyed to the Supreme Lama Terchen the last testament of his master, mentioned above. When he proclaimed, "This is my lama," Apang Terchen replied: "This child is a girl, therefore she is no use to you. Nonetheless, when she grows up, you can come back and ask her."

Then, at the age of one, the Supreme Maiden traveled to Lhasa with her parents and a retinue. Dudjom Rinpoche Jigdral Yeshe Dorje from Kham recognized her as an emanation of the ḍākinī Sukhavajra, who is Yeshe Tsogyal in person. He held her in his arms and, displaying her before the wish-fulfilling jewel Jowo Śākyamuni, made extensive aspirations that she accomplish the vast benefit of beings.

Next, when the Supreme Maiden had grown up, according to oral accounts, the attendant Alogowa returned to claim his previous master. With regard to that, her eminent father Terchen Rinpoche said to the Supreme Maiden, "You may become a venerable nun or remain a householder." She replied, "I am determined to be both venerable and a householder." Thereafter, the attendant offered her the possessions, such as liturgies and a ḍākinī bell, entrusted to him according to his previous master's wishes and command. The Supreme Lama Terchen said to the attendant Alogowa, "At this time, it's not proper for you to take her home. What would be the point?"

Regarding this eminent protector of beings, from a young age, she was free from the faults of ordinary women[19] and had uncontrived compassion and spontaneous mastery of mind. She had faith in deities and lamas and experienced extensive visions of them. In particular, just by uttering the name of the Great Orgyan, the hairs of her body would stand on end and tears would well in her eyes. Again and again, she experienced visions and prophecies of the king of victors, the Lotus-Born One, and oceans of the infinite three roots. As it is said:

The emissaries of Padma, who retrieve treasures,
Have great faith, discipline, and magnanimity,
Extensive learning and a liberated mindstream.
Holders of the view and meditation, precise in conduct,
They have great compassion and little negative emotions,
Having rejected saṃsāra and cast off worldly concerns.
Gentle and conscientious, they realize the sphere of reality.
Pacifying an evil mindset, witnessed by demons,
Skillfully they benefit and ripen the teachings and beings.
A source of benefit to anyone who encounters them,
The emissaries of Padma are wish-fulfilling jewels.
Supplicate them one-pointedly—whoever establishes
a connection
Will be led to Lotus Radiance in Padma's pure land.

At the age of seven, in the presence of her eminent father, she received the *Nyingtik Yabzhi* and the entire transmission of his own treasure revelations.[20]

When she reached the age of nine, the physical sphere of her eminent father, Terchen Rinpoche, dissolved into clear light for a short while and then dissipated into the expanse of *dharmakāya*.[21] For her father's inwardly luminous youthful vase body, for the great expanse of primordial peace, and for his attainment of buddhahood, with a grieving heart, the Maiden—using as a base her own necklace and gold bracelets—completed the construction of a reliquary stūpa for him of immeasurable value.

Around that time, she traveled to Dodrupchen Monastery to attend the sacred dances. The great lord of siddhas Rigdzin Jalu Dorje showed the Supreme Maiden a mask of Ne'u Chung from among the costumes of female deities and said, "You are an emanation of her."

Several stories from youth, not found in *Spiraling Vine of Faith*, likewise illustrate her forthright character and tenacity from a young age. These come from the newest and recently published namthar of Tāre Lhamo, *Wonder of Divine Music*, composed by Rigdzin Dargye, a cleric-scholar from her father's monastery.[22]

After her father passed away, she traveled on pilgrimage with her mother Damtsik Drolma to various monasteries and sacred sites throughout the region. One time while her mother conversed with Rigdzin Jalu Dorje, the fourth in the eminent Dodrupchen incarnation line associated with the monastery,[23] Tāre Lhamo and a childhood friend set off to explore the terrain. As they were leaving, Damstik Drolma cautioned them to be careful around the rock outcroppings. Defying her mother's warning, Tāre Lhamo climbed to the top of a rock outcropping and thought to herself, "If I am the disciple of Dodrupchen, then even if I fall off a precipice, what harm can come of it?" She and her friend leapt and fortuitously remained unharmed. Later when they returned to the place where her mother and Rigdzin Jalu Dorje were conversing, he casually commented that he had envisioned the two girls gently falling to the ground.

Another childhood tale shows Tāre Lhamo using clairvoyance to win at a Tibetan version of "hide and seek." She and her friend were digging for *droma*, a bean-size herb sometimes called the "Tibetan sweet potato." They took turns hiding dromas and searching for them. After her friend hid some dromas, Tāre Lhamo went straight to the spot to retrieve them, stating: "Because I am the daughter of Apang Terchen, I know exactly where they are." Stories like this give us a glimpse into the youthful exploits of an exceptional being, where her talents are manifest in, as yet, immature form. Nonetheless, her exceptional nature was recognized by the great masters of her day. Rigdzin Jalu Dorje was one of Tāre Lhamo's two main teachers, and he identified her as an emanation of Ne'u Chung, as the passage above indicates, and as an emanation of Tārā according to *Wonder of Divine Music*, which reports that he praised her before a group of disciples as "the revered lady, noble Tārā actually appearing in human flesh."[24]

Treasures in Youth

From childhood hide-and-seek games, Tāre Lhamo progressed to the more serious endeavor of revealing treasures. Her propensity was awakened as a teenager while she was studying with great masters at Dodrupchen Monastery. Once while circumambulating the monastery, Tāre Lhamo inadvertently stumbled on a treasure while fighting off a pack of dogs. In Golok, as elsewhere in eastern Tibet, packs of dogs roam the area around monasteries and can be a menace. It is not uncommon for people to carry rocks in case of stray dogs, and there is even a special sling some use to hurl the rocks a distance.

On this occasion, when a pack of dogs started to attack, Tāre Lhamo threw rocks at them to protect herself and sought high ground on a boulder in an otherwise open meadow. There was a dark stone on top of the boulder that she grabbed to add to her arsenal of rocks, and when she got home that evening, she still had it in her pocket. Showing it to her mother, the rock had special markings and turned out to be a treasure meant for Rigdzin Jalu Dorje. Needless to say, Tāre Lhamo later turned it over to him—after a gentle nudge from her mother.

Treasures come in a variety of forms. They can be rocks with special markings, such as the one Tāre Lhamo found which was marked by the seed syllable VAṂ. More typically, they are described as symbolic script written on yellow scrolls, tucked away inside a treasure casket along with ritual objects, medicinal substances, and relics. The symbolic script provides a mnemonic cue to recall a set of teachings from Padmasambhava or comparable master, which the tertön received in a previous lifetime.

Treasures can appear in any number of forms, including directly in the mind of the tertön.[25] Namtrul Rinpoche once said that symbolic script appeared on Tāre Lhamo's arm as she approached death, while music emanated from her body. Otherwise, as displayed by Namtrul Rinpoche for visitors, the treasures of the couple were, for the most part, specially marked rocks and ritual implements.

On another occasion, Tāre Lhamo revealed a treasure with the daughter of her second main teacher, Dzongter Kunzang Nyima. Like Tāre Lhamo, his daughter Lhacham Chökyi Drönma was considered an emanation of Yeshe Tsogyal and Sera Khandro. In the Nyingma tradition in Golok, multiple identifications for the reincarnation of great masters is common. Needless to say, the great tertön Dudjom Lingpa had three reincarnations, including the revered Dudjom Rinpoche, who fled into exile, as well as his own two grandsons, Kunzang Nyima and Sönam Detsen.

Once Tāre Lhamo joined the encampment of Kunzang Nyima at the shore of Lake Ngöntso in the sacred mountain range of Nyenpo Yutse. Lake Ngöntso is one of two sacred lakes in this vast mountain range, and local lore depicts it as the origin point of the Golok tribes. There, he instructed the two teenage girls, Tāre Lhamo and Chökyi Drönma, to go and find a treasure site called "tigress fortress" where Padmasambhava and Yeshe Tsogyal had practiced. Presumably, they would remember the site from their shared previous lifetime.

However, as they set off into the mountains, in fact, neither knew where to go. Fortunately, Lingtrul Rinpoche had previously provided Tāre Lhamo with a clue when she visited him at Dodrupchen Monastery. He had taken a handful of *tsampa*, the Tibetan staple food of roasted barley, and placed it inside a crystal glass to produce a magical illusion of Nyenpo Yutse and gave her a "virtual tour" of the site. When the teenagers came upon the location, she immediately recognized it and placed a long-life arrow to mark the spot.

The *Wonder of Divine Music* goes on to say that the two revealed a longevity sādhana there, which Tāre Lhamo later used to bestow a long-life initiation on Buddhist masters surviving the Cultural Revolution.[26] Her early treasures are recounted in *Spiraling Vine of Faith* as follows:

> At the ages of twelve and thirteen, she studied with both Dodrupchen Rinpoche Rigdzin Jalu Dorje and the omniscient Thubden Trinley Palzangpo and served them through offerings, service, and practice. On at least two occasions, she received from them the esoteric precepts of instructions that ripen and liberate for the *Nyingtik Yabzhi*, *Two Sections*,[27] and so forth.
>
> At the age of fourteen, while staying in the Do Valley, once she went to circumambulate Dodrupchen Monastery. In a great open plain, a pack of dogs attacked her. As they were chasing her, the Supreme Maiden without hesitation gathered up lots of rocks and threw them at the dogs. Specifically, on top of a large boulder, there was one dark stone. Fearlessly, she grabbed it to throw at the dogs.
>
> That evening, when she returned home, she still had the dark stone in her pocket. When she showed it to her mother, it turned out to be a treasure casket with a red syllable VAṂ protruding on top. "How amazing!" her mother said, "Last night I had a sign in a dream that a marvel would occur. This is good for the most part." Saying that, she affixed the dark stone around the Supreme Maiden's neck out of sight. From that point forward, having awakened the karmic propensity for profound treasures, she revealed various material treasures, including statues, caskets, and yellow scrolls.
>
> One time, she arrived in the presence of the great adept Lingtrul Rinpoche, who said, "Now I am very pleased. I will introduce you to Nyenpo Yutse, the supreme site of the eight great deities of the glorious sādhana section." Inside a crystal glass, he poured a handful of tsampa, which rose into midair like a magical illusion. A joyful land appeared. Lingtrul Rinpoche pointed out the great

> treasure site, Nyenpo Yutse, and the particulars of it, saying "This is the tigress fortress," and so forth. "One day, the time will come when this will be useful," he concluded.
>
> When she reached the age of eighteen, the Maiden stayed at Rizab in the Do Valley along with a retinue. Later, Dodrup Rinpoche Rigdzin Jalu Dorje arrived and asked her, "Do you have my treasure allotment from the fortress site?" Without hesitation, the Supreme Maiden answered, "I didn't take it." But then her mother inquired, "That casket you showed me earlier, did you find it some time ago on top of a boulder in the great open plain?" Rigdzin Jalu Dorje replied with great delight, "Oh, that's it!" Then, the Supreme Maiden offered the treasure casket to Dodrup Rinpoche. Later the great *vidyādhara* Dzongter Kunzang Nyima set down as a treasure the dharma cycle of the *Gathered Intent of the Ḍākinīs*.[28]
>
> Next, she journeyed to the banks of Lake Ngöntso at the sacred mountain range Nyenpo Yutse along with the encampment of Dzongter Rinpoche. On the occasion of offering a profound and extensive *gaṇacakra*, Terchen Rinpoche Kunzang Nyima said to his daughter Lhacham and Khandro Rinpoche, "You both resided here in the tiger fortress together with Guru Rinpoche and his disciples. There is the treasure door to the *Gathered Intent of the Ḍākinīs*. Whatever you find, be sure to insert this long-life arrow in its place." Although she did not know this place at all from the past, according to her magical introduction by Lingtrul Rinpoche,[29] the Supreme Khandro identified the site. As a result, the auspicious coincidence came about for Chagtrul Rinpoche to set down a praise to the *dralas* at that place.[30] Exerting herself solely in practice at all of the great and small sacred sites, including Chakri Öbar and Tashi Gomang, her realization became equal to the sky.

Her early training culminated in her traveling on pilgrimage to practice at the sacred sites in and around Golok, accompanied by her mother, Damtsik Drolma.

The *Wonder of Divine Music* contains a few other accounts of her early revelations. The most unusual is a father-daughter treasure, revealed at Drongri. Drongri is the sacred mountain and local protector deity of Serta and also a favorite site for Apang Terchen to set up his encampment. One day Apang Terchen requested his daughter to accompany him on an excursion to one of the holy sites at Drongri, a rock cliff that today is decorated with prayer flags. There, he traced a circle on the rock with his finger and then struck it around the edges with his palm to reveal an opening. He asked Tāre Lhamo, with her small hands, to reach in and remove a batch of the medicinal pills stored for posterity inside the cavity. Apang Terchen then retraced the circle and restored the rock to its original state.

Later, according to *Wonder of Divine Music*, Tāre Lhamo revealed a treasure on her own at Drongri. It was a vajra or ritual scepter, which she placed at Tsimda Monastery, her father's monastic seat in the Mar Valley. Apang Terchen saw this as a sign that great beings born there would have to go to another land to be of widespread benefit to others. This incident foreshadowed her later life with Namtrul Rinpoche, based in his homeland where they rebuilt Nyenlung Monastery.[31]

Such stories are important testimony to her visionary capacities in youth, well before her union with male tantric partners.

Marrying into the Dudjom Line

Tāre Lhamo's first marriage was arranged on her behalf when she was twenty years old. Her teacher Dzongter Kunzang Nyima received a treasure prophecy regarding his own son's fortuitous union with her, and elders in the Dudjom Line as well as her brothers approved of the match. His son, Mingyur Dorje (1934–1959), locally known as Tulku Milo, was four years older than Tāre Lhamo and considered an emanation of Vairocana, a great translator of the imperial period.

This was a marriage between prominent families among the Nyingma in Golok. Kunzang Nyima was the grandson and speech emanation of Dudjom Lingpa, the great tertön in the region who generated a prestigious religious lineage. Dudjom Lingpa had eight sons and four daughters with his three wives, and many of them became revered teachers.[32] Some of his scions across the generation became tertöns in their own right, including Kunzang Nyima.

As newlyweds, Tulku Milo and Tāre Lhamo lived at Kunzang Nyima's encampment at Rizab, in the rugged hills outside of Dartsang, the location of Dudjom Lingpa's monastery. In Golok and surrounding nomadic areas, disciples often gathered around the hermitages of charismatic teachers, living in the black yak-hair tents used by nomads in the region. These could turn into sizeable encampments, and Rizab had up to one thousand in residence at any given time.

Not all who stayed there studied and practiced the same material; the teachings depended on their abilities and progress on the Buddhist path. Only the inner circle, including Tulku Milo and Tāre Lhamo, received the highest teachings on Dzokchen, or the Great Perfection. In addition, Tāre Lhamo received the entirety of Kunzang Nyima's treasure teachings, and he specially appointed her the trustee of his treasure cycle on Yeshe Tsogyal. This meant that she was the official dharma heir and transmitter for that set of rituals and teachings.

> At the age of twenty, according to a symbolic prophecy that Rigdzin Nuden Dorje (Dzongter Kunzang Nyima) received from the ḍākinīs, and in consultation with the wishes of Tulku Dorje Dradul and Sönam Detsun,[33] and her own brothers, Wangchen Nyima and Gyurme Dorje, the Maiden was offered as the eternal companion to the reincarnation of the master Vairocana, Tulku Milo, alias Pema Ösal Nyingpo. Celebrating a great festival, the activities of auspicious coincidence increased.
>
> At the age of twenty-one, she performed the accumulations and purifications, such as 100,000 prostrations, and alongside that practiced the sādhana of the noble queen Tārā. Terchen Rinpoche, Rigdzin Nuden Dorje, wholly bestowed to her the transmission and esoteric precepts for the entirety of his profound treasures as well as supplementary religious services. And he appointed her the trustee for the sādhana cycle of Yeshe Tsogyal.

This is all the reader learns from *Spiraling Vine of Faith* of her first marriage. Indeed, we know little about the short time that Tāre Lhamo spent with Tulku Milo, other than that they had a son who would not survive the Cultural Revolution. They spent just one or two years together, practicing and studying the dharma, before tragedy struck.

Turbulent Times

Less than a decade after the People's Liberation Army marched into Tibetan areas in 1950, the Chinese Communist government shifted its policy away from a gradualist approach in minority areas, tailored to local conditions. In the late 1950s, the socialist transformation of Tibetan areas began in earnest. This meant the collectivization of the pastoral economy and closure of monasteries.[34] Tibetan elites were rounded up as "class enemies" and put in prison, including the heads of wealthy families, former chieftains, and prominent religious figures.

Tulku Milo and Tāre Lhamo's three brothers were all imprisoned in the late 1950s and died shortly thereafter. Her beloved teacher, Rigdzin Jalu Dorje, suffered the same fate, and many descendants of Dudjom Lingpa were similarly laid to waste at this time; some dying naturally, others in prison.[35] Doli Nyima, one of Tulku Milo's cousins who was twelve years his junior, survived this first wave of persecutions and became a special source of solace to Tāre Lhamo.[36] But even Doli Nyima would eventually be arrested, and he disappeared shortly after Tāre Lhamo found a way to send a letter to secure his release.

Terrible famine spread across China between 1959 and 1961, precipitated by the failed policies of the Great Leap Forward. This greatly compounded the tragedy for Tibetans facing the dismantling of their way of life and led to widespread malnutrition and death. The destruction of most visible signs of Tibetan culture, including Buddhist monasteries and temples, ensued during Cultural Revolution (1966–1976). During this time, Tāre Lhamo's only son died, and the main Vajrasattva temple at Tsimda Gompa was destroyed. *Spiraling Vine of Faith* glosses over these tragedies in order to focus on the heroic activities of Tāre Lhamo during this period.

Tāre Lhamo was spared the fate of her first husband and others of their generation, likely due to gender. Alongside the younger reincarnate lamas, like Namtrul Rinpoche, she was not viewed as a threat and so spared imprisonment in the late 1950s. For the next two decades, Tāre Lhamo was consigned to manual labor as part of a work unit in her homeland of Markhok in Padma County. Alongside other locals, she was forced to do various grueling tasks, such as digging trenches, carrying heavy rocks to construct pens for yaks, chopping wood and loading it, all the while tending to the herd of her work unit.

Amid such hardship and loss, Tāre Lhamo kept the benefit of others in the forefront of her mind. *Spiraling Vine of Faith* suggests that, during this period, her mind was "brimming with *bodhicitta*," the enlightened intent to save all beings from suffering. Indeed, she is depicted as a tantric siddha with supernormal abilities and a bodhisattva whose compassion focused on her local community even as misfortune was widespread across the Tibetan plateau. Miraculous in tenor, the tales of her compassionate intervention that likely circulated at the time provided a beacon of hope amid the devastation. For her local community, her presence showed that the buddhas and bodhisattvas had not abandoned them in the midst of crisis.

Time and time again, Tāre Lhamo came to the rescue when local Tibetans were in distress. During famine, Tāre Lhamo multiplied the supply of rice allocated to her work unit to feed more than its eighteen members. When a rockslide threatened to fall on a group of people and animals, possibly a road construction crew, Tāre Lhamo made a tantric gesture toward the rockslide to bring it to a halt. When the signs of death were everywhere, she still summoned the vultures needed to provide a sky burial. The high alpine conditions of Golok, with its permafrost, rolling grasslands, and few forests, makes cremation or burial difficult, so Tibetans have traditionally disposed of corpses by ceremonially chopping them to feed to vultures at special sky burial sites. That the vultures were full while everyone else starved is a devastating image of the times.

In this way, *Spiraling Vine of Faith* sets her heroic deeds against the backdrop of the mayhem of this period:

> From the ages of twenty-two to forty-one (1959–1978), because of the extreme turbulence of the times, the Supreme Khandro experienced a mix of myriad joys and sorrows. Nevertheless, she was able to embrace misfortune. Whatever her activities, inwardly she approached them with the discipline of a bodhisattva. Her mindstream was brimming with bodhicitta, and she took up with singular earnest the benefit of others, directly and indirectly.
>
> At the age of twenty-three, by the force of group karma, the whole land was devastated by widespread famine. Because the Supreme Khandro was a female siddha who commanded the inexhaustible treasury of the sky, each measure of rice that she cooked multiplied to be more than enough to feed eighteen people. Everyone was in a state of amazement.
>
> One time, a horseman named Norbu died. In general, during these times, because of the human and horse corpses strewn across all the mountains and valleys, there were no vultures to dispose of the body. Before the Supreme Khandro arrived, there was nothing to be done. Once she arrived, she commanded two corpse cutters

named Zangkyong and Tenzang, "Place the corpse on top of a boulder." They did as she said, and five vultures appeared—who were the emanations of five ḍākinīs—and partook of the corpse without leaving any remains.

According to a policy prior to the Cultural Revolution, the people were ordered to kill dogs and rodents. There was no way out of it. When ordered to kill, through the abundant strength of benevolence in her mind, fierce compassion arose toward all sentient beings without bias. The Supreme Khandro thought to herself, "I would rather die myself than kill those creatures." Following from that thought, during an agitated night of sleep, the tantric protectress Dorje Rachigma appeared to her. "Don't be sad. Before morning, I will provide a dog corpse for you to present. It is not yet time to die! Since you must accomplish great benefit for the dharma and beings, you are not allowed to die." The protectress stamped her foot, and the ground shook, vibrating throughout the area and rousing everyone from sleep. In that way, according to prophecy, the next morning there was a dog corpse and the Supreme Khandro was freed from the horror of that policy.

Another time, a rockslide was underway that included one large boulder. On the road, animals were injured. When she arrived, the people there were ready to flee. By merely pointing her finger at the rockslide, the Supreme Khandro rendered the large boulder unable to move. All were amazed.

On yet another occasion, having gathered eighteen measures of wood earlier in the day, she was able to load it onto yaks that never before had been burdened with a load. At the time, she appeared fatigued by the effort. However, while constructing a pen for the livestock, the Supreme Khandro lifted a boulder that could not be carried by eighteen people and added it to the stone wall, leaving her handprint on it. This was perceived in common by all.

During this period, treasure teachings and songs of realization effortlessly burst forth. Currently, her collected works are contained in more than five volumes, all of which possess the quintessence of the view of the secret mantra and Dzokchen. If examined by the wise, they are profound. And if studied by the foolish, they are easy to understand.

The Supreme Khandro was never sullied by the dirt of broken

samaya. Her many miracles continued to occur, said to be the swift power of blessings and lingering breath of the mother ḍākinīs.

In these miracle tales, Tāre Lhamo is depicted with superhuman capacities, such as the ability to turn back a rockslide or place her handprint in stone. Such tantric feats can be found in the namthars of great Buddhist masters across the centuries. Yet this mode of storytelling takes on new significance in the context of the socialist transformation of Tibetan areas. In the midst of calamity, the compassion and heroism of surviving Buddhist masters remained.[37] Sharing these tales at the time, Tibetans could affirm their faith in Buddhism and resist state-imposed political reeducation compelling them to regard their spiritual teachers as "class enemies."

Spiraling Vine of Faith mentions her ongoing revelations and songs of realization but says nothing about her continued practice in secret.[38] This is likely because the work was published in conjunction with the Serta County Office of the Bureau for Cultural Research. Since religious practice was forbidden for almost twenty years, from the late 1950s through the end of the Cultural Revolution, Pema Ösal Thaye had to be careful about what he included. This helps to explain the focus on Tāre Lhamo's heroism while her own losses and hardships are elided.

By contrast, her newest namthar, *Wonder of Divine Music*, emphasizes her continued practice during these two decades, reciting prayers while engaged in menial tasks and even giving esoteric Dzokchen teachings to a select group of disciples.[39] It goes even one step further to depict Tāre Lhamo as the female bodhisattva Tārā herself appearing in various guises, akin to the well-known verses of praise to the twenty-one forms of Tārā. Only here Tāre Lhamo is the goddess Tārā appearing as a milkmaid, dung collector, herder, woodcutter, and so on. While outwardly doing the work of an ordinary nomad, inwardly she was a bodhisattva at the ready to benefit others in crisis. In these guises, she was "no different from Green Tārā as the emanation basis for all of them."[40] Green Tārā is especially connected to protection from life-threatening danger, and so too, in stories about her life, Tāre Lhamo is depicted rescuing others.

Apparition in the Sky

During these devastating decades, Tāre Lhamo interacted with other Buddhist masters in person and in visions, both giving and receiving encouragement. *Spiraling Vine of Faith* shows her encountering the tertön

Do-ngak Tenpe Nyima in the form of an ordinary farmer who delivers a series of prophecies and liberating Sang-ngak Lingpa from the confinement of prison by appearing to him in the sky in a dream to deliver a prophecy of her own. Despite their consignment to manual labor, Buddhist masters who survived this period found ways to express their visionary capacities.

> Furthermore, when Garra Gyalse departed for another realm,[41] he bestowed the remains of his beer to the Supreme Khandro. Once, when drinking this, she demonstrated a state of drunkenness and mentioned that someone named Dalö Sungdar, connected to her by previous dedications and aspirations, was falling to hell. With her unobscured eye of wisdom, she saw the reasons for his fallen condition, and thereafter she performed rites and provided the means to liberate him from hell.
>
> At the age of twenty-five, she went to visit Terchen Do-ngak Tenpe Nyima, encountering him while he ploughed a field in the vicinity of Banak Monastery. The Supreme Terchen extracted an earth treasure of Guru Zahorma and offered it to Khandro Rinpoche. He uttered the following prophetic verses:
>
> In a former life in Tibet, you were Yeshe Tsogyal,
> Who satisfied the king by emanating as his consort.
> Named Machik Zhama, the lamp of Shelkar,
> Do you remember the liberation story of the activity lamp?
>
> And:
>
> From the coincidence of having tamed the earth and
> negative emotions,
> You will meet with supreme knowledge and treasures.
> How wondrous!
>
> And next:
>
> Honored one who coalesces all buddhas and accomplished
> ones,
> The lord of Ngari, crown ornament of Tibetan scholars
> and adepts,
> I supplicate Pema Wangyal, the heruka who performs
> yogic discipline.[42]

Take me as your disciple, inseparable in the succession
of lives.
Just so, you are my karmically-bound lama across lifetimes.

This prophecy indicated that one day the Supreme Khandro would meet with an emanation of Ngari Paṇchen.[43] Accordingly, she later converged in one residence with the glorious dharma lord and precious great tertön, Orgyan Namkha Lingpa (Namtrul Rinpoche).

Another time, when the incarnate lama, Rigdzin Sang-ngak Lingpa, remained in prison in Serta, Khandro Rinpoche appeared before him in the sky by means of a magical emanation. "I have come to pay a visit to Wangpo and you," she said, offering him a sapphire.[44] Then she prophesized: "Not long from now, you will be free from jail and we will meet." Later, in accordance with the vision of her prophecy, the supreme precious incarnation was released from prison like the sun freed from clouds.

Once again, at the time when the Supreme Khandro lived as a herder, she got upset with her disciple Pegyal. She took a cup full of tea and threw it at a stone slab in front of him. As a sign of her accomplishment, the cup broke but not even a drop of the tea spilled. The cup of tea spun on top of the stone for a long while. This was witnessed in common by all present.

Another time, in accord with a state decree, she had to travel between Drakchö Gabma and Chugar Tsachu for a gathering. Outpacing a number of men on horses, she traveled via swift-walking.[45] Those with great faith toward her said it had to do with the constitution of her subtle body, and ordinary people remarked on her swiftness.

These are the miracles attributed to Tāre Lhamo during the years leading up to and including the Cultural Revolution. From multiplying the supply of rice to breaking a cup without its contents spilling, she defied the laws of nature and endured the effects of state persecution.

Tāre Lhamo's resilience is further linked to her compassion in a poignant story in *Wonder of Divine Music*. It occurs while Tāre Lhamo was being beaten, presumably during a struggle session. Her body struck a wood-burning stove but she remained unharmed by keeping compassion in the forefront of her mind and by calling on Tārā, her namesake. As a miraculous flourish, Tārā's ten-syllable mantra, OṂ TĀRE TUTTĀRE TURE SVĀHĀ, appeared as a self-arisen image on her garment, tinged with green.[46] In a slightly different version, recounted by an elderly woman at Tsimda, when her body struck the wood-burning stove, Tāre Lhamo imagined the greater suffering of beings in the hell realms and, because of that, she had no scar.

From stories like these, it is clear that Tāre Lhamo instilled faith in those who witnessed and learned of her deeds, providing a beacon of hope in troubled times.

A New Day Dawns

With the death of Mao, Tibetans must have sensed a shift in policy, though the effects of liberalization in economic and cultural terms did not make its way to Tibetan areas until the early 1980s.[47] According to one of her friends, by the mid-1970s, Tāre Lhamo was ready to give up, feeling that she could not be of benefit during this life. But then, while offering a feast of meager tsampa to Padmasambhava, she received a prophecy that times were changing for the better. *Spiraling Vine of Faith* signals this by declaring 1978 the dawn of a new day for the renewed propagation of the Buddhist teachings.[48] It shows Tāre Lhamo on par with other lamas in the region, extending their lifespan at this crucial turning point. Their names provide a veritable who's who of the surviving masters in Golok—cleric-scholars and reincarnate lamas from monasteries throughout the region.

Tāre Lhamo's resilience and capacity to heal comes to the fore. In one vignette, she remains unscathed during a hailstorm in which everything around her is burned to the ground. This is a poignant allegory for surviving the devastation of the Maoist period. In another, she is able to revive a young girl, brought to her on the verge of death, by pronouncing "It is not yet the time for her to die." The brief account points to the healing power of her prophetic speech. Read allegorically, it highlights her capacity to revive what is on the brink of death, which at that historical juncture could be understood more broadly to refer to Tibetan culture itself. Such a possibility is significant, given that her treasure revelations with Namtrul Rinpoche were meant to "heal the damage of degenerate times."

> In the Earth Horse Year (1978), in accordance with a symbolic prophecy of the sphere-of-wisdom ḍākinīs, the Supreme

Khandro set down a revelation of The Indestructible Knot Longevity Sādhana in order to clear away the physical impediments of Abkong Khenpo Lozang Dorje. She bestowed the initiation to the great scholar himself—as well as to Getse Khenpo Wangchen, Gartrul Rinpoche and others—extending their lifespan.

Furthermore, she extended the lifespan of various defenders of the Buddhist teachings and beings, such as: Choktrul Rinpoche Rigdzin Sang-ngak Linpga, Khenchen Jigme Phuntok Jungne, Dodrup Rinpoche Thubten Trinley Palzang, Lama Rigdzin Nyima, Khenpo Munsel, Khenpo Chöthun, Palyul Karma Chagme, Tshophu Dorlo, and Shukjung Lama Tsedzi.

One time, when the Khandro herself was resting in bed, suddenly there was a fierce hailstorm. A bolt of lightning struck. The whole house collapsed into a heap of ashes, including her bed and mat. Having doused her clothing in water, her indestructible body remained without any harm whatsoever. All were amazed.

A new day dawned in the meritorious sky of the Snow Land of Tibet for a renewed propagation of the Buddhist teachings. And around the same time, a girl named Soza Dröpo fell severely ill and seemed certain to meet with death. A stallion was brought before the Supreme Khandro (in order to request the transference of consciousness). She pronounced, "It is not yet the time for her to die," and returned the horse to the family. People say, because of this, the girl survived.

One day, while staying in Padma County, the Supreme Khandro had a dream as a luminous experience in which a bearded Chinese man said to her: "Previously I died and took on the body of a mongoose as my rebirth. Because tomorrow I will be killed, do not be mistaken." The next day, in accordance with that, suddenly a Chinese worker killed the creature. Even though the Supreme Khandro could not save its life, together with the Dharma Lord (Namtrul Rinpoche), she performed dedications and aspirations, including the transference of consciousness.

Furthermore, she offered a maṇḍala of auspicious coincidence and good fortune before Khenchen Jigme Phuntok Jungne Palzangpo, the sun of the teachings for degenerate times. On the occasion of her receiving the transmission for the three roots, he took great delight and said, "You are the one who opens the one hundred doors of mastery, the origin for my activity to benefit others. Previously, at Thramoling, you were Nechung Yuyi Drönma. Do you remember?" Speaking spontaneously, he praised her as a display of the noble *khecarī*:[49]

E ma ho! Khecarī, only mother of buddhas of the three times,
Taking the form of a woman for the sake of worldly beings,
Friend who opens the gate of measureless benefit and joy,
Tāre Devī, I supplicate at your feet.

Ripening the coarse body as the indestructible luminous essence,
Placing the body's agitated winds in the womb of the central channel,
Maturing wandering thoughts as the essence of dharmakāya,
Grant your blessings so that I may be equal in fortune to you.

May you who possess the seven changeless vajra qualities
Enjoy prosperity and vitality, watched over by Amitāyus.
May the sunray garland of your noble activities
Fill the vast expanse of the sky and realms of beings.

Then, her activities to benefit others swelled like a lake in the spring. While her great and many deeds were of immense benefit for the teachings and beings, I will not speak of them here, since they are already clear from the biography of His Eminence Namtrul Rinpoche.

Khenpo Jigme Phuntsok was a towering figure in the revitalization of the Buddhist teachings on the Tibetan plateau and a key figure in authorizing Tāre Lhamo and Namtrul Rinpoche as tertöns. In this passage, he and Tāre Lhamo traded compliments: she made an offering to receive teachings from him after extending his lifespan, and he praised her tantric practice and blessed her future activities.

This is where her own story ends. The rest of her life, traveling and teaching with Namtrul Rinpoche, is narrated in his namthar, *Jewel Garland*.

2. Early Life of Namtrul Rinpoche

The Dance of Emanations

As a reincarnate lama, Namtrul Rinpoche seemed to have a well-worn pathway to Buddhist training and mastery. Prophecies accompanied his birth, and by the age of eight he had been enthroned as the Namkhai Nyingpo emanation of Zhuchen Monastery in eastern Tibet. However, his studies at Zhuchen were interrupted by the socialist transformation of Tibetan areas in the late 1950s when he was still a teenager. Spared imprisonment at the time, due to his youth, he found ways to continue his practice and study in secret, even though public religious expression was prohibited at the time.

His story of liberation, *Jewel Garland*, presents him as an enlightened being engaged in a dance of emanations, taking birth in order to intervene during degenerate times. Characterized as a mahāsiddha and *cakravartin*, or "wheel-turning" king, he was said to manifest the three secrets—the indestructible body, speech, and mind—of the eighth-century Indian tantric master Padmasambhva (alt. Padmakāra). After the opening verses of praise, his story begins:

> Thus he is praised as the mahāsiddha and cakravartin, Nubchen Namkhai Nyingpo, and furthermore in the miraculous dance of emanations as the three secrets of Padmākara. He is a great tertön and dharma king, sovereign over an oceanic maṇḍala. While it is difficult to recite all of his epithets, to state his name, he is the glorious, unrivalled Orgyan Namkha Lingpa, otherwise known as Namtrul Rinpoche Jigme Phuntsok.
>
> This is the narration of his activities—which are the three secrets of that great lord himself whose white parasol of fame shimmers

high above saṃsāra and nirvāṇa. Yet, like an ocean, how can one speak of them? They are the exclusive domain of wise sages. As it is said:

> Remaining on earth, the three secrets of a great being
> Emanate as an inexhaustible cycle of ornaments.
> Described in that way, they transcend the sphere
> Of those like me, ensnared in an iron cauldron of suffering.

Although fools like myself with immature intellect have no ability to evaluate the qualities of a master, one can reliably follow the invincible treasure prophecies and the candid speech of trustworthy people. Dispensing with distortions, such as exaggeration, deceit, bias, or adulation, I present this story in plain words to serve simply as the seed of faith. It is meaningful to behold. From the tantras:

> Instead of meditating for a hundred thousand eons
> On the deity possessing the signs and marks,
> To recall the lama for one moment is supreme.
>
> Instead of reciting a million times
> The approach and accomplishment,
> To supplicate the lama once is supreme.

According to the master Jigme Rigpe Lodrö:

> From the numberless victors of the three times,
> Whatever praises reach the ears of the lama
> From offerings made with musical songs of praises,
> Such greatly meritorious speech brings delight.

Similarly, according to numerous tantras, scriptures, and instructions, to recollect the qualities of a glorious lama is the root of virtue. By supplicating with fierce devotion and making offerings with praises, one accumulates heaps of merit. It is particularly exalted above other methods.

In this statement of intent, author Pema Ösal Thaye is careful to articulate the worthiness of his endeavor and, at the same time, downplay his own claim to being an authority on the topic. According to cultural dictates of humility, Tibetan writers typically disparage their lack of qualities while holding the object of their erudition—whether a philosophical treatise, advice on esoteric meditative techniques, or the biography of a tantric master—in high esteem.

The Fourth Namkhai Nyingpo

Namtrul Rinpoche was first and foremost an emanation of Namkhai Nyingpo, venerated as one of the twenty-five chief disciples of Padmasambhava. Padmasambhava has played a key role in the lore surrounding the advent of Buddhism in Tibet in the seventh to ninth centuries, and Nyingma lineages trace many of their revealed teachings directly to him. As the emanation of one of his close disciples, Namtrul Rinpoche was well positioned to serve as a tertön, bridging time and space to bring forth teachings and relics with an ancient pedigree.

Zhuchen Monastery already had an existing line of Namkhai Nyingpo emanations, and Namtrul Rinpoche became the fourth in that line. At the age of eight, he was recognized as the reincarnation of Namtrul Jigme Ösal Rigpe Dorje, the third in this line and an heir of the prominent family stock of Ngadak Nyang descending from the twelfth-century tertön, Nyangral Nyima Özer. Prophecies by well-known local masters confirmed Namtrul Rinpoche's status, and during his youth he lived and studied at Zhuchen.

Beyond this, Namtrul Rinpoche is correlated with a series of enlightened buddhas and past masters, including the illustrious tertön Rigdzin Gödem, founder of the so-called northern treasure tradition. *Jewel Garland* links him to significant people and places in Buddhist myth and history from India to Tibet, further validating his authority as a tantric master. While there is no effort to be comprehensive in terms of accounting for each and every past life, the list of names given in his garland of past lives is impressive.

> In terms of the definitive meaning, the precious Dharma Master, the supreme incarnation, reached original enlightenment innumerable eons ago as the primordial essence of the all-pervasive original protector Samantabhadra, peaceful, free from elaboration, transcending mind. Ceaselessly, in the saṃbhogakāya realm of densely arrayed Akaniṣṭha, he arose as the sign endowed with the five certainties, great Vajradhara, the teacher free from limitation

and partiality. As an emanational display, he performed immense benefit for the teachings and beings to tame living creatures in various realms, pure and impure.

From *The Garland of Lives, A Beautiful Strand of Lotuses*:

> Long ago, in the eon called Glorious Ornament,
> In the presence of the original protector, Dundubhīśvara,[1]
> He was known as the brahmin Bodhikara.
> In the presence of Śikhin, he was Mahābodhi.
> In the presence of Vipaśyin, he was Bhevaṇā.
> In the presence of Kāśyapa, he was Māṇava Tāraka Prabhā.[2]
> In the presence of Śākyamuni, he was the śrāvaka Aniruddha.
> In the noble land of India, he was mahāsiddha Kṛṣṇācārya.
> In Oḍḍiyāna, he was the mahāsiddha Lavapa.
> In the presence of Padmasambhava, he was Nubchen Namkhai Nyingpo.
> At the time of the warrior Ling Gesar, he was Yulha Thogyur Tsal.
> Next he was the lord of siddhas, Thangtong Gyalpo, the iron bridge builder;
> The holder of the profound storehouse of treasures, Rigdzin Gödem;
> Dudul Dorje Raga Asya; and Tāranātha Dudul Rolpa Tsal.
> In the region of Lhorung, he was Shepa Dorje and Tsayul Natsok Rangdrol.
> In Lhodrak, he was Lekyi Dorje; in Nyagyul, one named Dharma.[3]
> In Do Kham, he was Dharmadhātu Vajra.[4]
> The one now known as Pema Drime Lodrö,
> I supplicate you, the holder of the great secret treasury.

Accordingly, in the various dominions of the world and in the infinite buddha realms as numerous as dust motes, emanations of expedient activity manifest as numerous as the rays of the sun and the sands of the Ganges with mastery over an inexhaustible abundance of qualities of the three secrets. Performing immense benefit for the teachings and beings, they manifest ceaselessly to undertake the activities of buddhas and bodhisattvas.

From the *Uttaratantra*:

> Just as the reflection of the deity's body
> Appears on the pure ground of *vaiḍūrya*,
> In the same way, the reflection of the buddha's body
> Appears on the pure ground of the minds of living beings.

The master Jigme Rigpe Lodrö stated:

> In this regard, in the mirror of the pure
> And impure dominions of the world,
> Millions of reflections, which are emanations,
> Appear, the expressive power of bodhisattvas.
>
> Though indifferent to worldly existence,
> Which they have long since renounced,
> Because the waves of the ocean of compassion stir,
> Intentionally they take up the display of existence.
>
> In this way, like the reflection of the moon,
> As shimmering patterns in distinct water vessels,
> Playful manifestations arise in myriad forms
> To spontaneously accomplish activity.

Furthermore, in these degenerate times, regarding the manner of manifesting for the glory of the teachings and beings and emerging as an illusory wisdom body or *rūpakāya*, Rigdzin Taksham Dorje stated:

> The regent of Padma, lord of the victors, protector of beings,
> And emanation of Gödem,[5] born in the Monkey Year with the name, Tse,[6]
> He will open the gates to the coffers of the sky, the profound treasures,
> And lead those connected to him to the Glorious Mountain on Cāmara.[7]

Thus it clearly indicates the name of this very Master during childhood (Tsedzin) and his birth year. From Padma Garwang Tsal:

> From the south, an emanation of Namkhai Nyingpo
> Will appear in the Monkey Year to restore the profound treasures
> And lead those connected to him to the Glorious Mountain.

And from Rigdzin Kachö Dorje:

> The son of wisdom deities, the supreme support,
> Emanational display of the master Namkhai Nyingpo,
> E ma, the enlightened activity of one named Ayu,[8]
> If freed from the clouds of harm at age sixteen,
> Is medicine to heal the damage to teachings and beings.

And Godzi Terchen foretold "an emanation of Nam-Nying named Pema in Zilung." Regarding that statement, "Zilung" is the birthplace of this very Master. "Nam-Nying" (Namkhai Nyingpo) is his emanational basis, and "named Pema" refers to his name, Pema Drime Lodrö.[9] In that way, the excellences of taming activity such as the time, place, teacher, and retinue are indicated quite clearly in the prophecies of profound treasures.

Furthermore, Zhutrul Rinpoche Kunzang Nyima stated:

> As for the descent, the lineage of Ngadak Nyang[10] will manifest
> In an unbroken line of siddhas for forty-nine generations.

In accordance with that, in the unbroken family lineage of the great transmitter of the *Assembly of Sugatas*, Ngadak Nyang, arose as if in a procession of hundreds of thousands of great beings, who were knowledge-holders of mantra. Within this line of descent, an illusory wisdom body emerged: the emanation of Nubchen Namkhai Nyingpo and the third in an incarnation line of Namrol Zhuchen Orgyan Namkha Dorje, namely Namtrul Jigme Ösal Rigpe Dorje who manifested as the master of the teachings for glorious Nyenlung Thekchen Chökor Ling.[11]

In that capacity, he bestowed the complete teachings of both Rigdzin Dudul Dorje and Rigdzin Longsal Nyingpo[12] as plentiful elixir, vast and profound, to mature and liberate beings, including the empowerments, reading transmissions, instructions, and auxiliary teachings. In addition, he set down various cycles of pure visions and newly established seasonal practices and a Vajrakīla retreat center there. When the conditions to remain at Nyenlung for a long period of time did not arise, in order to generate auspicious circumstances, he made a prophecy: "In the future, I will

> return and cause the Buddha's teachings to flourish at this monastery like the rising sun."

These last two paragraphs focus on his previous life as Namtrul Jigme Ösal Rigpe Dorje, the third in the line of Namkhai Nyingpo emanations at Zhuchen. *Jewel Garland* ties this figure to Nyenlung in Namtrul Rinpoche's homeland, the monastery that he and Tāre Lhamo rebuilt and made the main seat of their teaching activities. Though the Third Namkhai Nyingpo's stay was short, the prophecy of his future return to Nyenlung portends the birth of Namtrul Rinpoche.

Namtrul Rinpoche's Birth

The account of Namtrul Rinpoche's birth begins with his parents and clan affiliation. On his father's side, he descended from the Buchung clan within the illustrious line of Mukpo Dong, and on his mother's side the Getse clan. Clan affiliation has been a central to nomadic society in Golok and neighboring regions, forming an important aspect of the identity and social networks for Buddhist masters alongside reincarnation schemas, monastic affiliation, and transmission lineages for esoteric teachings. The clans of Golok trace their ancestry to the mountain deities in the region, especially Amnye Machen in the northwest and Nyenpo Yutse in the southeast, linking themselves palpably to the landscape.

Thus Namtrul Rinpoche, known as Tsedzin (abbreviated as Tse) in childhood, came from good family stock and an eminent incarnation line, and these factors facilitated his early training before the social fabric of Tibetan areas came under attack by Chinese Communist state policies.

> According to a prophecy by Zhuchen Wangpo Gangshar Rangdrol, "As for one named Tse, due to the intention of the departed lama, if your household sponsors a guru feast with ten million recitations and a sādhana ceremony at Lhagtse Monastery, a holy being will be born in your household. It is certain."
>
> Regarding his birth in accord with that and other prophecies, his father's family descended from the royal line of the Mukpo Dong from the youngest son of Palshul Phurba Kyab, forming the clan division known as Buchung. From him, in succession,

> appeared great holy men like pearls on a thread such as Dodrupchen Jigme Trinley Özer and Jigme Phuntsok Jungne. As the crown of an unbroken family line, his father Namlo of Buchung became a tantric yogi with perfect demeanor and unshakable faith toward deities and lamas. Constant in his tantric commitments, his mind overflowed with loving kindness, compassion, and one-pointed clarity regarding the profound and secret Dzokchen, the Great Perfection.
>
> As a maiden of the Getse clan, his mother Drokyi was honest and naturally good having compassion and generosity for the destitute, as well as great faith and pure vision toward deities and lamas, and never lacking in social graces such as getting along with others.
>
> As the son of this happy couple, he was born in the Wood Monkey Year of 1944 in the morning at the Dragon Hour of dawn. His birthplace lay to the north of Bodh Gaya in the noble land of India and belonged to the Zalmo Range in Do Kham in Tibet, a valley of medicines that is the cool domain of the noble Avalokiteśvara. He was born at the base of Gyalrong Draklha Gonpo, on the right slop where the Do River gently descends, in the valley of Gakyil.
>
> At that time, both night and day, springs of light red medicinal water newly bubbled forth and rainbow light spread all around the inside and outside of the house and formed a dome in the sky. The water flowing in the valley also swelled up and turned into a lake in the middle of Gakyil. Thereafter it became a delightful playground of various animals—terrestrial and aquatic. White, gold, red, and green flowers newly blossomed alongside thickets of plants, including peepal and tamarisk trees. Several days following his birth, the Master himself looked into the sky and, with a smile, pronounced the king of gnostic mantras, A RA PA TSA,[13] three times. There were many auspicious signs like this, seen and heard by all present.

As in any story of a great master, dating back to accounts of the Buddha, a series of miracles accompanied his birth. This prepares the reader to encounter an extraordinary being.

Childhood Games and Visions

Signs of Namtrul Rinpoche's exceptional character included his sensitivity as a child—he wept if he saw others kill insects—as well as his early visions and predilection for religious activities. Rather than playing ordinary games, the boy Tsedzin constructed Buddhist images in dirt and pretended to teach other children, thereby rehearsing his future role as a tantric master. In childhood, he had visions of Padmasambhava and Mañjuśrī, who are depicted as ever-present protective forces by his side. He also had a vision of the one hundred peaceful and wrathful deities, tantric expressions of wisdom said to appear in the *bardo*, or the intermediate state between death and rebirth. In Buddhist terms, the karmic propensities from previous lives were already visible from an early age.

> Just as from smoke, one knows fire.
> And from aquatic birds, one knows water,
> One knows wise bodhisattvas
> From pure qualities in their character.

At a young age, his sublime potential was awakened. Accordingly, in his mindstream, weariness toward saṃsāra and the wish to benefit others spontaneously arose. When he witnessed other children killing insects, the Master could only weep with compassion at how unbearable it was, and he endeavored to protect the lives of beings by whatever means possible. He also experienced sacred outlook toward the purity of the phenomenal world. When playing, he would pretend to teach the dharma to other children. Frequently, he would construct various shapes as representations of enlightened body, speech, and mind, such as a temple or clay statue and pronounce, "This is a monastery."

During childhood, the Master had a vision of the peaceful and wrathful deities appearing clearly in the midst of rainbow abodes at his cakras, like a heap of mustard seeds in bloom, including the Samantabhadra couple at his heart center. On his right and left shoulder, Padmasambhava and Mañjuśrī always remained. To illustrate, once there was a miserable demoness who started to violently attack the Master. Merely by gazing at the vajra of Padmasambhava and the flaming sword of Mañjuśrī, the demoness was driven away. Various pure visions such as apparitions of deities and lamas and confirming prophecies arose. All the joy and sadness of living and dying appeared just so with his stainless eye of wisdom.

At seven years old, he began learning to read and write with his maternal uncle Samtse. When he was studying the consonants and vowels and learning the *Gangloma*,[14] suddenly his uncle had to travel to Ngawa District. Distracted by play, the Master did not learn to write even one letter. Returning home after a month, his uncle asked, "Have you learned to write?" Without concealing anything, his family members explained the reason he had not been studying, and his uncle scolded him harshly. On that occasion, under the influence of his tender age, the Master cried a lot and then fell asleep.

In the morning, he chanted Karma Lingpa's revelation of the peaceful and wrathful deities from start to finish in an unimpeded way. All were amazed and developed irreversible faith. After that, he effortlessly knew all the letters and words without learning a single one. Furthermore, on his own, he learned how to write as well as draw an assortment of designs and perform healing arts. Each day he copied a whole volume of the extensive version of the *Sūtra of Great Liberation*[15] by hand until he finished it.

The theme of rapid mastery of reading and writing is a recurring feature in the biographies of enlightened masters, and here it is given a Nyingma flavor. Despite having neglected his study of the Tibetan alphabet while his uncle traveled, Namtrul Rinpoche was able to spontaneously chant revelations by Karma Lingpa, whose most famous legacy was the *Bardo Thödrol*, known in English as the *Tibetan Book of the Dead*.[16] From there he began studying on his own and copying out sūtras.

Though his education began at home, Namtrul Rinpoche was soon recognized as the Fourth Namkhai Nyingpo emanation of Zhuchen, and his training continued at the monastery under the tutelage of its esteemed tantric masters and cleric-scholars.

Enthronement

Zhuchen was a branch monastery of Katok in eastern Tibet, renowned as the oldest Nyingma monastery in Kham dating back to the twelfth century. For this reason, Namtrul Rinpoche became steeped in esoteric teachings and practices revealed by Rigdzin Dudul Dorje and Rigdzin Longsal Nyingpo, which belong to the Katok liturgical system. The theme of rapid mastery continued in his training at Zhuchen, where he received a thorough monastic education and also revealed his first treasures.

At the age of eight, in the presence of Khen Rinpoche Jigme Senge, he received the preliminary practices for Longsal Nyingpo's revelations. On the first day of that occasion, when he performed prostrations, as his right hand touched the ground, he revealed a treasure casket made from precious materials and marked by a sword at the center of a lotus and offered it to the lama. Since this signaled auspiciousness and good fortune, Khen Rinpoche said, "How wondrous!" and showered flowers of praise upon him. After that the karmic propensity for profound treasures was awakened, and he revealed many wondrous types of treasures such as a small chest, sword, and ritual implements.

From Khen Rinpoche Jigme Senge, Rigdzin Khachö Dorje, Khen Jigme Dechen, and so forth, he received treatises on sūtras and tantras, such as the explanatory text on *The Application of Mindfulness* as well as *Ascertaining the Three Vows*.[17] Whatever they taught, by hearing all of these just once, he realized them and his renown for learning shined forth.

Arriving at Zhuchen Vairo Mingyur Yeshe Dorje Monastery,[18] he was recognized as the reincarnation of Zhuchen Namtrul Jigme Ösal Rigpe Dorje. This was determined by Jamyang Chökyi Lodrö, alias Padma Yeshe Dorje.[19] With great affection, Zhuchen Kunzang Nyima accepted him as a disciple and bestowed on him the empowerment, authorization, instructions, and auxiliary teachings for *The Precious Treasury of Dharmadhātu*, the complete teachings of Rigdzin Dudul Dorje and Rigdzin Longsal Nyingpo, and the entirety of his own teachings like filling a vase to the brim.[20] He was enthroned on the fearless lion throne at Zhuchen Karmar Ling, the life-force pillar of the great secret teachings and the eastern reach of Katok Monastery. Thus, he was empowered as a master of all religious and worldly knowledge.

When he reached the age of nine, while attending a performance about the life of the dharma king Songtsen Gampo at Tsangchen Ngödrub Palbar Ling (Dodrupchen Monastery), the Master pronounced that his mother would die soon. His uncle scolded him, saying, "This is a sign of a naughty child." Then, after several days, according to his words, his mother fell gravely ill and passed away. On that occasion, with her corpse resting on a cushion, he granted her the extensive introduction to the ejection of consciousness and

> guided living creatures of the six classes, with his mother as the principal, on the path of liberation.
>
> That day, the Master had a vision that she departed for the southwesterly *rākṣasa* land of the Great Orgyan and thought, "Ale!"[21] to himself. In that year, he revealed sādhanas of both Jetsun Mañjuśrī and the Great Orgyan, and he performed ten sessions of fasting practice[22] to cultivate the root of virtue on behalf of his mother.

The power of prophecy is evident in Namtrul Rinpoche's prediction of his own mother's death. Although he was scolded by his uncle for presuming to know such a thing, his prediction came true. Thereafter, Namtrul Rinpoche took loving care to perform the funeral rites, including the ejection of consciousness in order to liberate her into a pure realm. While a rākṣasa or demonic land may not sound so pure, this is the very place where Padmasambhava (here the Great Orgyan) is said to have set up his paradise of Zangdok Palri, the Copper Colored Mountain. And so the reader glimpses Namtrul Rinpoche's dedication to his mother and his visionary capacities at a young age.

Monastic Ordination

Namtrul Rinpoche was ordained as a monk at the age of thirteen, though he would later disrobe as monasteries were disbanded and their buildings destroyed or put to secular use. *Jewel Garland* never mentions his first marriage or the birth of his son, Laksam Namdak, just as *Spiraling Vine of Faith* does not mention Tāre Lhamo's only child, who died young. Instead, the namthar emphasizes his early religious training and the prophecies he received from esteemed teachers confirming his later role as a tantric master. As depicted below, the Fourth Dodrupchen gave him an auspicious white conch to confirm the flourishing of the tantric teachings (also known as the Vajrayāna) at Nyenlung Monastery. And Shukjung Khandro, a female master from nearby Dodrupchen Monastery, gave him ink and paper to confirm his future vocation as a tertön.

> At just thirteen years old, he ardently roused the thought of renunciation from the world. When visiting Tagtse Samdrup Chökor Ling, in the presence of Khenpo Thubten Yarphel, endowed with the two qualities of constancy and learning, he received monastic

ordination and learned the ritual of the three bases of monastic discipline. With great affection, Zhuchen Phande Chökyi Nyima accepted him as a disciple. Giving him a blessed statue of Tārā, he stated, "You are empowered as a holder of the great secret teachings of tantra." While reciting prayers on the roof of the assembly hall, he had a vision of the great protectors of the teachings, Dudgön Zhingkyong and Nyenchen Thanglha, and received confirmation and praise from them.

Then the golden wheels on his feet arrived at and transformed glorious Nyenlung Thekchen Chökor Ling and, upon his advice, the monastery newly established a summer retreat. At that time, Dodrupchen Rinpoche Rigdzin Jalu Dorje visited this monastery and presented him with a white dharma conch, coiled to the right, along with a woven thangka (scroll painting) with images of the noble sixteen arhats. He stated: "At this place, if you construct a stūpa, the teachings of secret tantra, the Vajrayāna, will become as if illuminated by the sun." And greatly treasuring him, he also said, "Not only that, we two are manifestations of a single mindstream."

The Shukjung Khandro, Kunzang Chökyi Drolma,[23] stated: "One day you will need to set down many treasure teachings, so now if you prepare with ink and paper, it will be advantageous." Saying this, she offered him paper made from bark for writing and much ink. As a praise, she said, "Now, there are none who are greater in ability to guide than these two, the protector Gyalrong Drakla (Drongri Mukpo)[24] and this reincarnate lama. Emanating as a little golden bee, by traversing the intermediate state, each day he guides many millions of sentient beings."

Yukhok Tulku Karma Zangkyong[25] offered him many auspicious substances such as a vajra and bell, praising him repeatedly as the emanation of the victorious lord, the Great Orgyan. Furthermore, those possessing the stainless eye of wisdom, such as Sengtrul Ngedön Gyatso, Zhuchen Tulku Khyenrab Wangchuk, and Choktrul Lodrö Wangpo also delivered unmistaken prophecies of him as a reincarnate lama.

On the tenth day of the seventh month of the Monkey Year (1956), he had a direct vision of the Great Orgyan and received many prophecies about future events, which no longer exist because the documents were burned due to the force of the times.

Needless to say, "the force of the times" refers to the socialist transformation of Tibetan areas and explains why some of his early writings did not survive.

Protected by Yeshe Tsogyal

Beginning with 1960, this period of his life is characterized as a time of extreme hardship. *Jewel Garland* attributes the famine that beset Tibetan areas to group karma rather than state policy. The explanatory power of collective karma, here as elsewhere, serves as an important way for Tibetans to understand the seemingly random and tragic events of this period without losing their cultural sense of the world as a moral order.[26]

That same year, Namtrul Rinpoche had a vision of Yeshe Tsogyal in which she warned him of the bad times ahead and insisted that he would be spared the worst of it due to her own loving protection. After this vision, despite suffering from severe deprivation, Namtrul Rinpoche became more vibrant and youthful according to reports by those around him.

> In the Iron Rat Year (1960), by the force of collective karma, the region in general and all its specific domains were afflicted by famine, and the Master also underwent comparable anguish in connection with that. On the twenty-fifth day of the tenth month, he had a vision of the noble queen Yeshe Tsogyal, who said, "Even though the circumstances for suffering will occur, you will never be separated from me even for an instant." Feeding him elixir from her nipple to fortify him, she uttered, "From now on, you will never go hungry or thirsty or suffer from the cold." After that, the Master himself changed and, like a snake shedding its skin, all the accumulated experiences of pleasure and suffering were no longer the same as before. His mastery of the wisdom of bliss and emptiness increased. All the anguish of cold, hunger, and thirst were purified on their own. His physical strength grew unlike before, and he became quite radiant. All remarked about these wondrous transformations: how the Master's physique had improved and his youth was enhanced.
>
> On the first day of the new year, the Female Iron Ox (1961), he had a vision of the Great Omniscient One (Longchenpa), who delivered many prophecies, including one that the omniscient Dodrupchen Rinpoche Thubten Trinley Palzangpo would return

> to his homeland and monastic seat in the year of the Male Wood Mouse (1984/5).

Given that Namtrul Rinpoche was only a teenager when tragedy struck, *Jewel Garland* depicts him under the care of Yeshe Tsogyal among others. Whether visionary apparitions or local lamas who survived, these figures protected him, encouraged him with further prophecies, and helped him continue his spiritual training in secret.

Training with Rigdzin Nyima

Since his monastic training was cut short, Namtrul Rinpoche was fortunate to study surreptitiously with a local master, Lama Rigdzin Nyima. In this way, during the 1960s, he was able to receive empowerments and esoteric teachings despite the prohibition on religious practice. Rigdzin Nyima transmitted his own treasure corpus to Namtrul Rinpoche and authorized him as the trustee for his corpus of revelations. While his monastic training provided the basis for a standard course of study, Namtrul Rinpoche gained exposure to esoteric teachings within the treasure tradition through the ritual cycles of Katok and under his training with Rigdzin Nyima.

> At the age of twenty-three, once during the Male Fire Horse Year (1966–1967), for the first time he met Lama Rigdzin Nyima, the great tertön who emanated as the protector of saṃsāra. To the Master, he appeared as the guru, great Vajradhara manifest in bluish black form. Merely by meeting, realization dawned in his mindstream, and the mind of guru and disciple mingled as one. With great affection, the supreme lama and great tertön accepted him as a disciple. Rigdzin Nyima delivered a prophecy about his status as a mind emanation of the victorious lord, the Great Orgyan, and his unbroken line of emanations, including Loppön Namkhai Nyingpo, Rigdzin Jatsön Nyingpo, Tertön Nyida Sangye, Jangse Yulha Thogyur, Lhase Drala Tsegyal, and Jalse Maṇi Kara.
>
> Furthermore, from the *Crystal Mirror Symbolic Certificate*:
>
> Emanation of the minister Nyima,
> The rainbow body of Nyida Zangpo,
> The one endowed with the seven vajra qualities

> Of an auspicious buddha, an incarnation,
> His body emanates in all directions,
> His speech, the inexpressible resonance of sound,
> His mind, beyond arising and ceasing in the three times,
> He is the son, blessed by mother Tārā.

In accordance with this prophecy, Rigdzin Nyima bestowed in detail the esoteric precepts, the instructions that ripen and free, for his complete profound treasures and appointed him to be their supreme dharma trustee.

From that point onward until now, principally the Master practiced at various sacred sites and hermitages such as Sholung Gomkhang and Lhalung Bragkar.[27] He recited approximately thirteen million propitiations to the three roots and continuously offered gaṇacakra feasts. Internally, he struck the vital point of his tantric commitments in stabilizing creation and completion, thereby attaining realization along the paths and *bhūmis*. In particular, he put into practice the dharma cycles of esoteric precepts on luminosity according to Dzokchen, the Great Perfection. Purifying the patterns of intellectual fabrication and dualistic grasping, he attained spontaneous realization transcending conceptuality. Great mind treasures burst forth. Having loosened the knots in the channels at the head and throat, the transmission for teaching and propagating the sūtras and tantras of the old and new schools—as well as the orally transmitted and revealed teachings, the support for maturation and liberation—expanded forth as did the activities of the three spheres of dharma. Maintaining the continuity of the precious Buddhist teachings without faltering, he became a great holy man, holder of the teachings of all manners of dharma in an unbiased way with followers like constellations in the sky.

This is a powerful testament to Namtrul Rinpoche's realization under the worst of conditions. Somehow he managed to slip away and do extended retreats at sacred sites nearby his homeland and practice the profound teachings he had been fortunate to receive. *Jewel Garland* announces his realization in no uncertain terms and foreshadows his later acclaim by pronouncing the great number of followers "like constellations in the sky" that would eventually surround him.

Under Duress

In the early 1970s when he reached his late twenties, Namtrul Rinpoche spent two months in prison and the benevolent presence of visionary apparitions once again insured his protection. Nonetheless, this became an occasion for his own heroism to emerge. When Namtrul Rinpoche was asked by the warden to slaughter a female dzo, he refused, declaring, "Now I certainly cannot slaughter this dzo since I have taken a resolute vow never to harm even a hair of a living creature."[28] *Jewel Garland* implies that he suffered a brutal beating as a result. This story demonstrates the personal sacrifice Namtrul Rinpoche was willing to make to maintain his commitment to nonviolence and compassion. There is no miracle here, only a courageous act of maintaining integrity when the stakes for disobedience were high.

> On the twenty-fifth day of the eleventh month of the Earth Bird Year (1970), he had a vision of a ḍākinī from the sphere of wisdom, who delivered a prophecy: "Now, this time, due to previous karma and present conditions, you will enter into prison. Nonetheless, the protectors among the three roots will remain inseparable as your source of refuge and companions. You need not remain there for long."
>
> The Master explained in detail the situation to his attendant Gelek Nyima and others, and all grew distressed. When his attendant said, "I should accompany you as a way to ease the situation," he replied: "Since the two of us did not accumulate this karma together in previous lives, you may not go to prison with me. Previously, when I took rebirth as a great *geshe* (cleric-scholar) at Reting Monastery,[29] there was a fierce obstructing spirit—demonic and harmful—which I subjugated by wrathful action. Now as a result and due to conditions, I must go to prison, but not for longer than two months."
>
> Soon thereafter, on the twenty-ninth day of the eleventh month, as a misfortunate impact of the Cultural Revolution, he had to leave behind his attendant and others and, with a fellow named Nubzur Jamgön, enter into prison. Everyone talked about seeing the Master himself and that fellow surrounded by lances topped by swirling banners belonging to the protectors among the three roots as they entered prison.

At that time, the prison warden arrived leading a female dzo with cruelty. Addressing the two radiant ones, the Master and his inmate friend, he commanded: "You two must slaughter this dzo." In reply, the Master stated: "Now I certainly cannot slaughter this dzo since I have taken a resolute vow to never harm even a hair of a living creature." Witnessing a living creature like this, with not even the slightest freedom, strengthened the force of his compassion, and he made a great resolution, stating, "At Nyenlung this year, it should be forbidden to sell any weakened creature for the following day's dried meat."

Then his inmate friend also remained resolute saying, "Because we two love the dharma and do not believe in evil deeds like taking life, we are entering prison. Now I certainly will not slaughter the dzo." The warden was uncertain what to do. Because of the Master's public rank, the prison guards took particular pleasure in brutalizing and beating him.

However, the Master was free of hatred toward enemies and attachment toward friends. By the strength of precious bodhicitta naturally endowed in his mindstream, he remained peaceful, smiling and making playful comments at the prison guards for whom just the sight of the Supreme Dharma Master brought forth cruel thoughts and wickedness. After two months, he was released from prison, like the sun freed from the clouds.

When I first met him, Namtrul Rinpoche emphasized that he bore no grudge toward anyone. *Jewel Garland* likewise emphasizes that, even in the worst of circumstances, his mindstream was filled with bodhicitta, or the awakened intent to benefit all beings. The image of the sun freed from clouds upon his release further reinforces his virtuous character under duress. In this image, the unobstructed wisdom and compassion of Buddhist masters continued to shine despite the dark clouds of obstacles and hardships, the result of historical contingencies.

Miraculous Deeds

By the mid-1970s, as the age of thirty, Namtrul Rinpoche is remembered for performing small-scale but poignant miraculous feats. Though fewer in number, these are parallel to the miracle tales that permeate Tāre Lhamo's twenties and thirties as depicted in *Spiraling Vine of Faith.* Just as Tāre Lhamo had increased the amount of rice when cooking for her work unit during famine, here as secretary for his work unit, Namtrul Rinpoche miraculously multiplied the end of year allotments of butter, especially for those who did not earn enough to survive. Likewise, he performed healings and delivered prophecies to benefit his local community.

> At the age of thirty, while performing the duties of a secretary for his debilitated cooperative work unit, when dispersing the allotments at the end of the year, if a person had no more than five or six measures of butter, the Supreme Dharma Master—through conferring a tantric sky-treasury blessing—obtained for all whatever they desired when doing the allocations. By making everyone happy, he gained their admiration. Also, for a monk named Chinpal, he gave an extra measure of butter, which to his amazement lasted him many months, feeding him without end and enabling him to share it with others.
>
> Afterward, when Washul Khechok was suddenly struck by a grave illness that filled his mind with dread, his wife approached one of his relatives and requested, "Please ask the Master to perform healing rituals for his illness." He came in person to provide much guidance regarding illness. When this did not help to assuage the man's increasing dread, the Master assumed a wrathful manner and with a small knife pricked his torso, moving it back and forth, amid the sound of blood bubbling forth. As soon as he pulled the knife out, the wound spontaneously healed. When Washul Khechok awoke, he was free of illness.
>
> Next, a girl named Damme got lost on the way home to her black (yak-hair) tent. They looked for many days but did not find her. When they requested a prophecy from the Supreme Dharma Master, he said, "She isn't dead." He continued, "When you go home, make an offering to the eight classes of spirits." As a result, in the morning they found her body collapsed where the guard dog was tied. The Supreme Dharma Master gave a forceful blessing, and she slowly regained consciousness. She said that many Khampa riders carried her, dead or alive, off to a dusty mountain pass, where she came before the Lord of Death. She wept intensely as she lamented how she saw that her virtues were just about the

> size of a heap of kindling while her evil deeds were nearly the size of Mount Meru, the king of mountains.
>
> Once in the winter, when the Master was one-pointedly practicing the sādhana of Avalokiteśvara, outside across all the peaks and meadows, white flowers newly bloomed, while internally all conceptuality was purified into space. All sights, sounds, and awareness became the boundless display of the body, speech, and mind of the Great Compassionate Lotus Holder (Avalokiteśvara). At that time, the indestructible dharma protector, the Great Lion of the World (Gesar of Ling), descended in actuality and alighted without hardship. A fellow named Khedrub said that he saw a pearl held by Padmākara fall there and wondered why. The Master stated, "Do you think that he couldn't hold it?" When he threw the pearl, the pearl rose into the sky and lifted into space. He supplicated, "Please take hold of this."

The various healings that Namtrul Rinpoche performed, such as the knife healing for Washul Khechok or blessings over the weakened body of Damme, are part of the repertoire of healing practices by non-monastic ritual specialists in Golok. As fantastical as they may sound, there are oral accounts of similar feats by Tāre Lhamo and other tantric masters in the region.

Further Visions

Namtrul Rinpoche not only healed others, he himself was miraculously healed on several occasions. The most poignant occasion during this period of life involved a vision of a glamorous ḍākinī in a peacock cloak. Appearing in the sky when he was gravely ill, she descended down a crystal staircase to perform a violent healing cure, helped by a male sidekick with a large sword. Namtrul Rinpoche battled with illness much of his life, and one time he joked by saying, "My namthar is about illness." Illness likewise featured strongly in his correspondence with Tāre Lhamo, and she sent him a ritual and several locks of her own hair in order to heal him and also appeared in a vision to offer him advice about how to practice when ill.

Jewel Garland reports a curious episode at the outset of the Cultural Revolution, which presages his later teaching career. In it, Namtrul Rinpoche found two sheets of paper flying in the wind that contained a wealth sādhana by Apang Terchen. As a result of his practice, the namthar reports that the cattle and harvest were fruitful that year in his local area. This episode foreshadows his partnership with Tāre Lhamo and his recognition, later in life, as the activity emanation of Apang Terchen.[30]

> After that, when exerting himself in practice at Lalung Cave, he was struck by a grave illness. At the brink of being unable to remain, the Supreme Dharma Master had a vision of a ḍākinī who extended a crystal staircase to him. She was a white ḍākinī adorned in a peacock cloak and surrounded by a retinue of four ḍākinīs of the same color. From behind her, a great being with a moustache, adorned in leopard fur with a sword around his waist, approached. The ḍākinī stood next to the Supreme Dharma Master with friendliness, while the great being drew his sword and cleaved open his body. The ḍākinī took out his entrails, and the sickness was completely removed. Repairing his body, she said, "Now the sickness will not return even in the least." With a loud clap, she departed across the crystal staircase, and it appeared as if the crystal staircase retracted into the sky. After that, the illness gradually cleared.
>
> Once, the Master said to his attendant, "If these vultures are actual emanations of ḍākinīs from the sphere of wisdom, then we two should offer a gaṇacakra feast along with dough effigies; then the birds will come." While offering a gaṇacakra from the profound *chöd* practice, vultures who were emanations of the five classes of ḍākinīs arrived and enjoyed the effigies without leaving anything. On that occasion, he received a crystal casket as a treasure from Rakre Zhongko and set down a sādhana of Yeshe Tsogyal.[31] He conferred the aspirational empowerment and entrustment onto his attendant among others.[32]
>
> One evening in the Male Fire Horse Year (1966–1967), in the luminous appearances of a dream, the northern treasure-revealer Rigdzin Gödem appeared in person in front of the Supreme Dharma Master within a massive expanse of rainbow light and stated: "You and I share the same ground of emanation. In the future you will bestow on fortunate individuals the empowerment and authorization for the entirety of the profound treasures of the Apang Terchen Orgyan Trinley Lingpa. This will be sufficient if the continuity of the empowerment and authorization no longer

remains." Saying that he entrusted him with a sādhana (from Apang Terchen's corpus). With regards to the *Oḍḍiyāna Wealth Deity Sādhana*, when the Master wondered, "Is it permissible to practice this?" instantaneously he had a vision of the golden Oḍḍiyāna wealth deity holding a jewel and scripture in his hands, who said, "Because you have been introduced to this wealth sādhana, by practicing it, you will never be bereft of wealth."

After a few days, when he traveled to the village Kromkyil Lam along with several other people, two sheets of paper with writing on them were blowing in the wind and fell on his lap. Upon examination, this was the short wealth sādhana of Apang Terchen Orgyan Trinley Lingpa. The Master was extremely pleased. In order to eradicate destitution in his locale and the region as a whole, he devoted himself to practicing the sādhana one-pointedly. As a result it rained throughout the region. Spontaneous treasures of good fortune and wealth burst forth, such as a good harvest and healthy cattle. Many such signs of accomplishment appeared in actuality.

Also, at one point, the second section of the great sādhana of the eight command deities descended as treasure. He brought this before Lama Rigdzin Nyima, who said, "Last night I had a dream that you would bring me a second section, saying this is the treasure allotment of Khordong Terchen."[33] Then the Master said, "Is this it?" and offered him the text. Rigdzin Nyima replied, "That's it! This must be his treasure allotment."

Afterward, with respect to that, he performed great benefit, tangible and intangible, through various visions, prophecies, symbolic letters on yellow scrolls, treasure caskets, higher perceptions, and the inconceivable display of miraculous powers. But concerned with taking up too much space, this will have to suffice for the time being.

Author Pema Ösal Thaye chose to end the section on Namtrul Rinpoche's youth with this one episode out of chronological sequence in order to highlight his visionary propensities and treasure revelations prior to his courtship with Tāre Lhamo.

Letters of Tāre Lhamo

At this point, Tāre Lhamo makes a formidable entrance into Namtrul Rinpoche's life story. *Jewel Garland* includes excerpts from a dozen of her letters to announce the prophetic nature of their union. Here I include the excerpted portion either in full or in part to give a flavor of the prophetic passages included in his namthar.[34] In order to avoid duplication of much material, with longer passages, I refer the reader to the appropriate page number in this book where the letter continues.

> On the seventh day of the Rabbit Month of the Earth Horse Year (1978), the ḍākinī Tāre Devī (Khandro Tāre Lhamo), who is the human manifestation of the noble queen Yeshe Tsogyal, sent the Supreme Dharma Master symbolic certificates in letters indicating that the time had come to activate the entrustment conceived as deeds and aspirations made together before the proprietor of profound treasures, the victorious lord, the Great Orgyan.
>
> From her Letter 1:
>
> To the tulku of Namkhai Nyingpo,
> Free from extremes, removed from worldly concerns,
> In the dream of dependently arisen phenomena,
> There is nothing for the mind to gauge.
> In alpha-pure naked awareness-emptiness,
> No distortions from thoughts, good or bad, remain.
> (continued on p. 81)
>
> From her Letter 3:
>
> May prosperity and glory proliferate, benefitting the Land of Snow.
> May the lamp of the Buddhist teachings blaze in dark lands in the ten directions.
> May auspiciousness and the ten virtues pervade the three worlds.
> May coincidence click into place, completely victorious in all directions.
>
> From her Letter 6:

North, at the opening of Trachugmo Pass,
Recalling what we've discussed,
Reflecting again, it becomes clear in mind,
I recall vividly as if carved in stone.

Friend, at the top right of the ravine, there is a letter.
If you look at the dhāraṇī seed syllable, you will understand.
Now, the time has come. What is hidden cannot remain so.
(continued on p. 97)

From her Letter 9:

In our past lives, at the Rasatrul Temple (Jokhang),
Deeds and aspirations were performed by five heroes together:
Padma Do-ngak, who accomplished the welfare of all;
Hayagrīva, who propagated the thirteen profound treasures;
Dorje Tumpo, who magically subdued the foreign army;
Drime Lodrö, supreme in mastery over longevity,
The one named Tse, the favorable condition for revealing terma;
And the supreme consort with convergent aspirations.
(continued on p. 112)

From her Letter 11:

If karma and aspiration can be activated in time,
There are allotments in thirteen lands and districts.
When the *mewa* of vitality reaches the seventh island,[35]
The means to liberate manifests through our own treasures.
To accomplish the path, rely on the treasure certificates!
What a glorious occasion, as if millions of petals were to bloom.

From her Letter 12:

In the great city of a vast open country,
Where the golden mountaintop meets the sun,

In the south, where the elephant bears jewels on its back,
Treasures arise to satisfy the needs and wants of all.
(continued on p. 120)

From her Letter 13:

During our previous lives at Butsal Serkhang,[36]
The empowerment of profound command
was repeatedly bestowed,
Creating the coincidence for our karma and aspirations
to converge.

Our flowers of profound command fell together,[37]
When Padma bestowed the aspirational entrustment.[38]

From her Letter 17:

E e! In a previous life, to the east in India,
The male consort was all-knowing Jñānamati,[39]
The female life-bestowing Śridevī from Madhya,[40]
They dredged the depths for beings connected to them.

Just so are our conjoined deeds and aspirations,
Youthful companion, Namkhai Nyingpo.
Although the many coincidences are good,
At present, vicious heretics obstruct us.
(continued on p. 149)[41]

From her Letter 23:

At the sacred site, the golden cliff at Gyalrong,
At the center of its base, like an arrow feather,
Is the destined lot of Nam-Nying's emanation,[42]
Appearing at the sublime citadel of Jangyul.[43]

From her Letter 27:

A *nāga* princess bearing a necklace of jewels
Offered a symbolic certificate written in golden letters.
If there's no impediment, benefit will spread in the six
realms,
Bringing solace to beings across billions of domains.[44]

From her Letter 29:

In the powerful Monkey Year (1980),
At the perfect place, a naturally arrayed retreat,
To see, here, recall, and touch the sole refuge and protector,
The maṇḍala of immaculate dharma and great bliss opens
With a retinue of manifold male and female warriors,
To dredge the depths of the realms to guide beings.
An unmistaken method, hold it in the heart like a jewel.

To the south, at Dzatra Chakyung, the *garuḍa* forest,
Beneath, a symbolic certificate to tame the nāgas and spirits,
Between, at the jeweled treasure gate in the golden valley,
There is a treasure casket of the mighty Mahākāla,
Jewels on leather in the shape of a vajra.
To the west, at the glorious site of heaped ruby lotuses,
There is the vitality sādhana of the deathless protector Pema Karpo,
For transforming the body into an adamantine fortress beyond birth and death.

To the north, at Drakar Namchak, in the shape of a trident,
To destroy perverted views with the lion's roar of dharma,
In a casket with three offerings of vaiḍūrya heaped at the center,
Is hidden the sādhana of the lion-headed ḍākinī;
There are yellow scrolls containing symbols without breaks.
If the timing and conditions are right to decode the symbols,
The murky and poisonous northern lake will drain from its base.

From her Letter 31:

The joyful countenance of the maṇḍala of the mighty Hayagrīva,
Opens the symbolic gate of the noble queen Varjravārāhī.
The treasure casket in the form of a glorious knot of eternity
Is the allotment of the pair of us when the time is right.

> These letters were sent to the dharma master and great tertön with various symbolic certificates indicating that the time is right to gain dominion over the profound treasures of the victorious lord, the Great Orgyan.

These excerpts from Tāre Lhamo's letters draw attention to their past lives together and the locations of treasures awaiting them in the Tibetan landscape. These are key facets of their partnership, but not the whole story. In addition to prophecies and past life recollections, the correspondence contains love songs, folk imagery, heroic declarations, and tantric innuendos. All these point to their compatibility in different ways. For example, they used Tibetan imagery to illustrate their mutual reliance—as a snow lion relies on its mountain abode or a juniper berry on its branch—while their mastery of tantric techniques was necessary for them to access the visionary content of treasures as a couple. Indeed, their karma and aspiration from previous lives drew them together, but so did feelings of affection in this life. These complementary aspects of their courtship come out more fully in the translations of letters that follow.

Destined Partners

Namtrul Rinpoche received further confirmation regarding their connections over lifetimes in visions that indicated he would soon encounter a partner who is an emanation of Yeshe Tsogyal. Other great masters from the region lent their voices in support of his union with Tāre Lhamo through prophecies. This section ends with his journey to Markhok to spend a brief sojourn with her and her relatives, narrated through excerpted letters.

> On the twenty-fifth day of the sixth month of the Earth Horse Year (1978), he had a luminous vision of the Great Lion (Gesar), sovereign of the world, arriving in person, wearing armor and a helmet, and surrounded by a retinue. Leading the Master into a shrine room with many ritual bells lined up in all directions—left and right, front and back, the precious Great Lion said, "All these were in the presence of the Great Orgyan, the victorious lord. Choose the one from among these who was your female partner connected to you in previous lifetimes and with whom you conceived aspirations together." Accordingly, as he was about to choose from

among the bells, one was especially grand and blazing with light. It rose up into the sky and landed in the Master's lap, simultaneously transforming into a red Yeshe Tsogyal.

Again one evening, he had a vision of the Orgyan couple (Padmasambhava and Yeshe Tsogyal) in which Yeshe Tsogyal bore a sad expression on her face. The Master inquired, "Whenever I have had a vision of the Orgyan couple, you always appear joyful, yet tonight you bear a sad expression. Why?"

The noble queen Yeshe Tsogyal herself replied, "Not long from now you will fall gravely ill. By the power of previous deeds, although it will be difficult to reverse, I will come in person to nurse you back to health."

When he told his attendant, his attendant asked the reason, "How is it possible that Yeshe Tsogyal will nurse you to health in person?"

He replied, "This is a sign that later I will converge with a genuine emanation of Yeshe Tsogyal, Khandro Tāre Devī."

Thereafter, the lord of siddhas Lama Pelo, a relative of Dodrupchen Rinpoche Rigdzin Jalu Dorje, stated, "Because you were the Gyalrong Namtrul in previous lives, the two of us have strong connections from the past. And for the same reason, Khandro Tāre Lhamo is your karmic female partner across lifetimes; she is like an intermediary key for you. Now it is time for me to depart for another realm. Later on, if the two of you reside together, it will bring positive, restorative benefit to the teachings and beings."

After several days, Lama Pelo departed for another realm. On that occasion, the Master had a vision of the Jetsun, noble Tārā, who appeared in the center of rainbow clouds in the sky. As she gazed toward the expanse of the sky, pointing her finger, he witnessed the lama, amid flowers and rainbow clouds of five-colored lights, being guided across a rainbow pathway made of silken rope by an inconceivable gathering of ḍākinīs from the sphere of wisdom.

Also, once the Master went to meet the supreme Rigdzin Sangngak Lingpa, alias Sera Yangtrul Rinpoche Tsultrim Gyatso, the precious great tertön who emanated in the guise of a primordial protector and spiritual friend. On that occasion, the great tertön and precious lama said with great delight, "Naturally, the two of us came together from Zangdok Palri. Last night I visited Zangdok Palri, and Yeshe Tsogyal sent this as encouragement to you." Giving him many kinds of delicious sweets such as celestial jewels made of sugar, he said, "I had a vision of the protectress Tseringma in which your constant companion across lifetimes has been Khandro Tāre Lhamo. Based on this prophecy, if you two converge together, it is certain to accomplish great benefit for the teachings and beings."

Next, the Supreme Dharma Master received in his mind a symbolic prophecy from the mother ḍākinīs which he offered as a letter in reply. Reflecting on the declarations made by lamas and in his visions that if the two of them converge at a single seat, it is certain to accomplish great benefit, he exhorted the Supreme Khandro for further treasure certificates as follows.

From his Letter 3:

> E ma! Lake-born Lama, embodiment of all buddhas,
> And Princess of Karchen, who engenders bliss-emptiness wisdom,
> Bless us to be beyond meeting and parting in great bliss,
> And bestow good fortune and glorious auspiciousness.
>
> Noble one with shared karma and aspirations across all lives,
> Like the full moon, the beloved as radiant as a heart drop,
> Eternal constant companion, Dewe Dorje,
> I marvel at your letters and illuminating words.
>
> In a state of shyness, I never have encountered such words,
> Because of your great affection, I feel emboldened.
> Even if you won't rely on the speech of a reckless man,
> I imagine offering flowers of unwavering wondrous speech.
> (continued on p. 91)

Also, from the treasure certificate, *The Luminous Torch*, of Garra Gyalse Padma Tsewang:[45]

> According to a letter from the north in the Horse Year,
> There is one with the name "Tā," a smiling tigress by birth,
> At Tsizhung near the lake in Markhu (alt. Markhok).[46]

If one meets with her, the two benefits are accomplished
And the hundred gates of magnetizing activity will open.

Moreover, from a prophetic certificate of Apang Terchen Orgyan Trinley Lingpa about the twenty-five sacred sites:

In the hidden land of Do, a maṇḍala of three crescent moons are heaped,
And the arrangement of the twenty-four sites is perfectly complete.
At the site that convenes the millions of mother ḍākinīs,
Which is no different from Padmasambhava's palace Lotus Radiance,[47]
Will arise the emanational dance of the Protector Guru couple,[48]
The method and wisdom pair named Abhaya and Tāre.[49]
If they are able to come together based on deeds and aspirations,
They will spread treasures and teachings, old and new, in the ten directions.

In this way, the concordance of various treasure prophecies from the victorious lord Padmākara indicated with abundant clarity that the time for the entrustment in accord with deeds and aspirations had arrived.

Thus the Supreme Dharma Lord along with his attendant Gelek Nyima set off to visit the Khandro. All along the route there was a tremendous amount of snow and moreover the Master was ill, making travel difficult. For this reason, he said, "Supposing there is the coincidence up to this point, but we may not be able to go farther."

As they were about to turn around, the attendant pleaded, "By all means, we should go." Then, immediately upon entrusting themselves to the protectors from among the three roots, and the supreme lord of refuge, enormous hoof prints unlike others appeared on the path and they proceeded by following the tracks. For that reason, they traveled the rest of the way without hardship to the land of residence of the Supreme Khandro, Tsizhung in Markhu (alt. Markhok). At their meeting, the Supreme Dharma Lord stated:

OṂ, the empty nature, dharmakāya,
ĀḤ, natural clarity, the perfected saṃbhogakāya,
HŪṂ, ceaseless compassion, the nirmāṇakāya,
HRĪḤ, the Lotus-Born Guru, protect us!
In the crystal mirror, the lucid clarity of mind,
This arose as patterns, the play of appearance:

During the late spreading of Buddhism in this virtuous land,
In the joyful country Jang, among the Mukpos,[50]
At the pleasant site, Yudruk Gying Dzong,
A place of jewels, joyous and auspicious,
An emanation of the glorious Lord of Secrets arose
As the hero, Yulha Thogyur, the favorite son of Jang.[51]
(from his Letter 5, continued on p. 99)

Loving and affectionate one, radiance of my heart,
Our connection from previous lives dawns in mind.
Happy and sad, tears fall as a steady stream of rain.

In the turquoise valley of an unwavering mind,
The lotus of faith and stainless samaya blossoms,
Free from the harm of obstructing conditions like frost,
As the means, honey nectar of profound secret mantra.
(from his Letter 6, continued on p. 102)

The Supreme Khandro replied:

In a peaceful domain of enchanting lotuses,
When the five excellences naturally arise,[52]
At Dhanakośa Lake in Oḍḍiyāna,
Father, the lord and guru, Padmākara,
And the great mother, excellent Vajravārāhī,
Inseparable appearance-emptiness, beyond meeting and parting.
Reside at the crown of my head amid rainbow light.

Precious teacher, crown ornament of complete faith,
Won't you look compassionately upon us without refuge
  or protector?
Outwardly, harmed by enemies, demons, and obstructing spirits,
Inwardly, tormented from illness and the three poisons,[53]
And deceived by the confusion of conceptuality and delusion,

> Now, lacking freedom, we suffer in the city of saṃsāra.
> Omniscient precious master, please listen to my lament!
> This lowly one, your gullible daughter, offers this request;
> Please consider it in the ease of your unwavering mind.
> (from her Letter 17, continued on p. 148)[54]

This rather formal exchange shows the importance of their exalted identities and inseparability across lifetimes to their public persona as a couple. Yet it does not give a complete picture of their courtship, leaving aside for the most part the personal affection shared between Namtrul Rinpoche and Tāre Lhamo. The correspondence itself gives a fuller picture of how they forged a tantric partnership, seamlessly weaving together the personal and prophetic aspects of their relationship at this crucial juncture in modern Tibetan history.

In 1978, when Tāre Lhamo sent her first letter, the wave of communist fervor had run its course and more moderate voices in Beijing were coming to the fore. A policy of "reform and opening" set China on a course of liberalization in economic and cultural terms. By the early 1980s, the impact of this policy had reached the Tibetan plateau, and Buddhist leaders began to spearhead the reconstruction of monasteries and reconstitute Tibetan communities through large-scale teachings and rituals. In the intervening years, as they exchanged letters between 1978 and 1980, Namtrul Rinpoche and Tāre Lhamo charted their own collaborative course for revitalizing Buddhism in Golok. Their letters show resilience and courage—as well as the strength they drew from their connection across lifetimes—in order to love again and to establish anew the Buddhist teachings through their own revelations.

3. Letters of Tāre Lhamo and Namtrul Rinpoche

Tāre Lhamo | Letter 1

In the middle of the Horse Year (1978), Tāre Lhamo began an extended correspondence with Namtrul Rinpoche by sending a prophecy about their future revelations together.[1] Her first letter is formal yet direct compared to Namtrul Rinpoche's elaborate poetic reply. Tāre Lhamo refers to him by his tulku status, as the reincarnation of Namkhai Nyingpo, and his Buddhist name at the time, Pema Drime Ösal Lodrö Thaye, and her scribe signs the letter "Devī," meaning "goddess" or "lhamo" in Tibetan, the second part of her name. The letter demonstrates her knowledge of esoteric Nyingma teachings in a style that is reminiscent of a song of experience, relaying the results of meditative experience. The second half of the letter contains a prophecy about a treasure revelation awaiting them at Drakar Tredzong, a well-known Nyingma pilgrimage site in northern Amdo, and suggests rituals for them to perform at one of two sacred lakes in the Nyenpo Yutse mountain range in Golok.

On the seventh day of the Hare Month, in the Earth Horse Year of the sixteenth Tibetan era:

To the tulku of Namkhai Nyingpo,
Free from extremes, removed from worldly concerns,
In the dream of dependently arisen phenomena,
There is nothing for the mind to gauge.
In alpha-pure naked awareness-emptiness,
No distortions from thoughts, good or bad, remain.
While unobstructed experience, the cognizing aspect,
Flashes forth as the five lights manifesting wisdom,
Free from extremes of permanence or absence,

The sun of awareness, the definitive meaning, arises.
Recognizing the nature of awareness as clear light,
Just that is nonconceptual wisdom.

Through the power of our aspirations,
If coincidence makes it possible to meet,
In the powerful Monkey Year,
At the eastern Turquoise Peak's lakeshore,[2]
Sacred site of the Eight Command Sādhana,
If we are able to make aspirations together,
We will awaken the entrustment as a couple.
If we reach ten million feast offerings—
The material arrangement of five gems
Along with superior gold, silver, copper, and iron—
It is our fortune for circumstances to converge.

At the meditation site of White Cliff Monkey Fortress[3]
Are yellow scrolls of the one-hundred thousand ḍākinīs.

Offered to Pema Drime Ösal Lodrö Thaye
By Devī. Secret seal.[4]

Namtrul Rinpoche | Letter 1

Namtrul Rinpoche's reply follows formal epistolary conventions for Tibetan letter writing and uses an ornate Indic-based poetic style. He begins with elaborate praises of Tāre Lhamo as the emanation of Yeshe Tsogyal and an array of female tantric deities, while imagining himself as the lotus flower held by the bodhisattva Tārā, bowing with deference to whisper news into her ear. Namtrul Rinpoche goes on to make an extensive tribute to the Yeshe Tsogyal sādhana that Tāre Lhamo included with her first letter and concludes by asking her to send more letters like the flow of the Ganges River and wishing her long life in language reminiscent of a longevity chant to a Buddhist teacher: "May your lotus feet remain on a vajra throne." Along the way, he makes an artful innuendo with respect to their future consort relationship by referring to her as "the lady of bliss-emptiness" who is skilled in conjuring the "sport of attraction" and guiding to "the wisdom expanse of the four joys."[5] The four joys are engendered through the tantric rite of sexual union and provide access to a state of nondual bliss and the deep reaches of the mind where treasures are said to be hidden.

In the space of alpha-pure dharmakāya, Samantabhadrī,
In the realm of natural saṃbhogakāya, the mother Tāre,
Compassionate nirmāṇakāya, supreme goddess, the Lady
 of Speech (Sarasvatī):
Bear witness that the purport of aspirations by Yeshe Tsogyal—
These three aspects inseparable—be accomplished.

Before the *utpala* lotus at the ear of the celestial maiden,
Who arises as glorious among beings throughout space
From the sacred site, supreme Orgyan Khandro Ling,
Like the ornament of sun and moon adorning unadorned space,

I bow down laden with the fruit of my news,
Like the supple stem of the verdant utpala,
In a radiant lake of liquid emerald jewels;
Or an unforgettable fruit tree, blooming undamaged
In a lake of karma, aspiration and coincidence.

As soon as I heard the queen of drumbeats heralding your news,
My mind danced with delight like a peacock displaying its feathers
That the full moon of your physical elements
Is free from the harm of an eclipse.

Perfect maṇḍala of aspiration and entrustment,
The moon that increases the profound nectar,
You, special friend, swell the ocean of early translations[6]
And grace the eastern ridge with good fortune and merit.

Under the white parasol of refuge in the Three Jewels,
My physical aggregates are also comfortable at present.
When the flowers of faith, joy, and inspiration bloom,
I send a message of hope, playing a leaf flute.

A ho! The mother who gives birth to buddhas of the three times,
The embodiment of Sarasvatī, born into the family of Karchen,[7]
Intent on the teachings of secret mantra, activating the flow of realization,
Obtaining the dhāraṇī of total recall, you collected Padma's words.

The sādhana of Yeshe Tsogyal, chief among ḍākinīs,
Is the elixir of life, the core of the oral instructions,
Like a mighty wish-fulfilling queen, satisfying needs and desires,
Accompanied by a guru yoga invocation,
The best of medicine for the teachings and beings.

The manual, feast, amending and concluding rites,
All together, including the means to practice the four actions
And the empowerment, fire pūjā, offerings, and thread-cross,
Are the supreme elixir to purify downfalls, evils, and obscurations
In the worthy vase, source of blessings and siddhi.

Discovering the supreme and ordinary siddhis in this life
Is the essential heart-blood of the ḍākinīs.

In the palace of the immutable space of mind,
Resides the casket, a sphere comprised of five essences,

The supreme, profound certificate of the two knowledges.[8]
It is certain to open the treasure door of mind effortlessly.
Inheritance from the only father, the Lotus-Born Guru,[9]
It is the profound treasure, the secret elixir of mind.

The supreme Yeshe Tsogyal Sādhana Eliciting Siddhi,
Was previously entrusted to the prince Mutik Tsanpo;[10]
The best scholar and translator, the adept Namkhai Nyingpo;
And the consort of bliss-emptiness, Princess of Karchen.

Afterward, at supreme Orgyan Mindrolling,[11]
Although the aspiration and entrustment were ripe,
The coincidence to set it down was incomplete,
Even so, you clearly know this method.

Please bear in mind that I have great affection
For my inseparable companion across many lifetimes.

Just as vegetation bursts forth when spurred by the seasons,
So too with the karmic inheritance of Padma's profound treasures,
When pure deeds, aspirations, and coincidence converge.

With this message, I urge you, in the vast knot of eternity,
Please lay out the essential points to fulfill wishes and aims,
Whatever is needed to accomplish favorable conditions in this very body.
Without giving up, kindly do not forget this!

If it arises in the mind of the lady of bliss-emptiness,
Who is skilled in guiding to the wisdom expanse of the four joys,
With the iron hook that conjures the sport of attraction,
Please send letters continuously like flow of the Ganges,
Or like the dance of the sun and moon in the sky.

In this life, may your lotus feet remain on a vajra throne,
I request that the armor of your resolve never slacken.[12]

Tāre Lhamo | Letter 2

An invigorating call to action, Tāre Lhamo's second letter uses naturalistic images and Tibetan symbols of strength. In this way, she imagines them surmounting the challenges ahead by rousing their own skills and talents. In her encouragement, Tāre Lhamo acknowledges the contingency of their historical moment, suggesting that a show of strength and the proper karmic foundation are needed for them to move forward. The letter employs a folk style, called a "song of marvels" used on celebratory occasions.[13] The overall mood is optimistic.

A ho! Mirror of my heart,
Open your ears and listen to this.
A la! Dear friend, I sing a song of marvels:

On stalks of *bodhi*, the root of mind,
If the crops of virtue are not ripe,
It's difficult for Tibetans to be happy.

If the snow lion doesn't emit its valiant roar,
It's difficult to subdue the lowland beasts,
Now's the time to unfurl its mighty turquoise mane.

If the young garuḍa won't spread its sturdy wings,
It's difficult for us birds to reach the heavens
In a flight path so far across the lofty sky.

A la, how wondrous! Long life!
May the teachings spread far and wide.
May there be auspiciousness.[14]

Tāre Lhamo | Letter 3

An aspiration prayer in a single verse, this was likely not a stand-alone letter, so it is grouped together with her Letter 2 above. At one point, Namtrul Rinpoche mentioned that their letters were batched and sent by a secret messenger in batches. It was then a two-day journey by horseback between their respective homelands. Given that their correspondence is separated into two collections, his letters to her in *Adamantine Garland* and her letters to him in *Garland of Lotuses*, the ordering here is necessarily tentative. Composed in 1978, Tāre Lhamo's aspiration is for the Buddhist teachings to spread once again in the wake of the Cultural Revolution. In addition, she wishes for a host of good things, such as prosperity and auspiciousness, to similarly increase.

> May prosperity and glory proliferate, benefitting the Land of Snow.
> May the lamp of the Buddhist teachings blaze in dark lands in the ten directions.
> May auspiciousness and the ten virtues pervade the three worlds.
> May coincidence click into place, completely victorious in all directions.[15]

Namtrul Rinpoche | Letter 2

This brief letter starts with an invocation of the Nyingma progenitors Padmasambhava (here Padmākara) and Yeshe Tsogyal. Namtrul Rinpoche harkens to their past lives together and the enduring nature of their shared deeds, aspirations, and connection. He refers to Tāre Lhamo as Dewe Dorje here and elsewhere in the correspondence; this is one of the names of Sera Khandro, a female tertön of the previous generation in Golok and one of Tāre Lhamo's past-life identifications. There is a sense of urgency, as he suggests they act on the auspicious coincidence of their shared karma coming together with favorable conditions in order to reveal the "profound extract" of Padmasambhava's teachings. This extract, likely a reference to their own future treasure revelations, is attributed the power to "heal the damage to the teachings and beings" in the wake of the Cultural Revolution.[16]

Lord of victors, Padmākara, great holder of gnostic mantras,
Lady of speech, Tsogyal, who obtained the dhāraṇī of total recall,
Precious gurus, inseparable and merged into one,
Remain as witness to gaze on me with great affection.

Sublime jewel of my heart, over myriad lives,
Our deeds, aspirations, and connection are everlasting.
As the famed presence of the celestial Dewe Dorje,
You replied with a letter that resounded like a lute.

E ma! The profound extract
Of the lord of victors, Padmākara,
Is the sublime heart essence of ḍākinīs,
The wish-fulfilling jewel that heals
Damage to the teachings and beings.
The coincidence that obtains is fleeting—
Yes, yes, just at the present moment.
Afterward, we can speak of good fortune.

May your life be eternal and constant!
Three roots and protectors, please accomplish
Favorable conditions for whatever mind desires![17]

Tāre Lhamo | Letter 4

In another "song of marvels," Tāre Lhamo begins by honoring the divine above, the terrestrial guardians in between, and nāgas or water spirits below.[18] After that, she uses the parallelism specific to Tibetan folk songs to call to mind her "youthful friend," whereby "friend" can connote an amorous liaison.[19] In the final three stanzas, Tāre Lhamo depicts three auspicious things that are unforgettable. The first two provide analogies—the sacred Jowo image in Central Tibet and the melody of the cuckoo bird heralding spring—while the last stanza provides the referent, none other than her youthful friend, Namtrul Rinpoche.

On the eight day of the Dog Month, in the Earth
   Sheep Year,
Beloved, I sing a song of marvels:

In voicing it, I invoke the sound of a flute,
Making each word into vajra speech.
As a result of such words, I draw in the silk cord.

Ya la! When I saw Lhasa with my own eyes,
Did I meet the golden face of the Jowo?
Please grant your blessings, Lord Jowo.

Today, I sing a song to the divine above,
The divine I sing to is the sublime Three Jewels.
The referent of my song is the virtuous companion.
May glorious dharma spread throughout the world.

Today, I sing a song to the mighty one,
The mighty one I sing to is the sublime Drala Takmar,
The meaning of my song is the virtuous companion.
May glorious dharma spread throughout the world.

Today I sing to the serpentine spirits below,
The meaning of my song is the Wish-Fulfilling Jewel,
The treasure to dispel the misery of all beings.

When traveling among dharma assemblies in Lhasa,
Meeting, meeting the golden face of the Jowo,
I cannot forget the potency of the Lord's blessing.

When wandering among thickets of juniper bush,
Warbling, warbling, the call of the cuckoo bird,
I cannot forget the tune of its melodious song.

When meandering in the sublime six districts of Ling,
Sustained, sustained by the affection of a youthful friend,
I can never forget your unwavering mind.[20]

Namtrul Rinpoche | Letter 3

In his reply, Namtrul Rinpoche shows off his mastery of ornate poetic style. This style is based on the influential Indian classic, the *Kāvyādarśa* by Daṇḍin, which became a prestigious model for Tibetan poetry over the centuries. Marveling at the affection expressed in her letters, Namtrul Rinpoche artfully shifts from an Indian scene of a lotus grove with a bee enjoying nectar to an eighth-century tantric context at Samye, Tibet's first Buddhist temple. There he conjures up the scene of a tantric initiation in the which the couple, in their previous lives as Namkhai Nyingpo and Yeshe Tsogyal, receive the prophetic entrustment of treasures from Padmasambhava. Referring to the "consort who liberates through touching,"[21] he alludes to the tantric rite of sexual union, said to open access to the depths of mind and treasures stored therein. Asking Tāre Lhamo if she remembers too, he casts her in a gendered role as the "supreme consort who gives rise to the wisdom of bliss-emptiness" even though in their later partnership they contributed equally to the revelation process.[22]

E ma! Lake-Born Lama, embodiment of all buddhas,
And Princess of Karchen, who engenders bliss-emptiness wisdom,
Bless us to be beyond meeting and parting in great bliss,
And bestow good fortune and glorious auspiciousness.

Noble one with shared karma and aspirations across all lives,
Like the full moon, the beloved as radiant as a heart drop,
Eternal constant companion, Dewe Dorje,[23]
I marvel at your letters and illuminating words.

In a state of shyness, I never have encountered such words.
Because of your great affection, I feel emboldened.
Even if you won't rely on the speech of a reckless man,
I imagine offering flowers of unwavering wondrous speech.

In the azure sky, a vast expanse of vaiḍūrya,
When the smiling sun emits rays of radiant emptiness,
The utpala blooms as a smiling white lotus,
Emitting the fragrant perfume of causation and coincidence.

In the vast terrain of a splendid turquoise meadow,
Newly sprouted plants blossom into a lotus grove of delight.
The bee who sings a melody of six-fold tones enjoys
Sweet dew of honey nectar, its legacy from the past.

At the profound, secret, eternal, and glorious palace of Samye,
The master Padmākara and disciples, lord and subjects,
Assembled for a feast of *vidyādharas* and ḍākinīs.
Do you recall the samaya of the initiation, aspiration, and entrustment,
When the elixir was distributed at this festival of great secret dharma?

Illustrious disciple Chokgyur Nubchen Namkhai Nyingpo
And Yeshe Tsogyal, who attained the dhāraṇī of total recall,
Actualized bliss-emptiness, the wisdom of the four joys,
Through the profound dharma of Anuyoga, the shortcut
Of union with a consort that liberates through touch,
Sublime path of means to ripen the illusory body into divine form.

Do you recall the conferral of the fine vase of profound elixir?
The Great Orgyan, Lord of Victors, Great Holder of Gnostic Mantras,
Thereby bestowed the garland of eternal, adamantine command.
Please protect the samaya unimpaired over all lifetimes like an eye.
May we be forever blessed not to be separated, even for a moment.

In the future, in the Zalmo range of Do Kham,[24]
At the time of the Earth Tiger Year, when the sun is near,
To amend faults of weak samaya and coincidence—
External conditions of barbarians, internal conditions of torpidity—
It's key to recite the OṂ YE DHARMA mantra 100,000 times
And perform atoning rites and feasts as needed.

In the Month of Taurus in the year to accomplish all aims,
When the auspicious day arises, offer a ḍākinī feast. If performed,

It will awaken the power of deeds, wishes, coincidence, and the
entrustment.
At that time, in the east at the turquoise lake, in a jewel casket, is:
The Secret Path of Four Joys, the Profound Extract, Bliss-Emptiness.[25]

In time, a prophecy of the ḍākinīs will arise,
When acquired in hand, it is vital to keep it secret.
Like a tree of paradise growing on the golden earth,
It is the oath of the ḍākinīs, accomplishing our wishes.
This is their final testament etched in gold.

Keep this in mind, sublime companion Dewe Dorje,
The iron hook that transforms the channels and winds
With the blazing and stirring of bliss and joy.
You guide to the wisdom expanse of the four joys, great bliss,
Supreme consort who gives rise to the wisdom of bliss-emptiness;
Blissful one, how wondrous that you reside in the Zalmo Range.

Just as the golden-eyed fish and verdant lake are inseparable,
And vultures and white cliffs overlooking valleys are inseparable,
And the radiant sun and moon in the azure sky are inseparable,
Due to the initiation, aspiration, and samaya, we can never be
separated.

The Lake-Born Guru is the nature of skillful means, the apparent
aspect;
And Tsogyal, the wisdom ḍākinī, is knowledge, and the empty
aspect;
Their nondual union is the supreme child, the play of great bliss.
E ho! This is the maṇḍala of great purity and equality, vessel
and contents.

Your lovely face that enhances the youthful splendor of wisdom
Is like a crystal wish-fulfilling jewel, smiling with loving
affection.
Please send letters in a steady stream of moonbeams and elixir,
Bestow 100,000 resplendent light rays to merge our minds as one.

Friend, my inseparable companion until awakening
With the power to heal all the damage to the teachings and beings,
May we become sublimes guides to lead anyone connected to us,
Whether by good or bad, especially the host of *māras*.[26]

From the lowly Pema Drime Lodrö.[27]

Tāre Lhamo | Letter 5

Opening this letter in a more ornate style, Tāre Lhamo describes the emotional impact of hearing Namtrul Rinpoche's letter read aloud to her. His words are compared to sonorous music and the melodic strum of a lute, filling her with delight. As elsewhere, images of fertility convey good fortune, such as thunder, rain, and the blooming lotuses of their shared intention. A flirtatious tone emerges as Tāre Lhamo shifts into a folk style midway, flashing "sidelong glances" toward him and characterizing their courtship as a sport or even a hunt.[28] For this, she uses the image of the tigress—referring to her birth in the Earth Tiger Year of 1938—which circles the monkey, referring to his birth in the Wood Monkey Year of 1944.

On the tenth day of Sagadawa in the Earth Sheep Year—

E ma! A fresh day, the new moon brandishes a smile
Emitting sonorous music of delight and affection.
Hearing your message so agreeable and pleasing to mind,
May the bud of our aspiration to meet bear fruit!

The echoing rumble of thunder without end,
Our intentions, like an array of lotuses, bloom.
Bright lights spread across the earth in ten directions;
The deep waters swirl in rings in the turquoise lake.

The dance and play of the water-born goddess Sarasvatī
Issues a scented mist of offerings of the five sense enjoyments.
In a cleansing pool possessing the eight pure qualities,
Our good fortune playfully rains down as a shared lot.

If one knows how to draw out the elixir of esoteric instructions,
Its profound essence liberates into a body of light in
one life.

Joy like a bird circling the pleasant scent of a tree
Elicits the rustle of leaves, a mind invigorated in response.

Sweet, sweet words, I am delighted by the sound.
Flashing, flashing sidelong glances to your virtuous face.

Dear, dear, the clouds of mind are cleared by your affection.
Melodic lute, I always love the sound of its strum.

Circling, circling, the mind of the tigress circles the monkey.
The wheel of yogic practice is the root of joyful bliss.[29]

May you enjoy bliss-emptiness that perfects the six elements![30]
Sukha writes to the secret friend Mati.[31]

Tāre Lhamo | Letter 6

From their exchanges, Tāre Lhamo describes inspiration bubbling in her mind that allows for a profound clarity and gives rise to the process of visionary recollection. This letter indicates a treasure awaiting them on the side of a cliff at Trachugmo Pass to the north. In this sense, it is similar to a treasure certificate, which provides the location of a treasure in the landscape awaiting the one destined to reveal it.[32] This particular treasure is characterized as a vast casket, the contents of which has the power to "reverse the strife of degeneration."[33] Tāre Lhamo emphasizes that the time has come for the two of them to join together and awaken the entrustment of Padmasambhava, given long ago in their past lives as Yeshe Tsogyal and Namkhai Nyingpo.

Within the palace of ravishing joy, for the guest
Who makes the mind bubble with inspiration,
I sing a song from the depths of my heart:

North, at the opening of Trachugmo Pass,
Recalling what we've discussed,
Reflecting again, it becomes clear in mind,
I recall vividly as if carved in stone.

Friend, at the top right of the ravine, there is a letter.
If you look at the dhāraṇī seed syllable, you will understand.
Now, the time has come. What is hidden cannot remain so.

Within the white cliff is a golden casket of nectar.
Above at Trazhung, it is hidden as treasure,
Now at this time, if we make effort in offerings
To the assembly of ḍākinīs, great benefit will occur.

Now, to obtain the inheritance of Padmasambhava,
The time has come for the entrustment of us pair of friends.
Now if we proceed according to his command, it is good.

In the vast casket of the inner sanctum of the mind
Is the heart certificate of the 100,000 mother ḍākinīs,
Expressly the means to reverse the strife of degeneration.

In a punctuation-free missive in ḍākinī script,
Definitely there is a prophecy of the ḍākinīs.
Friend, it is the key of the vidyādharas![34]

Namtrul Rinpoche | Letter 5

As one of his past lives, Namtrul Rinpoche links himself to the lore of King Gesar of Ling through the figure of the Prince of Jangyul. Yulha Thogyur was a "converted hero,"[35] meaning that he became a leader in Gesar's army during the conquest of his own kingdom Jangyul. In this letter, framed as spontaneously arising from the "crystal mirror, the lucid clarity of mind,"[36] Namtrul Rinpoche further links Yulha Thogyur to the process of treasure revelations, discovering weapons and tantric teachings with the beauty Metok Lhadze as his consort. In the epic, Metok Lhadze is a princess from Mön to the south, another kingdom conquered by Gesar, and one of Tāre Lhamo's past-life identifications in their correspondence. Fast-forwarding to the present, he predicts several treasures to be revealed with Tāre Lhamo.

OṂ, the empty nature, dharmakāya,
ĀḤ, natural clarity, the perfected saṃbhogakāya,
HŪṂ, ceaseless compassion, the nirmāṇakāya,
HRĪḤ, the Lotus-Born Guru, protect us!
In the crystal mirror, the lucid clarity of mind,
This arose as patterns, the play of appearance:

During the late spreading of Buddhism in this virtuous land,
In the joyful country Jang, among the Mukpos,[37]
At the pleasant site, Yudruk Gying Dzong,
A place of jewels, joyous and auspicious,
An emanation of the glorious Lord of Secrets arose
As the hero, Yulha Thogyur, the favorite son of Jang.[38]

From the kingdom of Lodrak to the Chinese city of Trithung,
Their troops fell and were consolidated under control.
In mid-life he became a "converted hero" of Ling,
Made the leader of the thirteen fallen districts.[39]
Late in life, he practiced the two stages of meditation.[40]
Whoever has a karmic connection, he leads to Ngayab Palri.[41]

First, the pleasant valleys of Jangyul,
Second, the great fortune of its 10,000 people,

Third, the son Yulha Thogyur, brave and fierce,
Their convergence is the legacy of our forefathers.

In Mön, at the jeweled treasure door at Sheldrak,
He retrieved a variety of armor, helmets, and weapons,
As precious treasure, along with a seven-faceted jewel
And thirteen caskets of precious substances.
He set down the tantra, *Essential Drop of Molten Gold*,[42]
And four *Nyingtik* cycles of profound dharma.[43]

At the time of receiving teachings and initiations
From the protector Padmasambhava in a previous life,
Deeds, aspirations, and the entrustment were sown
Together with a supreme emanation of noble Tārā.

As the lady of Mön, the divine beauty Metok Lhadze,
She became a consort on the meditative path of bliss-emptiness,
Providing the key to the dharma of profound secret mantra,
Releasing the entrustment of profound nectar of oral
instructions.

With blissful-bodied lady of Mön, Metok Lhadze,
At the renowned mountain gorge, Takrong,[44]
The hero, Yulha Thogyur performed benefit.
Accomplishing the wishes of the great lion, Gesar of Ling,
He turned the lands of Jang and Mön toward the noble dharma,
Spreading the teachings of scripture and realization indivisible
And practicing the profound skillful means of secret mantra,
Leading those karmically connected to Dhumathala.[45]

Connected by samaya, inseparable through all time and lives,
Beloved companion, in the confluence of bliss and joy,
Now, at this time, in the Zalmo Range of Do Kham,
Together let us awaken deeds, aspiration and entrustment,
Quickly and powerfully during the Monkey Year.

To the east, at the lake shore of the Turquoise Peak,
If we are able to make sublime aspirations together

And offer 100,000 feasts to the Padmākara couple,
We will receive a casket of fivefold precious substances,
And thirteen repositories of profound *Yangtik* teachings.

Through the power of yogic exercises to elicit the four joys,
Bliss-emptiness, the sprout of Nuden's emanation is matured,[46]
And torrential storms are quelled by Phurba.[47]
When the jewel possessing the power of nāgas is offered
By one named Akyung Dharma to the north,
Favorable coincidence arises to accomplish aims.

When the ears of the guard dogs perk up,[48]
In order to purify the stains of faults and downfalls,
The sādhana of Vajrasattva and its ancillary rites
Descend from the maṇḍala of the vast expanse of mind.

He will found retreat hermitages in the thirteen districts
And, each day, give teachings on the deity Vajrasattva.
Twenty-five fortunate disciples will gather
To pursue the path of liberation according to their connection.

For a brief moment, these symbols self-manifest just so.
As they unfold, vital aims and needs will gradually be clear.
Then the potent vision in symbols dissolve into space.
Hold these words in mind as a knot of eternity. That is all.[49]

Namtrul Rinpoche | Letter 6

Namtrul Rinpoche ventures to express his affection more fully for Tāre Lhamo in his sixth letter, calling her "loving and affectionate one."[50] He stakes a claim to spontaneous composition in this regard, referring to himself as an "impetuous madman" who scribbles whatever arises in mind.[51] The letter is full of praises for her and indicates his overwhelming emotion at realizing their connection through past lives together. There are several tantric references as Namtrul Rinpoche characterizes the two of them as "spiritual supports": her as the "lovely goddess of emptiness" and himself as "supreme method, the vajra liberating all."[52] One of the standard phrases to describe tantric consorts is "method and wisdom" in union,[53] where the female represents wisdom and the male method or skillful means. Though supports to each other, Tāre Lhamo is positioned in the role of the consort here, as the one who increases his life, merit, and sphere of influence.

Loving and affectionate one, radiance of my heart,
Our connection from previous lives dawns in mind.
Happy and sad, tears fall as a steady stream of rain.

In the turquoise valley of an unwavering mind,
The lotus of faith and stainless samaya blooms,
Free from the harm of obstructing conditions like frost,
As the means, honey nectar of profound secret mantra.

An array of disciples and attendants
Is the wish of the unequalled father guru,
The aspiration of protector Orgyan Padma,
The oath of mother warriors and ḍākinīs.

These are scribbles, whatever arose in mind,
By the slightly impetuous madman priest, Tse.
Incomparable friend, Tarpo, steady in intent,[54]
Please speak frankly, whatever comes to mind, no secrets!

With shared karma and wishes, we are spiritual supports:
The peerless companion, lovely goddess of emptiness,
And the supreme method, the vajra liberating all.

By the power of your immeasurable kindness,
My life, merit and sphere of influence are increased.
Faith is an ever-ripening of fruit on the tree of compassion.

E ma ho! As the result of the two benefits
One obtains the jewel of the twofold noble family.[55]
Friend, even though I don't mean to flatter you,
The meaning is: you have special qualities.

May your eternal body be protected by Amitāyus,
Your unceasing speech sustained by Sarasvatī,
Your unwavering mind guarded by Vajrapāni.[56]
May all your aims, wishes, and desires be fulfilled![57]

Tāre Lhamo | Letter 7

This is a short and sweet letter. Perhaps in response to Namtrul Rinpoche's request for her to speak frankly, Tāre Lhamo confesses to missing him a hundred times a day. Once again, she links her fondness for him to the clarity of mind able to recall their past lives and the location of future revelations. While acknowledging that their separation across province borders is unbearable, Tāre Lhamo gestures to their inseparability across lifetimes. For this reason, she states, sadness is not warranted. They need only trust the command of Padmasambhava and oath of the ḍākinīs while striving to fulfill their aim to be together.

> One hundred times a day,
> I recall the spiritual support;
> My congenial friend comes to mind.
> The sketch of past lives becomes clearer;
> Mind yearning, my fondness increases.
>
> "Separation" is like the heart being ripped out.
> Ah! It is just so. But there is no need to be sad.
> Hold in your heart the oath of the mother ḍākinīs.
> We must respect the Lord Padma's command.

May the sublime three jewels and guardians bless the congenial friend so that our wishes may be fulfilled.[58]

Tāre Lhamo | Letter 8

In this letter paired with her seventh above, Tāre Lhamo encourages Namtrul Rinpoche to visit her as the natural unfolding of their karmic connection. There is a musical quality, following a folk song style of eight syllables per line in couplets, with the added syllables *la* and *so* after the first and third syllable respectively. In the translation, I add the syllable "oh" mid-sentence in the second line of each couplet to create a comparable effect. The song is playful with images of fertility, imagining Namtrul Rinpoche first as a bee circling a lotus to enjoy its nectar and later as a monkey finding its dwelling place among the treetops, satisfying itself on the fruit. The nectar of a lotus is then homologized to the elixir inside the vase at a tantric initiation, which she invites them to enjoy together. This appears to be a sexual innuendo, implying the tantric practice of sexual union and linked to the generation of "inner heat" or *caṇḍālī*.[59] Overall, there is an upbeat tone and a sense of auspiciousness in the fulfillment of their aspirations.

Setting forth, friend? Do we have the chance to meet?
I am the maiden, oh, dispatched by the ancestors.

Without summons, the guest comes in the turning of karma.
Pining away, oh, I offer some words in a ditty:

Radiance of the past, it is heaven above.
Young friend, oh, Yuyi Lathöcan,[60]

In a pleasant grove, where we meet together,
With sweet speech, oh, I recall the lute strum.

With affection, now again, I recall our aim.
The distance is not far. Oh, I hope we meet soon!

Gold mountain, it bears a golden victory banner.
Radiance of the past, oh, it is our soul mountain.[61]

These days, it is behind the mountain, Roglo.
Friend, we two, oh, our aspirations converge!

Mind delighted! Now again, I recall our wish.
Auspicious valley, oh a lotus grove of delight.

Lotus juice, when longing to enjoy the nectar:
Hey you, the bee! Oh, if you circle, bliss!

In my mind, the etchings become clearer.
Do you recall? Oh, talk straight—no secrets!

At summer's onset, the dragon's rolling thunder;
Raindrops fall, oh seasonal rains, *tha la la*!

Yellow-hued gold, is the vase yours?
Splendid peacock, oh, its feather eye is mine.

Inside, fine juice. We sip the elixir together.
Means, bliss-empty, oh, it is caṇḍālī blazing.

White eastern tiger, its *bindu* of six stripes spreads.
Vast fortress of trees, oh, its leaves proliferate.

Life, merit, the Buddhist teachings, may they flourish!
The aim of us friends, oh, coincidence will fulfill it.

Above the white cliff, I am its changeless peak,
Dwelling place, oh, of the white-breasted vulture.

On the tips of trees, circling the cliff,[62]
Dwelling place, oh, of the powerful monkey.

Enjoying the fruit at the top, that is freedom;
When sated, oh, it is a festival of coincidence.

Your changeless body, may it be protected by Amitāyus.
Your ceaseless speech, may it be sustained by Sarasvatī.

Your unwavering mind, may it by guarded by Vajrapāni.
Auspicious joy, oh, may the good signs proliferate![63]

Namtrul Rinpoche | Letter 7

While delighted by her tidings, Namtrul Rinpoche appears unable to make the journey to her homeland in Padma County at this point. In the opening of his seventh letter, he describes his illness and requests help in an extended lament and supplication to Padmasambhava (referred to here as Padmākara) and Yeshe Tsogyal, mentioned in the opening as the Princess of Karchen. In the second half of the letter, he records a vision of Tāre Lhamo appearing to give him advice in the form of her previous incarnation, Sera Khandro, also known as Dewe Dorje. She is thereby exalted as a teacher and also placed in the role of consort who can help extend his life and health. The advice ends with a prophecy about their future treasures and coded warnings about potential obstacles in their midst.

E ho! How wondrous, this flower of your tidings.
Born on the great plains of intention, a turquoise valley,
On the ocean of mind, the basis of radiant clarity,
Are waves of thoughts, patterns of expressive power.

My nose bleeds profusely. While remaining, not knowing what to do, this arose in mind:

Kye kye, the blissful father, the guru Padmākara,
And the Princess of Karchen, mother giving birth to
bliss-emptiness,
In actuality, the nondual precious gurus
Reside as an ornament on the top of my head.[64]

The lowly one, I, Pema Lodrö,[65]
Although my mind is distracted by outer circumstances,
Inwardly, I am afflicted by the anguish of sickness.
My body's essential blood is overflowing from the nose;
My blood pressure rises like enemies gathering.
Because causes and conditions disturb my physical
elements,
Although words come to mind, I cannot get them out.
On this occasion, mind and memory are unclear.
Thoughts and speech fall from my mouth like leaves.

Within the terrifying domain of flesh-eating rākṣasas
Lies the supreme land, Oḍḍiyāna, sanctuary of ḍākinīs,
With glorious Padma at the center of a palace of light.
I recall the unparalleled kindness of the only father guru.

Without a refuge or protector, we beings of the dark age
Now, in an anguished lament, cry out to whoever.
We summon any and all who protect the destitute
As the iron shackles of karma and *kleśa* tighten their grip.

Those who are trapped in the prison of saṃsāra,
As if tethered by the noose of suffering,
Sovereign guru, liberate swiftly by your compassion!
Supreme teacher, apart from you, there is no refuge!

Padmākara, we have no other protector than you.
Precious Lotus-Born One, with constant kindness,
From this time forward until attaining awakening,
Please accept me and bless me as inseparable from you.

Sweetheart, friend with shared karma and aspiration,
I recall the queen of *dharmatā*, dear to my heart.
In this body, even if the mind grows weary,
You are my unforgettable companion, beloved.

Imagine if we were to reside in the same land,
Imagine if I could ask in person about your health.
Imagine if we could converge in a single household.

To the north, in the meadow, Trachugmo Pass,
I recall vividly our words: aspirations and promises.
The weary tale of me, Pema (Drime Lodrö), is like this.

Do you hear me, precious guru?
Do you get my meaning, constant fine companion?

This is what arose in mind. In the sky in front, in the middle of a dome of five rainbow-colored lights, a youthful beauty, the khecarī from Oḍḍiyāna, brandished a smile. The four classes of ḍākinīs in the four directions performed a dance as if shimmering. The smiling central ḍākinī gave me a gleeful sidelong glance. Here is what she said:

E VAṂ! A meaningful song of alpha-purity whose symbols
are self-arisen—
I relay these symbols, spontaneously manifest by expressive
power.

I come from Dhumatala, realm of ḍākinīs.
Foremost lady among the assembly of myriad ḍākinīs,
I am the medicine goddess, Dewe Dorje.
Sweetheart, companion, Drime Lodrö.

From the expanse of space, the unborn ground, dharmakāya,
Where there is no such thing as "separation,"

First are the outer elements, primary causes and conditions,
Second, within, are the two truths, unmistaken dependent
origination,

Third is the fulfillment of karma, aspirations, and words
of truth.
In actuality, we are beyond meeting and parting within
great bliss.

What is called "illness" has three: great, middling, and small.
In actuality, it is the expanse of awareness naturally arising as
the three *kāyas*.

Even if the body grows more ill, why be sad?
It is illusory phenomena, with dependent origination as the basis.

Even if the mind grows more weary, why be sad?
At its base, it is all-good, free from happy or sad in the vast
expanse.

Even if one grows happier, why cling to it?
In actuality, it is the sphere of the self-liberated adept, free
of desire.

Even if one were to die now, why panic?
Indeed, it is only the transformation of appearance.

Don't regard circumstances as faults; know them to be siddhi.
Don't regard spirits as obstacles; know them to be good qualities.

Bring circumstances like the pain of illness onto the path,
Indeed, this is the inheritance of bodhisattvas.

Regardless of what arises: enemies, ghosts, demons, turbulence,
In actuality, it is purifying the unimpeded display of awareness.

Do you know how to bring these onto the path, darling Tsebo?
Grasp the vital point of dispelling obstacles and enhancing
practice.

Even the sick body is encompassed in the dharmakāya,
Even the weary mind is space and awareness in union.

In actuality, it is the union of method and wisdom,
bliss-emptiness.
Relying on the blazing and dripping by A HAṂ,
Enjoy the actualization of awareness as wisdom,
Supremely joyous and preeminently co-emergent.

Take to heart the command of the protector, Padma.
Put into practice the meaning of the guru's instructions.
Friend, keep my heart advice in mind.
I dispel the obstacles of turbulent conditions;
I loosen the knots of the channels at the five cakras;
I heal the vital essence of the physical elements.

At this time, in the year of the smiling Sheep,
In the sixth division of the white horn,
To clear way obstacles of samaya corruptors,
Perform the approach and accomplishment of glorious
Vajrakīla.
If you complete up to 100,000 feasts, amending rites, and
confessions,
From the treasure storehouse of the turquoise lake,
That ravishing nāga beauty, Dungza Bumpa,
Will entrust a casket of jewels to your hand.

From the many cycles of profound ḍākinī teachings,
The sādhana of the lady khecarī will descend
As the allotment of the great being, Namkhai Nyingpo.
Then, in the potent year of the Monkey,

At the Glorious Cliff, sacred place of the divine protector,
You will find a turquoise vessel and beautiful white jewel.
In divine meadow to the east at the Turquoise Peak,
When the conch-white moon is newly arisen,
In order to reach our aim, the vital point of coincidence,
Endeavor in 100,000 OṂ YE DHARMĀ mantras
And recitations of the Spontaneous Accomplishment of Wishes.[66]

In the east is a flesh-eating *rākṣasī*, Tramigma,
Disguised as a member of a local family called Dong.
You, the hero Yulha are the one to subdue her.
Now, there is no time to delay. Don't be late.
In the south, in the land of Gad, in the house of Adra,
There is a golden tigress flaunting six stripes.
You, Yulha Thogyur, rely on this tigress.[67]

Past deeds and coincidences are clicking into place.
Now the moment has come, how wondrous!
Now is the time to fulfill the fruit of our aspirations!
Let us meet soon in bliss, joy, and happiness.

Emanated as a luminous messenger from the red tigress,
Isn't it, Tsebo, my dearest one?

After this a red drop, just the size of a pea, dissolved into my heart. The end.[68]

Tāre Lhamo | Letter 9

Tare Lhamo returns to prophecy in a short letter referencing the distant past, when the couple made deeds and aspirations as part of a group of five heroes. Namtrul Rinpoche is referred to as Drime Lodrö, his Buddhist name prior to meeting Tāre Lhamo, and by his childhood name Tse, from Tsedzin. There is reference to his past life as Atsara Sale, the Nepali consort to Yeshe Tsogyal, and to his being the "sprout of the Nuden tulku,"[69] potentially Taksham Nuden Dorje, the one who revealed Yeshe Tsogyal's best-known life story. Once again, Tāre Lhamo gestures to a treasure awaiting them at Nyenpo Yutse. The white cliff could refer to the cliff above Lake Ngöntso, the site associated with the origins of the Golok clans.

In our past lives, at the Rasatrul Temple (Jokhang),
Deeds and aspirations were performed by five heroes together:
Padma Do-ngak, who accomplished the welfare of all;
Hayagrīva, who propagated the thirteen profound treasures;
Dorje Tumpo, who magically subdued the foreign army;
Drime Lodrö, supreme in mastery over longevity,
The one named Tse, the favorable condition for revealing terma;
And the supreme consort with convergent aspirations.

In the east, at a white cliff in the vicinity of the Turquoise Peak,[70]
If there's the opportunity to meet once more
With the emanation of Atsara Sale,
And if the sprout of the Nuden tulku has ripened,
There's good fortune to come together based on merit.

The master and his retinue of disciples rejoice.
I beseech you: please visit my homeland!
Those connected by sight, sound, memory, and touch,
I vow to guide to the celestial realms!

The *kapāla* marked with good aspirations
Is entrusted to the envoy for the holder of this dharma.
May there be auspiciousness to fulfill karma and aims!
This is offered to my dear friend.[71]

Tāre Lhamo | Letter 10

This is a duet that Tāre Lhamo composed between Devī and Pema.[72] Devī means "goddess" in Sanskrit and translates the second part of her name, Lhamo, and Pema refers to Namtrul Rinpoche's name in youth, Pema Drime Lodrö. This duet was performed in 1979 for a small group of her followers during Sagadawa, the month-long celebration of the Buddha's *parinirvāṇa*. To begin, the mood is tinged with the sorrow of being separated from the beloved. Yet overall it portrays a sense of optimism and good fortune. The devastation of the recent past is implicitly referenced as demonic forces and enemies that destroy the dharma. Despite this, there is a triumphal tone. The demons have been vanquished and the sun of the Buddhist teachings is poised to rise once again.

On the fifteenth day of Sagadawa in the Earth Sheep Year—

Devī:

Congenial friend, these etchings on mind,
Engraved on the stone of selflessness,
Cannot be altered, even in death;
It is samaya, the oath of the past.

In a splendid garden on earthen meadow,
An utpala of exquisite beauty blooms.
Its nectar is the allotment for the little bee
As an elixir for memory that liberates through taste.

The resonant plucking of the lute
Has sorrow in its melody,
So that I never forget the words of my friend.
This is the accumulation of past deeds.

The sun is your handsome face,
Decorated with the help of rainbow-colored clouds.
A drizzle of cool rain is the field of disciples.
This is coincidence, shared in common.

In reply, Pema:

The luster of my youthful friend, like a conch-colored
moon,
Traversing space alongside the constellations,
Its radiance clears away the murkiness of sorrow.
From prior aspirations and samaya, the time has come!

Devī:

Above, the Indian peacock bearing a crown,[73]
Its voice like the melodious *kalaviṅka* bird,
Flaunts its plumage, spread out like a parasol,
And dazzling form, like a hollyhock in bloom.

Pema:

The mottled rocky peak with a conch seal
Is the den of the white snow lioness and her cubs,
Not the thoroughfare of lesser, ordinary beasts.
This is the way of the world, according to karma and
dominion.

Devī:

There is yellow gold in the depths of the ocean;
But the conch crocodile left without acquiring it.
I, the fish, so supple and so flexible,
Retrieved the nāga vase for my own gain.
Inside is the merit of all we need and desire.

Pema:

Great Lion Gesar established on the golden throne,
The six divisions of Ling are settled like ice on a lake.[74]
The fortune of Ma[75] is replete with cattle, goat calves, and sheep,
And the mothers and aunts offer liquor to gladden.

Devī:

Lord Norbu Rinpoche,[76] the supreme victorious one,
Has destroyed the doctrine of dark demons at the borders.
The sun of the teachings of sublime Śākyamuni shines.
I offer the choice draft to convene a festival of delight.

Pema:

You, fortunate men and women gathered here,
Like a city of divine male and female warriors,
I am from the auspicious site, Lhalung Sumdo,
Signifying in my sovereign form that the benefit of beings will
be accomplished.

At a time of plentiful good fortune, the month's start,
To open the maṇḍala of the profound path of secret means,
Friend, the lineage of many vidyādharas are arranged in rows,
And the powerful warriors of Ling perform the dance.

Hundreds of thousands of mother ḍākinīs sing songs of praise.
Above, the wisdom deities disperse blessings to consecrate.
In between, all eight classes of gods and spirits provide aid.
Below, the earth lords and nāgas spread luck and fortune.
The great kings of the four directions protect and nurture.

This is a song to eat the lungs and hearts of vicious demons,
Enemies that harm the dharma, the teachings of Buddha.
In order to heal the demise and misery of destitute Tibetans,
This is a song to swirl the lasso at auspiciousness and fortune.
This is a song to gather whatever deeds have been undertaken.

Retinue of chief, ministers, and subjects, remain here now;
The time has come to bring down the eighteen fortresses.[77]
Coincidence clicks into place without obstructing conditions!
Instigate the joy of dharma, the teachings of Buddha!

With faith and respect for the teachings of Lord Śākyamuni,
With confidence in the speech of the divine lama,
Value the command of the sovereign king.
Heed the advice of the kind father and mother.
Tell the truth: don't muddle karmic cause and effect.
Not entrusting enemies, bring them down headlong.

Without inwardly taming negative emotions, the five poisons,
There is risk of ruin in both this life and the next.
With supreme compassion for all mother sentient beings,
Lovingly protect the lowly, weak, and destitute.

Welcomed by smiling friends, relatives, and neighbors,
Conversing in the exchange of pleasant words,
Enjoying the sweet nectar of delicious food and drink,
Dressed in fine wools and jewel ornaments,
Body, because it is a maṇḍala, I present it as an offering.
Speech, because it is symbolic dharma, I sing melodiously.
Mind, because it is dharmatā, I invoke the vast expanse.

Because this place, through pure vision, is a buddha realm,
Today is the time, under the auspicious sun,
For the coincidence of glorious good fortune to converge.
The gods and humans are happy. Oh bliss! Oh joy!

However long, from now until attaining enlightenment,
To forge the happiness of the six realms of mother beings,[78]
And so that dharma, the Buddha's teachings, does not
disappear,
Carry the burden of others' benefit at the risk of your life
And don the mighty armor of rousing bodhicitta.

May I be a guide to one day lead all mother beings
To the self-arising citadel of Zangdok Palri,
Into the presence of the sovereign, Lord Padma,
Gathering as one assembly, never to part ways.

As a result of this aspiration in song and verse,
May the aspirations of the divine lama be accomplished.
May the mighty dominion of the ancestral chiefs increase.
May the mothers and aunts be meritorious and elegant.
May auspiciousness in accord with dharma be fulfilled.

This was spoken at the pleasant grove of Tashi Lhathang Norbu for the enjoyment of a gathering of disciples, the glory of a delightful ocean.[79]

Namtrul Rinpoche | Letter 9

Here Namtrul Rinpoche delivers one of the most lyrical love songs in the correspondence.[80] Starting with the standard Indian poetic image of bee and lotus, he then moves into scenery specific to the grasslands of Golok with its snowy peaks, open meadows, and abundant wildflowers. He declares his love for Tāre Lhamo in no uncertain terms: she is dearer to him than his own eyes and heart. In line with praises to the beloved found in Amdo love songs, he compliments her body, speech, and mind, though they had yet to meet during their correspondence.[81] The song has an eight-syllable meter in verses divided first into three lines and later into couplets. The syllable *so* falls after the first three syllables in each line early in the letter and extends the meter, adding a musical quality. Again, I use "oh" in my translation at roughly the same point in most lines. While this reads as a complete letter, it is only the first half; his ninth letter continues with a cryptic prophecy not included in the translation.

Shall I also sing a song?

Dharma valley, oh, the auspicious jewel land,
Happy flowers, oh, in a lotus grove of delight,
Quivering hum, oh, it belongs to the little bee.

Melodious song, oh, recurring strum of the lute.
Sweet dew, oh, enjoy the extract of honey,
Yes little bee, *a bu lo lo wo*!

Quivering hum, oh, through this sweet melody,
I refresh the memory of my beloved companion.
I cannot help, oh, but hum a tune!

Singing this song, it reaches the snowy peak.
Snowy peak, oh, how could it possibly tremble?
Sweetheart, my mind is more firm than that.

Singing this song, it reaches the depths of the lake.
Verdant lake, oh, how could one possibly judge its depth?
Sweetheart, my devotion is more deep than that.

In past lives, deeds and aspirations were good.
At present, the shared coincidence is good.
In the future, come! Oh, the final aim is good.

The three goods, oh, aspirations and wishes fulfilled.
Friend, I am caught on the iron hook of your loving affection.
My three gates, oh, I delight to see you amidst the crowd.

First and foremost, the inner and outer elements,
Second, the power of prior vows and aspirations.

Because of my faith and yearning fondness,
How could I dare to be apart from you, friend?

Do I cherish the eyes on my face that let me see?
You dear friend, I cherish more than that.

Do I cherish the heart that upholds the mind?
You dear friend, I cherish more than that.

When wildflowers bloom across grassland meadows,
The beautiful form of my beloved comes to mind.

When the cuckoo bird emits a melodious call,
The musical speech of my beloved comes to mind.

When sunrays shine at the break of morning's dawn,
The affectionate mind of my beloved comes to mind.

Splendor of high peaks, though I've seen hundreds, thousands,
You are the queen of the snowy range; there is none higher.

At this juncture, due to the oaths of the past,
I promise to honor you always and forever.

I feel shy to say any more than that.
That's the point, darling, nothing else.

Though fatigued, the distance is not far.
Whatever the means, it's certain we will meet.

Only friend, whose mind is stable as the snow mountain,
Please remain within the radiant bliss of my heart.[82]

Tāre Lhamo | Letter 12

Likely paired with the next letter, this short and cryptic note describes the site of a future revelation at Magyal Pomra, which is the mountain range of Amnye Machen in the northwest of Golok. This is framed as a prophecy by Manene, a female protector and aunt figure in the Gesar epic. Its visionary nature is signaled by the origin point for the prophecy in the "crystal palace of mind's radiant clarity,"[83] a poetic way to depict the clarity of mind accessible to realized masters. To further signal its prophetic nature, the letter is marked with the special orthographic mark at the end of each line, called *tertsek*, to indicate its status as treasure.[84]

From the crystal palace of mind's radiant clarity,
Manene, none other than Yuyi Drolma,[85]
In the powerful aspect of unceasing awareness,
Uttered this, the music of ḍākinīs in symbols:

In the great city of a vast open country,
Where the golden mountaintop meets the sun,
In the south, where the elephant bears jewels on its back,
Treasures arise to satisfy the needs and wants of all.

To the north, in the vicinity of Magyal Pomra,[86]
The white peaks and turquoise dragon touch the sky.
Splendid, without decay, its pure color shines forth,
The descendants of the monkey utter a joyful cry.[87]

At the splendid meadow of the striped tigress,
Adorned by crystalline moonlight,
To the right, like beautiful hair ornaments,
Nectar-laden golden gesar flowers bloom.

At glorious Palri in the southwest,[88]
As guests not summoned by karma,
We have cultivated the seeds of good aspirations
On the ground of pure samaya.

When there is fortunate karma, it is like this.
Do we have a chance? It depends on the actions of others.
Will our aims be fulfilled? Within myriad domains,
The mindset of the local people will determine.

Has the vital point been struck?
Only my darling knows.
These symbols are advice to my companion;
Hold these words in the maṇḍala of mind.[89]

Tāre Lhamo | Letter 13

A whimsical song in which Tāre Lhamo suggests the folly of springtime and love.[90] In successive stanzas, she depicts a series of natural convergences—bee and lotus, storm clouds and rain, her "youthful friend" and herself—in which good fortune is the "legacy of past deeds."[91] There is a sense of the natural unfolding of events set in motion long ago, particularly their entrustment of treasures by Padmasambhava. On that occasion, Tāre Lhamo states that the flowers they tossed into the maṇḍala while receiving tantric initiation fell together, suggesting a shared karmic propensity. Presenting herself as confused by this "infatuated talk,"[92] she nonetheless affirms their inseparability as a couple in naturalistic terms, like the snow lion and craggy peak or the golden-eyed fish and verdant lake.

Now I sing a song:

Joyful valley, oh, in a garden of lotuses,
Delicious juice, oh, the sweetness of nectar.
I sing a song, oh, the melody of a circling bee.

In this open valley, when the lotuses bloom, the folly!
The bee's compulsion to circle is the legacy of the past.
Oh joyful valley! Among turquoise juniper branches,
Here its body with powerful wings delights to stay.
Its sonorous hum echoes through Tibet.

When the cuckoo emits its melodious call, the folly!
Its sweet melody is the legacy of the past.
Oh joyful valley! A land of increasing abundance
For the six clans within the sublime districts of Ling
On the occasion of the waxing moon.

Youthful friend, when singing and dancing, the folly!
The method companion is the legacy of Padma.
Within a palace of rainbow clouds in the sky,
The turquoise dragon emits roaring thunder.
With the sound, the earth knows what's in store.

When storm clouds hover in the sky, the folly!
However much rain falls, it is our worldly destiny.
Blue sky is inseparable from the clouds.
Ya ya! Just so is the congenial friend.
Storm clouds are inseparable from the rain.
Just so is the coincidence of us two friends.

The rocky peak and snow are inseparable;
The snow lion and its cubs make tender companions.
Just so is the wistful mood of us two friends.

Upon the foliage, flower petals grow;
For the bee, the nectar is from deeds of the past.
Just so are the deeds and aspirations of us two.

Verdant lake, treasure store of the nāgas,
It is the worldly legacy of the golden-eyed fish.
Just so is our connection from aspirations in former lives.

During our previous lives, at Butsal Serkhang,
The empowerment of profound command was repeatedly
 bestowed,
Creating the coincidence for our karma and aspirations to
 converge.

Our flowers of profound command fell together,[93]
When Padma bestowed the aspirational entrustment.[94]
Friend, do you see this clearly in your mind?

I am confused by this infatuated talk.
Can we fulfill our aims? You discern, Pema Lodrö.
If there's karma and coincidence, it will click.
May teachings to benefit beings spread far and wide.[95]

Namtrul Rinpoche | Letter 10

In a tender letter, Namtrul Rinpoche uses the parallelism particular to Tibetan folk song styles to describe a series of natural scenes in which something grand and unmovable is made even more lovely when adorned by movement: rainclouds in the sky, ripples on water, plants swaying on a mountainside. These serve as the analogies for the referent in the final stanza, his beloved whose expressions of love and affection adorn her unchanging intention and render her even more lovely.

Joyful dear companion, vine of my heart,
I offer a message of good tidings in song
On the stainless base of a vast white lotus page
With ink etchings, beautiful like anthers.

Look at the page, like a bee enjoying nectar,
Listen to my song, like receiving a transmission,
Hold the meaning in mind, not forgetting our aim.

In the expanse of heaven above, without center or limits,
Rain clouds gather to the north, adorning the sky.
More lovely still when the sprinkle of rain falls.

On the great lake without increase or decrease,
Lovely ripples gather to ornament the lake,
More lovely due to the movement of waves.

On majestic mountains, unmoving and unshakable,
Grasses, shrubs, and trees grow to ornament them,
More lovely when undulating en masse.

For my beloved with a changeless mind,
The inspiration of love and affection adorns you,
More lovely due to heartfelt words in your remarks.[96]

Namtrul Rinpoche | Letter 11

This is a song of remembrance concerning their past lives and the locus of their future revelations. Namtrul Rinpoche begins by recounting their lives together in medieval Nepal and in eastern Tibet during the reign of Gesar, gesturing to a total of seven lives together in Tibet. From there, he proceeds to describe several treasure sites, naming their distinctive features. The emphasis is on the act of recalling, used repeatedly at the end of each line (which I transpose to the start of each line for emphasis). While the same term can refer to "mindfulness," it means simply "to remember" and can also have an affective connotation, "to miss."[97] This range of meaning allows his recollections of deeds in the distant past to seamlessly blend into his statements of longing and affection for Tāre Lhamo in the present.

In this blissful domain, joyful dharma-holders,
Both I, the divine prince Yuyi Thortsuk,[98]
And you the smiling goddess, Sarasvatī,
Came together in a delightful garden of flowers.

In the auspicious place, the blissful country of Nepal,
For me, the royal prince Karmavajra,
You, Princess Kālasiddhi, acted as my companion
In practice on the path of bliss-emptiness.

In the cool domain of Tibet, the Land of Snow,
We came together across seven lifetimes.
We practiced the profound path of secret mantra,
Engaging in the four joys, the means to bliss-emptiness.

Keep in mind the command of father Padma,
Do you remember, joyous heart companion?

First, this body of flesh and blood is born from the womb,
Second, it is clothed in the stains of habitual propensities;
Due to broken vows and tantric commitments,
I don't sufficiently remember all seven lives.[99]

Friend, consider the truth of this clearly in mind.
As the faults of the degenerate age burst forth,
Thinking that there's no time to waste,
Now vanquish enemies and protect allies.

Not falling under the sway of the eight worldly concerns,
In isolated retreat, at meditation sites of Padma, the protector,
As partners, method and wisdom, we forged a worthy union.
When practicing the path of spontaneous union,
Truly, we matured the result of the two benefits.

Recalling the naturally arising sun over the Yarlung Valley,
Recalling the solitary mountain, Padma's crystal fortress,
Recalling the jeweled treasure gate at the white cliff, Sheldrak,
This is the sacred place where we two friends made aspirations.

Recalling Kokonor, the queen who destroyed ten thousand,[100]
Recalling the place of great bliss, the garuḍa fortress of
Padma,[101]
Recalling the divine protector of the cliff at golden Gyarong,
Recalling an auspicious site, the dharma throne and coil of joy,
Recalling the majestic heights of the great tigress fortress,
Recalling the cave of the sun and moon and the blood lake.

Recalling Nyenpo Yutse, the place in Ma of great bliss,
Recalling the storehouse of treasures in the turquoise lake,
Among all of these sites, it's particularly glorious and supreme,
The jewel terrain granting whatever one needs and wishes:
Heaven, the eight-spoked wheel in the sky above,
Earth, the eight beautifully arrayed petals of a lotus,
Between, rocky peaks with eight auspicious symbols.

Recalling Drakar Tredzong, the site of awakening,
Recalling the cave of flowers at that mighty fortress,
Recalling the treasure gate and auspicious white conch,
Recalling the many cycles of profound ḍākinī treasuries,
Now I also recall the aspiration of the father Padma.

Recalling the treasure certificate of protectors and lords of
mantra,
I especially recall the entrustment to us pair of friends.
I specifically recall your loving affection and yearning.

This is the convergence of deeds, coincidence, and aspirations,
Even more happy than journeying to a lovely place.
The etchings on my skull are becoming clearer,
My joyful faith and longing are becoming stronger,
This is the destiny of the succession of previous lives.
Of course, affectionate beloved, darling,
You are my spiritual support, impossible to forget.

Jewel of the heart, don't have an attitude of separation.
It's not possible to be separated; we have Padma's intent,
We have the blessings of the sublime protectors and lamas,
We have the companionship of the ḍākinīs and heroines,
We have the power of dharma protectors and guardians.

Not long from now, the sun of happiness will shine.
At this point, if we offer 100,000 ḍākinī feasts
And practice 10,000 times the Seven-Line Supplication
And the Spontaneous Accomplishment of Wishes,
In the casket of *citta*, the innermost mind,
There is a heart certificate for the 100,000 ḍākinīs,
Which heals the damage to the teachings and beings
And guides those who have a connection.[102]
Hold the meaning in your mind's knot of eternity.[103]

Namtrul Rinpoche | Letter 12

In this short and cheerful song, Namtrul Rinpoche encourages Tāre Lhamo to remain steady in her affection in anticipation of his journey to her homeland, Markhok. He uses natural imagery to convey his meaning: a rock outcropping that does not wobble, a lake with a constant water level, and a snow mountain that does not tremble. In these analogies, he imagines himself as a series of animals returning home to their natural habitat, in the same way that he hopes to return to Tāre Lhamo, his companion across lifetimes. In other images of mutual compatibility, Namtrul Rinpoche imagines himself as the stripes of the tigress, referring to her birth year; the golden eyes of a fish; and a ritual vase capped with a peacock feather. The letter ends with a tantric reference to "bliss emptiness" and his anticipation of favorable conditions ahead.

This time today, oh, auspicious sun.
Words of tiding, I offer a little song:

White crag, oh, it must not give way or wobble.
For the bronze-breasted vulture, this is where it alights.

Verdant lake, oh, its water must not rise or fall.
For the golden-eyed fish, this is its swimming hole.

Snow mountain, oh, it must not tremble now.
For the mighty lion, this is its stomping ground.

You, powerful one, oh, the variegated tigress
And I, the six stripes, the confluence of past karma.

You, dazzling one, oh, the fish with six fins
And I, its golden eyes, the confluence of past karma.

Golden yellow, oh, I am the vase.
Splendid peacock, you are its feather.

The deathless elixir, oh, we drink it together.
Means of bliss-emptiness, caṇḍālī naturally blazes.

Above, throne and parasol,[104] oh, rays of sunlight,
Below is Padma, flashing a radiant smile.

Between cool rains, oh, favorable conditions.
To glimpse the friend, oh, eternal gratitude.

Now, today, this is all, because you asked.
There is still time, so I offer this happy song.

Please send letters frequently.
Joy upon joy, oh *tashi delek*![105]

Tāre Lhamo | Letter 14

Labelled as a "song of sorrow,"[106] this letter articulates Tāre Lhamo's feelings of sadness and longing. She wrestles with the paradox of being ultimately inseparable due to their karmic connection across lifetimes and yet separated in relative terms across province borders at a time when travel was severely restricted. Nonetheless, Tāre Lhamo imagines a bright future with the two of them surrounded by disciples like clusters of stars, propagating the dharma together. She also anticipates their tantric practice together to access the "wisdom of the four joys."[107] Unable to sleep at night, she confesses to recalling Namtrul Rinpoche a thousand times a day and again encourages him to visit her.

On the twenty-fifth day of the Ox Month of the Earth Sheep
Year—

E ma! Supreme companion, radiance of my heart,
When I sing a song with a sorrowful mood,
Friend, you're an incomparable spiritual support.

Even if we have not been separated for an instant,
Within my miserable life in the snow mountains,
Not even one day has passed without sorrow.
Just so is the manner of my despair.

Jewel palace in the deep blue heavens,
The golden sun spontaneously shines forth,
The turquoise dragon meets its retinue there.

Cluster of stars circled by hundreds of thousands.
May rain drops continue to pour down without end.
Just so is the destiny of two eminent selves.

Between, in the happy sphere of this human world,
Sublime lamas remain for the benefit of beings;
Naturally we meet in the practice of creation and completion.[108]

Surrounded by hundreds of thousands of the populace,
May dharma teachings and all knowledge flourish;
The benefit to beings of us two friends is like this.

Offering this song, both happy and sad,
Signs of coincidence arise as a result.
Friend, may we happily meet soon
To accomplish great benefit for the teachings and beings.

Performing the secret path of means, bliss-emptiness,
Frees the knots and seals of the channels at the five cakras.
Means of bliss-emptiness, the blazing and dripping of caṇḍālī,
It is the actual method to the potent wisdom of the four joys.

Of course, we will spend our life together,
Dear friend, the affectionate radiance on my heart.
Recalling you a thousand times a day, what need I say.

In bed at night, it's not possible to fall asleep.
A brief encounter won't console my mind.
With weariness, if I look far into the distance,
Is there a way for you to come? Think it over!
When a good time comes, whichever day or month, I'll be happy.

Your tender affection is unforgettable.
Just so I remember the promise of my companion.
These are the steadfast words, changeless and firm.

Spiritual support, never separate for even an instant,
Dear Tsebo, unforgettable and close to my heart,
Please remain within the radiance of bliss.[109]

Namtrul Rinpoche | Letter 13

At long last, Namtrul Rinpoche set forth to visit Tāre Lhamo in Markhok. In this letter, he portrays himself in heroic terms as various animals flaunting their qualities and skills en route. As a complement, she is the natural habitat to which each animal returns, and their reunion is celebrated in each stanza. The pairings of each animal with its habitat provide the analogies for the final stanza in the series about the couple themselves. In line with dictates of humility in first-person speech, Namtrul Rinpoche refers to himself as "lowly me, Drime Lodrö,"[110] using his Buddhist name at the time. The letter is infused with a sense of joy, underscored by the triplication of "joy" and "bliss" in the closing stanzas.[111]

Beloved, vine of my mind, great affectionate companion,
I offer auspicious words and good tidings at setting forth.

Stay well, invincible turquoise lake of wealth!
Golden-eyed fish with six fins, setting out across the ocean,
Flaunts its skills in the middle of the vast ocean.
Without delay, fish and lake shall happily meet.

Stay well, Indic terrain of sandalwood forest!
Powerful red tigress, setting out for the meadows,
Flashes its six stripes on a grassy hilltop overlook.
Without delay, tiger and forest shall happily meet.

Stay well, pristine snow mountain!
Splendid snow lion, setting out for the craggy peaks,
Unfurls its turquoise mane atop the dark boulder.
Without delay, snow lion and white peaks shall happily meet.

Stay well, dear friend, jewel of my heart!
Lowly me, Drime Lodrö, setting out to your homeland,
With the good intention to benefit the teachings and beings,
Without delay, friend, we shall happily meet.

Joy, joy, joy: the power of deeds, aspiration, and samaya.
Joy, joy, the source of joy: the kindness of the Three Jewels.
Joy, joy, the site of joy: the journey along the paths and bhūmis.
Joy, joy, the joyful supreme friend: the goddess liberating all.

Bliss, bliss, lifetime of bliss: may your lotus feet remain firm.
Bliss, bliss, bliss-emptiness: enjoying the glory of the four joys.
Bliss, bliss, bliss-bestowing: the three roots and guardians.
Bliss, bliss, supreme bliss, our wish to fulfill the two benefits.

E ho! I offer this white lotus of speech as good tidings.
E ma! May it delight us two supreme companions.[112]

Namtrul Rinpoche | Letter 14

In another short letter using pairings of animals and their natural habitat, Namtrul Rinpoche emphasizes the "stable and steady" character of each habitat, in reference to Tāre Lhamo's steadfast intention.[113] Complementing this, each animal is characterized as "changeless," suggesting that Namtrul Rinpoche has likewise not changed his mind about joining together.[114] Such pairings offer a palpable way for the couple to offer each other assurances of their mutual compatibility and steadfast commitment before and after their meeting in Markhok. The ending asks her to maintain her steadfastness and compliments her as Mount Meru, the center of the Buddhist universe, to which he now journeys.

Amid rain clouds of auspiciousness,
The turquoise dragon fulfills its aims.

Wondrous seasonal rain falls,
And the lotus of goodness blooms.

On the stable, steady white snowy mountain,
The changeless snow lion unfurls its turquoise mane.

In the stable, steady invincible turquoise lake,
The changeless golden-eyed fish flaunts its myriad fins.

In the stable, steady sandalwood forest,
The changeless tigress flashes its myriad stripes.

In verse, like Mount Meru, king of mountains,
I wish you to be unshakable and steadfast.[115]

Namtrul Rinpoche | Letter 15

This next letter appears to have been written in several stages. The first part is formal, with Namtrul Rinpoche casting himself as the youthful prince Yuyi Thortsuk, writing to Tāre Lhamo as the goddess Sarasvatī. He describes his immutable intent and longing to meet her. Next it appears that he is on his way, depicting the challenges of journeying to Markhok to meet her. After that, there is an abrupt reference to a person-to-person encounter. I hypothesize that Tāre Lhamo ventured out a distance to greet Namtrul Rinpoche, as is customary in Tibetan culture, but then felt too shy to say much. He teases her, asking if she failed to recognize him. In her fifteenth letter, Tāre Lhamo apologizes, suggesting that she hesitated out of a concern for gossip. Thereafter, his letter ends hastily on an encouraging note.

> *At this juncture, although appearing to be the marks of mental elaborations, this letter was composed while immersed within the great expanse of Samantabhadra. Thus, as the all-creative divine youth Yuyi Thortsuk, I offer these words as flowers of wondrous speech to smiling Sarasvatī.*

E ya ya! This land is a bejeweled and divine valley,
Supreme site for mantra blessed by our forefathers.
As an upholder of dharma, feeling delighted here,
I am the youthful prince, Yuyi Thortsuk.

Supreme companion, who generates bliss-emptiness,
Please listen with the ears of smiling Sarasvatī.

These etchings of mind, so pleasing,
Are stamped with the seal of my immutable intent,
Unlike etchings or designs made on rock,
Which are perishable and subject to decay.

The command of Padma is without deception,
So too past deeds, aspirations, and coincidence.
Constant friend, unforgettable jewel of my heart,
I am overjoyed that you remain in good health.

Amazingly, I remain in good health together with my retinue.
With gratitude, the union of sun and moon brings joy.
The coincidence to fulfill our wishes is clicking into place.

A la la! The divine and modest prince,
I hold in mind the tender words of your speech.
Dear, my heart breaks with yearning and devotion,
Hoping soon that we can meet face to face.

Though my physical elements are disturbed, I do not despair.
With the forceful gate of my horse, Öchung Kyangbu,
Though the peaks rise higher, I don't give up.
Though the river has swollen, I don't cower.
Though the weather blizzards, I'm not distressed.
Isn't it my wish to meet my companion? It is just so.

At the base of the auspicious divine valley,
I am grateful that you came to receive me in person.
How wondrous that you looked for me with squinting eyes!
When you did not speak, I thought: "What's the matter?"
I wondered: "Did you not recognize me?"
A la la, just kidding about all that!

The Do and Mar valleys are close together,
But even if I had to circle the world,
Even if my body were exhausted,
I would have no regrets!

The bronze-breasted vulture alights on the white cliff;
Rejoice in the good health of the changeless cliff.

The wild yak wanders among variegated boulders;
Rejoice in the good health of the changeless boulders.

The golden-eyed fish swims in a lake, pure and vast;
Rejoice in the good health of the changeless lake.

These words, wishing you well,
I offer to my companion, Sarasvatī.[116]

Tāre Lhamo | Letter 15

This is an extensive letter, written in sections.[117] The first part is a heroic song in the style of the Gesar epic, which Tāre Lhamo titles "The Eight Auspicious Gateways to the Fortress of Songs: A Jewel to Enhance the Intent to Accomplish Aims."[118] With its source in ḍākinī symbols from the vast depths of mind, akin to a treasure revelation, it proclaims the power to vanquish enemies and demons and to enable the flourishing of Buddhism once more. The heroic song ends with an acknowledgement of her first encounter with Namtrul Rinpoche. After that, Tāre Lhamo apologizes for her reticence and describes some of the challenges facing her, such as state policy restricting movement across province borders and reluctance on the part of her relatives to see her leave Markhok to join him at Nyenlung. Next, she records a visionary encounter with Namtrul Rinpoche in the form of a *werma*, a type of "war god" in Tibetan ritual and myth. In this encounter, she feigns ignorance and places a series of visionary recollections of their past lives into his mouth as his memories. The letter ends with her detailed instructions regarding the route to Markhok.

On the eighth day of the Hare Month, in the Earth Sheep Year—

From the vast casket of my innermost mind, this is called, "The Eight Auspicious Gateways to the Fortress of Songs: A Jewel to Enhance the Intent to Accomplish Aims."

E ma! Like the music of a melodic lute,
Knots freed in the channels at the throat,
The treasure door of speech is opened.

I sing a song to the divine as foremost,
A song of praise to the glory of divine ancestors.

I sing a song to the mighty spirits in the middle,
A song to befriend the mighty war gods.

I sing a song to the nāgas below.
A song offered to their king, Tsukna Rinchen.[119]

It is a maṇḍala offered to the divine Three Jewels.
It is a song and dance to delight the mother ḍākinīs.
It is a song in ḍākinī symbols, naturally powerful.

It is a heroic song to conquer the enemy, hatred,
A song to heal the damage of degenerate times,
A song to vanquish conditions of disease, plague, and famine.

It is the song HUṂ to expel unruly demons.
It is a song to lasso valuables, auspiciousness, and luck,
A song to increase life, merit, and the domain of power.

A song to spread the precious teachings of Buddha, the protector,
A song to remove the gloom of countless negative conditions,
A song to gather the lord king, ministers, and retinue of subjects,

A song to convene the monastic assembly,
A song to spread the teachings of the sublime Śākyamuni,
A song to increase the profound nectar of Padma, the protector,

A song to recall karma and aspirations of previous lives,
A song to recall our seven lives as companions,
A song for coincidence to click from actions done,

A song of abundant fortune for the time, today,
A song to recall counsel from a loving friend,
And to recall amorous words upon parting!

Though suitably sad, there was no choice but to go.
Let me leave these words as a spiritual support:
As a talisman to place around the neck,

As strands of yarn entwined inseparably,
As a reminder not to forget the samaya of the past,
As a circular ring to keep in mind present deeds.

If you said, "let's go," I could not extricate my mind.
If you said "stay," I could not be happy in this situation.

First is the forceful policy of the Chinese authorities.
Second is the chatter among country folk.
Third is sharp dissent from the old aunties.

If the felicitous means to benefit beings doesn't occur
And if the coincidence for our union is reversed,
I suppose it will not work out.

Imagining there would be local gossip, I did not ask you to stay.
Reflecting that the road is long, I did not ask you to go back.
Thinking of the great physical hardship, I did not dare.

During the cheerful waxing moon of the Ox Month,
On the evening of the thirteenth day, in sleep,
The mother and son clear light merged.

A werma appeared with pennants flapping.[120]
In a terrifying place, a forest with rocky crags,
The treasure guardian, a *tsan* spirit,[121] rode on a deer.

Behind, banners swirled and lightning flashed.
It was as if he was escorted by a powerful fire tigress,
Your own guardian protector. This vision arose.

In the vicinity of a cliff like a standing rākṣasa,
On the full moon, the Namkhai emanation
Rode swiftly on an invincible little horse.

I dreamt that you appeared in the form of werma,
Who, with radiant smile, looked around delighted.
My mind bubbled with joy; my eyes cast sidelong glances.

Our minds, clear and radiant, mixed like water and milk.
I dreamt that auspicious words of truth were spoken.
Your envoy riding on a white horse,
Had arranged provisions for you two travelers.
At that time, I spoke these words:

I am a maiden with an emanational lineage.
Outwardly, this maiden's form is encased in flesh and blood.
Inwardly, I am the noble queen Vajravārāhī,
Supreme mother of the buddhas of the three times.
My name is Trinley Kundrup, All-Accomplishing Activity.
I am the consort of glorious Hayagrīva,
And I have come to this place as a manifestation.
In general, my purpose is the teachings of the Buddha.
In particular, I think of the joys and sorrows of all beings.
Also, I remember the friend who made aspirations,
Not knowing who you are, obscured by haze,

When I see the two of you, I wonder:
Who are you? Where are you going? What's your purpose?
Speak frankly the truth—no secrets!

I am a gullible lady with thick latent tendencies,
Whose transgressions and violations of samaya are great.
I have only glimmers of recollecting past lives and deeds,
The mirror of my mind is tarnished and unclear.
Explain without holding anything back.
I am a lady from the borderlands
With many undertakings to accomplish.

Not leaving out of lack of food and clothes,
Not roaming because I failed as a householder,[122]
Not cast aside for lack of affection from kin,
Not tossed away because a relationship didn't work out,
Not distracted by actions of the eight worldly concerns,[123]
Not thinking of destroying enemies and protecting friends,
Not attached to worldly activities in saṃsāra,
Not deceived due to the confusion of inner emotions,[124]
I am bound by the visionary prophecy of glorious Padma!
The time for the oath of the mother ḍākinīs has come!

Of course, you remember, youthful one.
Please explain—talk straight, no secrets!

Then, friend Pema Lodrö thought, "Since I aspire to recollect past lives and now the signs of the ḍākinī appeared in this vision in a dream, I think that I should respond." His reply went like this:

Oh beautiful woman with delicate feet,
To explain where, how, and why to go,
The way for me to go is to the north;
The time for me to come is the break of dawn.
Reflecting, I recall the latencies of the past.
My body and thoughts are drawn to you.

Regarding our past lives and deeds in India:
Friend, the princess with a garland of blue lotuses,
Whose mother was the beautiful Devī Kumāra

And father, Lekdrup, a warrior accomplishing his aims;
Friend, the princess smiled like a joyful utpala.

In the noble land of India, in the region of Kashmir,
With a noble body, you attained the freedoms and favors.[125]
My name was the brahmin Dheha,
A student of the protector Hūṃchenkara;
I was a yogin of the glorious Vajrakīla.
You were an emanation of Korlo Gyedeb,
And the noble queen Vajravārāhī.
We had the chance to meet as wisdom-method couple.

I could not see beyond that;
Then more previous lives and deeds came.
You, Metok Ladze, and I, Munchen Thökar,[126]
Together the two of us made aspirations.

Now that I've remembered our past lives,
With faith in the teachings of sublime Śākya,
I practice the meaning of his profound intent.
Friend who accomplished buddhahood,
Our aspiration is to connect again and again.
There's no time to explain, I have to leave soon.
Hold these words in mind.

In the presence of eminent Padma, we made aspirations.
I, the priest of Nub, Namkhai Nyingpo,
And you the ḍākinī, Shelkar Dorje Tso,
In the place of practice, Kharchu in Lodrak,
We accomplished life mastery beyond birth and death,
And obtained the siddhi of glorious immortality.
Do you remember? Keep this in mind, friend.
There are many deeds but no time to speak of them.

In Utsang at the Serkhang at Samye,
Master, scholar, and dharma king converged.[127]
Glorious Orgyan Padma bestowed the aspiration,
Commanded the oath of the mother ḍākinīs,
And conferred an allotment of thirteen profound treasures.
The opportunity to benefit beings exists

In the Ser, Do, Mar, and Ma valleys.[128]
We can also be of benefit to the east in Gyalrong.
In the sacred site, White Garuḍa Fortress,
Is a casket of symbolic script for glorious Mahākāla.
There are eighteen texts of Chinese astrology;
It is the key to the eight great nāga fortresses.

You were the lovely nāga maiden Metok Drön,
and I was the youthful nāga prince, Karma.
Do you recall? Is it clear in your mind?
This year, the time has come for action.
Don't say that you don't know or remember.
Do you realize the purpose of my traveling?

In the auspicious divine valley of Sabong,
The sublime joyful friend, called Devī,
I recall the virtuous smile of youthful beauty.
I recall the elixir of her melodious speech.
I recall the old inclination toward sorrow.

The profound samaya of the past is irreversible.
The Tsangpo River does not flow uphill.
An avalanche doesn't go back up a mountain.
A cool north wind doesn't change course.
The oath of the ḍākinīs cannot be reversed.
Friend, our aspirations cannot be reversed.
We have the fortune of karma and coincidence converging.
Lady, don't say that you don't remember.
Please reply with conviction.

At this point, in the maiden's own mind: "It is the power of aspiration that karmically connects me to this person across past lives. Since the past becomes clear in mere glimmers, I don't know exactly how it is. Now that I realize that the causes and conditions for our convergence is not due to gods and demons or non-human interference, I think that I should pretend to know."

Ya ya! Well said, divine son,
But I'm not sure the meaning is clear.
If I consider your words, I may think I'm something.
Where this all leads, I don't really know.

Now, if you and your attendant come my way,
I can tell you in detail what to look for on the path.
From the border, it's not far, just one day.
Cut across the high waters of Do River.
Keep Akyung Chakmö Budzong to your right.
Keep the sacred site, Doyi Chongri, on your left.
Keep the glorious peak, Tsal Dradul Chak, ahead of you.
The main path is through the Kyir Valley at Lhalung Ringmo.
Take the easy route, Lakkan Karchungmo.
Don't mistakenly go along the wide course of the Bö River.
To the right, the valley has an eight-petal lotus, where the sun rests.
To the left, there are rocks of good fortune and a pleasant lotus grove.
In front is Lhathang Ringmo where the water lily blooms.
It is a sacred site of Mahādeva, magnetizing the three spheres.

When you see the red mountain before you, its form is Umadevī;
The shape of her iron hook captures the mind and perception.
The mark of her lasso binds apparent phenomena into servitude.
She is in union with the all-mighty lord, guiding by means of great bliss
And taming the three spheres of existence through passion.
She is the counterpart in every way to the grandeur of Mahādeva's site.

In the area around the supreme sacred site, Lhathang Ringmo,
It's safe for humans and nonhumans to travel day or night.

Banners of the dharmapālas, dralas, and werma flutter;
Protective guardians, who serve as attentive friends,
Bring ghosts, demons, and obstructing spirits under control.
They guide beings through life and death along the path to liberation.
They always satisfy guests with four types of generosity.[129]
They always make effort for the benefit of beings, self and others.

Do not lose courage due to hardship or fatigue!
I took the form of a woman to fulfill the hopes of beings high and low,

Posing as the girl who remembers a previous life as Karchen,[130]
In pure perception, wondrous and more beautiful than
others,
The mother of all buddhas, the best of guides,
Who knows how to lead whoever is connected to
Dhumathala.

Speaking in that way, the nonhuman wisdom ḍākinī arose as the display of magical emanation. Within the abundant and joyful Lhathang, her dwelling place is the sanctuary of mastering mind. That is it.[131]

Namtrul Rinpoche | Letter 16

A short prophecy in just seven lines, this letter depicts the release of symbolic script by the ḍākinīs in the process of treasure revelation. Namtrul Rinpoche records receiving a "symbolic certificate" from the ḍākinīs and refers to it by the name, "bundle of jewels."[132] But he does not specify if this certificate contains the location of a future treasure or a list of its contents.

SAMAYA PHAT!

Ai! The wisdom ḍākinī of bliss-emptiness
Releases the treasury of signs to emanate what arises.
When the clouds of the past are dispersed,
Primordial buddhahood, free from deception!
The symbolic certificate, called "bundle of jewels,"
Has been released by the treasury of blissful ḍākinī.[133]

Namtrul Rinpoche | Letter 17

In this praise for Tāre Lhamo, Namtrul Rinpoche expresses his eagerness for them to join as a couple. At the outset, he uses both formal and informal modes of address, referring to her as the female bodhisattva Tārā and using the nickname "Tarpo," based on a local convention of taking the first syllable of a Buddhist master's name and adding *po*, *bo*, or *lo* to it. Adding to the letter's sense of intimacy, Namtrul Rinpoche addresses her with several terms of endearment: "friend, dear to my heart," "congenial loving companion," and "bindu of my heart," where *bindu* means "vital drop" referring to seminal fluids in the subtle body.[134] Namtrul Rinpoche praises her body, speech, and mind in amorous terms: her graceful movements, heartfelt words, and light rays of affection. Gesturing to the initial secrecy of their exchanges, he asks her not to share his letter with others. Overall, his words are encouraging, suggesting that the time will come soon to fulfill their aims.

Tarpo,

Friend, dear to my heart, Tārā of bliss-emptiness,
On earth's fertile treasury, joyful and auspicious,
Congenial loving companion, you are the bindu of my heart.

Your body, the graceful dance of bliss-emptiness;
Your speech, melodious words issued from the heart;
Your mind, emanating heat of a thousand rays of affection;

When can we be carefree at play with delight?
Winter, once its early months have passed,
Not long from now, the time will come!

Outside, don't let others hear this secret talk.
Squinting at the early morning sky,
Clouds drizzle with tears; dense clouds hang.

Now, don't say. A la, explain later!
Is it so, vine of my heart?[135]

Tāre Lhamo | Letter 17

Another extensive letter, this was composed while Namtrul Rinpoche remained in Markhok. Five sections are excerpted in *Jewel Garland* and framed as her direct speech during the visit.[136] Tāre Lhamo begins with an invocation to Padmasambhava and Yeshe Tsogyal in the form of Vajravārāhī, followed by an extensive tribute to her father, Apang Terchen, here giving his tertön name, Orgyan Trinley Lingpa. At several points in the letter, Tāre Lhamo confesses a sense of shame in not living up to her father's legacy yet makes no reference to the historical devastation of the last twenty years and prohibition of religious practice that made it impossible for her to do much. Perhaps as a way to convince her reluctant relatives to allow her to join Namtrul Rinpoche at Nyenlung in Serta, she laments not being able to benefit even a single creature, build even one stūpa, write even a single book, or bring even one student to liberation. Despite all this, Tāre Lhamo exercises her visionary capacities by adding several more identities to their series of past lives as a couple and highlights their samaya, or vow of tantric commitment, as a binding factor connecting them across lifetimes. The letter is regarded as a treasure text and marked in publication with a tertsek indicating its status as such. A short cryptic section containing prophecies and ritual prescriptions is omitted in the translation.[137]

> A song in the melody of Magadha, its meaning is free of elaboration:[138]
>
> In a peaceful domain of enchanting lotuses,
> When the five excellences naturally arise,[139]
> At the Dhanakośa Lake in Oḍḍiyāna,
> Father, the lord and guru, Padmākara,
> And great mother, the excellent Vajravārāhī,
> Inseparable appearance-emptiness, beyond meeting and parting,
> Reside at the crown of my head amid rainbow light.
>
> Precious teacher, crown ornament of complete faith,
> Won't you look compassionately upon us, without refuge or protector?
> Outwardly, we are harmed by enemies, demons, and obstructing spirits,

Inwardly, tormented by illness and the three poisons,
And deceived by the confusion of conceptuality and delusion.
Now, lacking freedom, we suffer in the city of saṃsāra.
Omniscient precious master, please listen to my lament!
This lowly one, your gullible daughter, offers this request:
Please consider it in the ease of your unwavering mind.

Father and guru, born into an esteemed lineage,
Within your inconceivable sphere of influence,
You guided disciples through sight, sound, memory, and touch,
Establishing them at glorious Zangdok Palri[140]
And bringing benefit to beings in millions of domains.
As the results of deeds performed in previous lifetimes,
Unable to pass your fiftieth in the great rosary of life,[141]
You slipped away suddenly, due to irreversible karma,
As if struck by the venom of a flesh-eating demoness.

Eminent master of the assembly, north at Kailash,
Raudracakrin,[142] tamer of 3,700,000,000 beings and realms,
Guides many fortunate ones who have made aspirations.
Especially noble is the lord of the three realms,
The glorious Orgyan Trinley Lingpa,
The protector, said to be an omniscient buddha.
Engaging in the means, bliss-emptiness, of union and liberation,
You are the heruka who practiced yogic discipline.
Bellowing the sound "Ha" of eminent Hayagrīva,
You have subjugated the minds of beings in saṃsāra.
The benefit to beings is rebirth in Shambhala.
In brief, this is my father's sphere of influence.

Ha ha! I am the fifth sibling born to this noble family.[143]
Emanating various bodies, I have the aspiration
To benefit beings to the north, south, east, west, and below.
Prior deeds, aspirations, and the pure water of samaya,
Although we have drunk this together with many siblings,
Since causal factors from actions and emotions are strong,
The surface of the stainless mirror, the radiant clarity of mind,
Is tainted by the remaining dirt of karmic and emotional obscurations.

Inwardly, I'm ashamed, having not severed duality.
From that the body and soul of the father lama are sold.
From that doubts about the master and retinue emerge.
From that causal factors of good and bad deeds arise.
From that, the boundary of saṃsāra and nirvāṇa is drawn.
From that pure lands and hell realms arise.
Karma is like the etching of joy and sorrow on water;
It emerges continuously without interruption.

When bound by the confusion of duality,
By means of the mighty sword of *prajñā*,
With a sharp tip to pierce self-clinging,
I sever self-clinging within the space of selflessness.

E ma ho! With buddha nature as the ground,
We two friends mingle as one in basic space,
The inseparable union of method and wisdom,
Knowing the extent of confusion up until now.

Never separate from the primordial nature.
Friend, Pema Lodrö, keep this in mind!
If your mind strays into confusion, confess it.
If my talk is senseless, please be patient.

By releasing confusion in its own place, thoughts are liberated as they arise. They are pervasive, but powerless. At this point, due to an entanglement, I am speaking this way.

E e! In a previous life, to the east in India,
The male consort was all-knowing Jñānamati,
The female, life-bestowing Śridevī from Madhya.
They dredged the depths for beings connected to them.

Just so are our conjoined deeds and aspirations,
Youthful companion, Namkhai Nyingpo.
Although the many coincidences are good,
At present, vicious heretics obstruct us.

In the past in India, in the vicinity of Drokye,
The female consort, the life-holder Devī Tārā,[144]

And the protector Matikirti, emanation of Akaśagarbha,[145]
Led those connected to us to Lotus Radiance Palace.[146]

Arriving at Orgyan's celestial realm,
I, the venerable and noble Tāre,
And you, the friend called Pema Lodrö,
Together made aspirations for coincidence.

Method and wisdom couple, inseparable due to samaya,
E ma ho! Our connection from former lives and deeds!
Ya ya! The youthful companion, known as Lodrö,
Profound command's coincidence strikes the vital point.

In the white month of the fortunate year,
The red tigress flaunts her six stripes from the depths,
Flowers bloom on the lake of mind for the powerful
monkey.[147]
I recall the legacy of deeds from the past.

I recall building a temple at a lovely hermitage,
Thinking of the harvest sown in the field there together.
Our retinue of disciples, however many, are clear in mind.
We all drank the elixir of immutable life.

Internally, we are relatives of one samaya.
You are the heart friend who holds my vital pledge.
We are like twins inseparable due to karma.
It is the master's immutable words of aspirations.

It is the samaya of undeceiving command.
Repeated reflections of the unconfused mind
Burst from the space of primordially-arisen insight,
Creating causal factors for the practice of bliss-emptiness.

In joyful Samling, site of abundant good fortune,
Coincidence from accumulated deeds and wishes clicks—
As many favorable conditions for us companions to converge!

Now, don't let the coincidence to strike the vital point disappear!
Let's restore the teachings and beings, praised by Vajra![148]
The symbolic certificate of the ḍākinīs in thirteen verses
Contains many profound practices to be decoded.

If we're diligent, the two benefits of self and other will be fulfilled.
Think again and again, consider the time we have.
It's not enough to only care for oneself.
It's not enough to amass food and clothing.
It's not enough to pursue solitude.
It's not enough to secure the eight worldly concerns.
Pretention does not lead to liberation.

If the body bleeds, it's a purification.
There's no way to escape even a serious disease.
Whether happy or sad, it's fleeting experience.
If the body is fatigued, it's a thick mist.
Whether born in a decent place or not, it's a dream.
Don't grasp at sounds as good or bad; they are like echoes.
Inwardly, I'm ashamed, not having tamed the five poisons.

En route to the great benefit of beings and the teachings,
First, I did not fulfill the promise of samaya to the lord.
Second, I did not delight nor appease the mother ḍākinīs.
Third, I did not perform activities to protect the teachings.
Fourth, I did not accomplish the wishes of my father guru.
Although praised as a person benefiting mother beings,
I did not accomplish the benefit of a single creature.
In terms of supports, I did not build even one stūpa.
In terms of speech, I did not write even a single book.
In terms of mind, not even one student of mine attained liberation.
I don't want to stay; I feel sad and ashamed.

In these thirty years, the youthful nirmāṇakāya
Has arisen in a mired swamp and narrow gorge.
Although worn out by joys and sorrows,
The crops, previously sown, are now ripening.
It is experience in accord with the cause.
It is the undeceiving dictate of Lord Buddha.
With confidence in the sublime guru's speech,
Hold in mind the oath of the mother ḍākinīs.

Like the masters of yore: Marpa, Mila, and Gampopa,
The six ornaments and two supreme ones,[149]
Keep the benefit of beings in mind,

Especially eradicating hardships and weariness
Following the example of the prince, Drime Kunden,[150]
Who gave his glorious wealth and body.

I will protect those in need with compassion;
In this way, I will pursue the way of buddhas.
How could I abandon mother beings?
I will remain until saṃsāra is emptied.

Ha ha! This is a song about the confusion of saṃsāra,
A song of symbols, the secret talk of ḍākinīs,
A song of invincibility unlike most.
If one grasps the meaning, it is wondrous illusion.
It self-liberates the mind not fixated on permanence.
We are beyond meeting and parting from the very
beginning.
Friend, hold these words in your heart!

You, sublime son of good family and pure origin,
And I the mantra-born woman, Devī, the two of us,
In order to rescue beings from strife in degenerate times,
We have been appointed by Orgyan Padmasambhava.
Awakening together past deeds, aspirations, and the
entrustment,
It is our promise to guide all mother beings.

Is my meaning clear, youthful nirmāṇakāya?
Do not forget these words! Hold them in your heart!
Friend, your contours are becoming a bit clearer.[151]

Namtrul Rinpoche | Letter 19

Written as he was leaving Markhok or shortly thereafter, Namtrul Rinpoche emphasizes the word for "affection" by repeating it at the start of three lines.[152] Here again he conveys fondness and intimacy through a string of terms of endearment: "consort," "bestower of bliss," "beloved," "vine of mind," and more.[153] Through a repetition of terms, he strikes an optimistic tone, portraying the "best" of circumstances and praising the steadiness of her "mind," while referring to himself as "lowly" in the humility required of first-person speech.[154] Again, naturalistic images of animals and habitats are used to emphasize their inseparability and mutual compatibility. With the quick beat of six syllable lines toward the end of the letter, Namtrul Rinpoche conveys a sense of urgency for their plans to move forward.

Consort, maturing the nectar of awareness,
Bestower of bliss, guide to a blissful mind,
Glorious partner, bestowing the four joys,
I make this offering of a letter to you.

Affectionate vine of the mind,
Affectionate lady, steady as a mountain,
Affectionate beloved, heart friend,
My reply to the message before me:

Best in the stainless vast sky above,
Best, the horse-drawn chariot of the splendid sun,[155]
Best, emanating a hundred clear light rays,
Best, to delight like finding great joy.

Lowly Pema Lodrö, in appearance,
Lowly by sickness, both hot and cold,
Lowly, while extremely ill,
Lowly, but not sorrowful.

Mind, steady as the king of mountains,
Mind, not worried or wavering,
Mind, radiant, a story of delight,
Mind, send letters to please the mind.

Snow mountain palace, bright white,
The snow lion unfurls its turquoise mane.
Mountain and lion are inseparable.
This is the power of previous deeds.

Invincible turquoise lake, in its midst,
A golden-eyed fish flaunts its six fins.
Lake and fish are inseparable.
This too is the legacy of the past.

Pleasure grove in a sandalwood forest,
The tigress brandishes its six stripes.
Forest and tigress are inseparable.
This too is worldly inheritance.

Love love—aim of my heart,
Joy joy—vine of my mind,
Dear dear—gleam of my heart,
Kind kind—I don't dare part.
Yearn yearn—sole support for mind.
Match match—shared deeds and wishes.
Steady steady—sole steadfast friend.
Beauty beauty—recalling your fine face.
Sweet sweet—recalling your lovely speech.
Clear clear—recalling your wise mercy.
Recall recall—I won't forget your words.
Joy joy—showing the play of the four joys.
Bliss bliss—wisdom of bliss-emptiness.
Arise arise—it arises in mind.
When when—my hope to meet you.
Again again—it's vivid in mind.
Sad sad—words of affection.
Write write—I set down what arose.

May your lifespan be stable and immutable,
May your wishes be fulfilled without exception,
Along with your hopes and aspirations.

Turquoise divine son, Karma Dorje,
Flashing playful sidelong glances,
Recalling heartfelt words of affection,
Within the joys and sorrows of affection,

On stainless Chinese paper,
My unsullied ink designs,
Writing these inexpressible words,
May they be blameless and worthy.[156]

Tāre Lhamo | Letter 18

The main section of this letter is dubbed a "Fortress Garland of Flowers."[157] It is regarded as a treasure, marked with a tertsek at the end of each line. Opening with a standard Tibetan formula—above, between, and below—Tāre Lhamo imagines the couple together in various settings in India, Tibet, and China. Acknowledging their karmic connection across lives, she also warns of moving ahead with their plans too quickly. The song goes on to recount the role of Yulha Thogyur, the Prince of Jang, in overthrowing his father's corrupt kingdom as part of Gesar's army.

Above, in India, at the indestructible seat, Bodh Gāya,
Friend, shall the two of us meet together there:
To spread the teachings of the sublime Śākya,
To debate the tenets of dharma, both sūtra and tantra,
To obtain the great result from training in meditation?

Between, in Utsang, with its three monastic seats,[158]
Friend, shall the two of us go there to make offerings,
A gold and turquoise maṇḍala to accumulate merit,
To the Jowo Śākyamuni, principal sacred support,
And to the monastic colleges like stars in the sky?

Below, in Do Kham, in the land of five valleys,
At the meditation place of Orgyan Padma,
Gathering place of the assembly of ḍākinīs,
Friend, shall the two of us hold fast to dharma there,
Wandering in isolated mountain retreat
And seeking buddhahood in one lifetime?

In the marketplace of the Chinese authorities,
Friend, shall the two of us go to see the sights:
Many warehouses with garments and such,
Like a dance for the sake amusement,
Or a little ditty with a sweet melody?

Dharma holders, content in this pleasure grove,
Dear compatible friend, us pair of sublime youths,

We joke and laugh at the peak of happiness,
And exchange heartfelt words, sweet to hear.

Recalling our pledge from the depths of sadness,
Recalling the gait of your fine horse's cantor,
Recalling the tender affection of the loving friend,
Recalling the escort of wind and rain clouds,
Knowing that the road is long,
I recall your patient kindness.

On the tenth day at summer's outset,
During the tantric feast of means, bliss-emptiness,
I recall the original face of the innate
Through the bliss of caṇḍālī, the site of A HAṂ,
The luminosity of four joys resulting from practice.

Tender and faithful, I have great inspiration;
The target is your affectionate heart.
With tender affection etched on my skull,
I recall again the strength of our connection,
It is our legacy from deeds of past lives.

The tree has sprouted shoots, *lo lo bo.*
Don't shake off the fruits too early.
Next year or the year after, in early summer,
When water-laden clouds shower rain, *tha la la*!
Branches of juniper bushes, *ya la la*!
Melodious call of the cuckoo, *kyu ru ru*!
When the turquoise dragon's thunder rolls, *di ri ri*!
These are natural guests, not invited by past deeds.
When karma and coincidence converge, it is like this.

Recalling our samaya of inseparability,
At a golden mountain ornamented by lovely lotuses,
With sheep and calves, the basis for wealth,
Where drinking milk and yogurt is an elixir,
This domain of influence is merit accumulated;
There one finds finely bred horses, known to soar.

There the youthful hero, Yulha Thogyur,
Is the life-force pillar of the Buddha's teachings.
His weapon is a sharp, blazing blade,
His armor fearlessness, an indestructible shield.
His lady is the beauty, Zilha Chödrön.[159]
This is the day to vanquish the dark teachings of Jang.[160]

Does this sound familiar? Newly bloomed flowers
In a nook by the white crag in the Melong Valley,
The sublime divisions of Ling gather for a festival.
In the midst of the assembly of male and female warriors,
This auspicious song is performed!
Again, we make aspirations to fulfill our aims.

Hey you, here today, there is good fortune.
Arrange the king and minister on tiger and lion thrones,
Heap enjoyments like a mountain of desirable things,
Bless them with the transformative power of *samādhi*,
And make offerings of select portions of liquor.
Bestow auspiciousness, expanding splendid radiance.

The repository of dharma,
Is the sanctuary of Ling's six districts.
The repository of wealth,
Is the three valleys of Ma, Yang, and Ra.[161]
The repository of treasures,
Is the majestic peak, Magyal Pomra.

Fulfilling the wishes of Gesar, the Great Lion,
The highland pastures are swiftly made happy.
First is the fierce fulfillment of the master's wishes.
Second is the converging of happiness for Tibetans.
Third is the taming of enemies of the four directions.

May all wishes be fulfilled! May there be auspiciousness!
May the benefit of beings be accomplished. Samaya.

This song, "Fortress Garland of Flowers," is complete.
Sarva Maṅgalaṃ![162]

Tāre Lhamo | Letter 20

Next is a playful letter repeating the term for "life," which is *tse* in Tibetan.[163] Not coincidentally, this term is the first syllable of Namtrul Rinpoche's childhood name, Tsedzin. Tāre Lhamo uses this to riff on various Buddhist longevity practices, the Tibetan custom of liberating the lives of animals, and their own connection across lifetimes as a tantric couple. She even refers to herself as the "long life goddess" to pun on her role in attending to Namtrul Rinpoche's health.[164] Tāre Lhamo was well-known for extending life and performed a longevity ceremony for the surviving Buddhist teachers and cleric-scholars in Golok at the end of the Maoist period.

Life, if you seek buddhahood in one lifetime,
Life, throughout it, exert in study and renunciation.

Life and accomplishment, if equanimity is possible,
Life, in this one, you will obtain liberation.

Life, its successions, practice the longevity sādhana:
Life, the Amitāyus sūtra, its dhāraṇī and recitation.

Life, please liberate the lives of animals as you are able.
Life impediments, dispel obstructing spirits.

Life empowerment, achieve the level of a vidyādhara.
Life, supreme, attain an adamantine lifeforce.

Lifelong friend, Tsedzin, my object of contemplation.
Long life goddess, I prolong its span with the longevity arrow.

Life, in all its successions, may we never be separated:
Life, in this, the next, and the three intermediate states.

Life and merit, may they shine forth!
A festival of tea and beer, it is happy!

Exchanging words in pleasant conversation,
Happier still, appearances get more vivid.

Better still, our life conditions improve.
Whatever you think, nurture as dharma activity.
Whatever you do, it's not just sitting around.
Whatever we wish, may auspiciousness make it so.

Sarva Maṅgalaṃ! Auspiciousness! Virtue![165]

Namtrul Rinpoche | Letter 21

In this letter, Namtrul Rinpoche writes of illness and asks Tāre Lhamo not to worry. Putting on a brave face, he interprets illness in a variety of ways: as a profound teaching on impermanence, as a means of exhausting negative karma, as the kindness of the guru, and as an indication of the illusory nature of reality. He concludes that the nature of illness, from the vantage point of the highest view, is "unobstructed alpha-purity."[166] Based on this, he generates a sense of equanimity and concludes the letter on a joyful note. Conspicuously, he refers to himself as the "mad priest Tse" here and elsewhere in the correspondence, invoking the authoritative model of the "holy madman,"[167] who engages in unconventional views and practices as the means to liberation.

> Source of refuge, the precious guru,
> Resides as an ornament on my head.[168]
>
> Dear friends, Karma Lhadrön and Kundrol Rigpe Dorje,[169]
> Connected by deeds, wishes, and coincidence,
> To me Karma Dorje,
> Outwardly, the elements are disturbed,
> Inwardly my physical health is weak,
> Oppressed by illness, both hot and cold,
> Please do not let me worry the two of you.
>
> He he! To this youth Rangjung Dorje,
> Illness is the kindness of the guru,
> Illness is the kindness of the *yidam*,
> Illness is the attainments of the ḍākinīs,
> Illness is the supreme actions of guardians.
> Due to illness, I know the challenge of finding the freedoms
>   and favors.
> Due to illness, I recall death and impermanence.
> Due to illness, I know that karma never deceives.
> Due to illness, I give birth to revulsion for sāṃsara.
> Due to illness, I bring adverse conditions onto the path.
> Due to illness, I give rise to devotion for the guru.

Due to illness, I recall the kindness of the Three Jewels.
Due to illness, I feel affection for my companion.
Due to illness, I cultivate compassion for beings.
Due to illness, I exhaust bad deeds accumulated in the past.
Due to illness, I am encouraged to perform virtue.
Due to illness, I realize that apparent phenomena are not real.
Due to illness, I realize that all phenomena arise naturally.
Due to illness, I clear obstacles and enhance practice.
Due to illness, I encounter my original face beyond concept.

The illness itself is unobstructed alpha-purity.
The location of illness is the primordial space of Samantabhadra.
The cause of illness is groundless and rootless,
The experience of illness is innate space transcending mind.
In the ultimate expanse of primordial space,
The expressive power manifests without clouds of illness.

View, in its expanse, is free from center and fringe.
Meditation mingles with the environment of luminosity.
Action is accepting and rejecting, free from hope and fear.
Result has surely been accomplished since the beginning.

Illness is a teaching on illusion and dependent origination.
Suffering pervades saṃsāra and nirvāṇa equally.
Death too is only the transformation of appearance.
And bliss, once realized, is the resting place of concentration.

In the vast space of ever-perfect dharmakāya,
All appearances—good and bad, happy and sad,
Arise infinitely as the pure primordial equality.
From bliss to bliss, happiness to happiness!

He he, supreme heart friend,
He he, assemblies of fortunate disciples,
Ha ha, this is a joyous song of Shukjung.
Ho ho, the mad priest Tse wrote this![170]

Tāre Lhamo | Letter 22

In this letter, Tāre Lhamo highlights her access to treasures in the sky and the wisdom expanses of her own mind. Depicting her own healing powers, she references tantric physiology, gesturing to the movements of the subtle body as well as the tantric deities and mantra syllables that fill it. Moreover, she links enabling Namtrul Rinpoche to complete his lifespan to their greater mission to pacify the dark age, revitalize the Buddhist teachings, and bring about good fortune for Tibetans. As her own treasure composition, in the second half of the letter, Tāre Lhamo includes a brief ritual to Mahāvairocana for pacifying illness, demons, evil deeds, and obscurations. Like her own strands of hair, the ritual is meant to cure him of illness and address adverse conditions. I omit a translation of the ritual here, out of respect for her own request within the letter itself: "Don't show this to just anyone. Keep it secret."[171]

On the 20th day of the Rabbit Month in the Earth Sheep Year—

Beloved, vine of my mind, before the nirmāṇakāya,
Flowers of tender joy, I imagine offering with delight.
In the one vast expanse, the all-pervasive sky,
There is one inexpressible, genuine meaning.

A thousand sweet melodies, the drumbeat of thunder,
You are the powerful elephant ornamented with jewels,
The inexhaustible result of the two accumulations.

Due to the kindness of the authentic guru
And the cool rays of compassion of the Three Jewels,
Relying on practice, one obtains realization.

Within treasure sites lie in the expanse of the sky,
And treasure objects hidden among the four elements,
The symbolic meaning echoes in the space of sound.

The key is discovered in the expanse of wisdom.
Treasure guardians exist as wisdom's expression,
No need to be commanded again by others.

The jewel of definitive meaning is found within oneself;
Not in ordinary earth and rock on some golden island.
It is like the gathering of all the rivers into the ocean.

If we have confidence and hope, it's easy.
Composing secret words for the secret friend,
I convey them in order to stir your mind.

Ha ha! The unforgettable flower of my heart,
The handsome youth in a verdant lotus grove.
Your unwavering intent is vividly etched in mind.
I recall each heartfelt word of counsel.

Within the mental tendencies of Tāre,
Apparition of the divine lady in human form,
Supreme consort of the *ratna* family,[172]
Is fine nectar to heal the physical elements.

A rain of medicinal camphor and elixir,
Incites the channels at the bliss-sustaining cakra.
The vivid self-radiance of the five wisdoms,
Ḍākinīs fill the major and minor cakras.

In the field, male and female warriors frolic in dance,
In the mind, mantra garland syllables, like a string of lambs,
Revolve like endless firebrand circles spinning.
The twenty-four sacred sites resound with *u ru ru*!

The means, enjoying the glory of the four joys, bliss-emptiness,
The path, completing two accumulations and purifying two
obscurations,
The point, actualizing the result of the four buddha bodies,
May we manifest the qualities along the path of purification.

To fulfill the lifespan of Yulha,
Lady of Ling, accomplish our aims without obstruction.

To conquer the foreigner's machine and tame by whatever
means
Those who harm the dharma teachings of sūtra and tantra,
May we pacify this dark age of suffering!
To kindle the lamp of the teachings in the Land of Snow,

And foster auspicious glory in every direction—
The welfare of Tibet, the world and deeds in accord with
dharma—
Accomplishing all virtue and goodness in this life and
the next,
May we gain dominion over profound treasures.

I have visions in the daytime and at night in dreams in which you appear, the companion from whom I have never been separated even for an instant. This morning, at the break of day, in a dream, a non-human wisdom ḍākinī appeared, wearing a green shawl and saying she was the messenger of the supreme consort, named Tse. Toward the aim of coming here, in order to reverse present conditions, this is a protection circle from among my own treasures and seven strands of hair that you requested. At this point, the Khandro loosened her own hair and removed seven strands.

In confusion, there is nothing to rely on;
Yet even in lies, there is the hope for truth.
I think we can definitely pacify present conditions.

Virtue! Sarva Maṅgalaṃ![173]

Namtrul Rinpoche | Letter 22

Containing an artful set of images to depict their partnership, this letter starts by invoking new beginnings: the morning sun ready to shine on the world and himself as the cuckoo heralding the onset of spring. Through these images, Namtrul Rinpoche expresses a sense of optimism and his eagerness for them to join together as a couple. The main part of the letter consists of four stanzas, using the Tibetan style of parallelism with a series of analogies and the referent in the last stanza. Here Namtrul Rinpoche depicts them as "partners in dance."[174] They are a pair of ravens squawking news across the sky, a pair of golden-eyed fish swimming in tandem, a pair of tantric adepts quivering in postures, and a pair in Do Kham (eastern Tibet) revealing treasures, none other than Namtrul Rinpoche and Tāre Lhamo themselves. Invoking their collaborative enterprise and shared aim, these images show a progression from the play of courtship to its consummation in the tantric rite of sexual union and its role in treasure revelation.

Lady, vine of my heart, with mind unchanged,
Stable friend who has realized the path of awakening,
Sole goddess, dearest beloved, emanation of Sarasvatī,
Friend, divine beauty renowned as Tārā,

In the midst of the vast vaiḍūrya sky,
Golden throne and parasol, the radiant rays of the sun,
Now descend toward the western continent.
Tomorrow morning, from the east, it shines on the world.

At the tip of the juniper branch, turquoise in color,
I, the cuckoo of Mön, issue a melodious call.
Now, having gone south to the land of Mön,
Next year, I'll return to find the juniper.

Ya, ya! In the east is Magyal, conch-white snow mountain.
In the jeweled palace of glorious Cakrasaṃvara,
The protector, precious Machen Pomra,[175]
Is a territorial guardian of us two friends.

Even if I die, still this will not change.
Isn't that it, constant and worthy companion?

Ah! Just so, the mind is untainted by sadness.
Such words of promise, I hide in the heart.

Friend, who accompanies me in every moment,
In this life and in the entire succession of lives,
May you remain in the radiance of bliss![180]

Tāre Lhamo | Letter 25

In a folk song in couplets, Tāre Lhamo reflects on Namtrul Rinpoche's previous letter and thinks over the timing of their union. The style is called the "congenial friend," which conveys the laments of lovers in separation.[181] It uses a seven-syllable meter, unlike the eight-syllable meter more typical of folk songs and bardic verse. To create a whimsical tone, Tāre Lhamo uses triplication of syllables as she articulates their mutual reliance in naturalistic images: thunder clap and rainclouds, hillside and grasses, river and golden-eyed fish, juniper branch and berries at its tip. Through these images, she expresses her reliance on Namtrul Rinpoche in parallel fashion to his reliance on her as animals returning to their natural habitat. By the end of the letter, she seems close to reaching a decision to leave her homeland.

Companion, the jewel who recalls the beloved,
I share heartfelt words with my joyful friend.

This year or next is a good time
Now that we have many allies.

With friends surrounding us,
With plenty to read, expressing inner feelings,
With a joyful gaze and smiling eyes,

With grand aims and enthusiasm in mind,
I cannot forget my constant beloved, dear to life.

Dragon thunder, clap, clap, you clap.
Rain clouds in sky, thick, thick, I'm thick.

Golden hillside, firm, firm, you're firm.
Grasses on top, grow, grow, I grow.

River water, flow, flow, you flow.
Golden-eyed fish, zoom, zoom, I zoom.

Juniper branches, grow, grow, you grow.
Berries at the tip, ripe, ripe, I'm ripe.

Lady friend for life, think, think, you think.
Kindness indeed, guard, guard, I guard.

Singing this little ditty expressing sadness,
Is a supplication from within saṃsāra.

If we think of the suffering of saṃsāra,
It's fine to keep the discipline of ten virtues.

If we think of the gossip of country folk,
It's fine to remain alert and heedful.

If we think of the welfare of ordinary people,
It's fine for us two friends to protect them with love.

If we think of the kindness of the sublime teacher,
It's fine to act in line with our tantric vow of samaya.

We two friends are inseparable.
Isn't that so, Tsebo *lo lo*?[182]

Tāre Lhamo | Letter 26

This is the opening of a letter that references their past lives at the time of King Gesar of Ling and provides a recipe for medicine to help cure Namtrul Rinpoche's ongoing bouts of illness. However, the opening stands on its own and is demarcated as a separate section in their correspondence, so I translate it here as a distinct piece. Sadness is the dominant theme as Tāre Lhamo reflects on his health and becomes nostalgic for the kindness of her own parents. Her affection, concern, and yearning for Namtrul Rinpoche are palpable. At the same time, she confidently asserts their inseparability and connection across lives.

Thoughts sad, mood sad, I feel sorrow for the master.
Recalling the Great Lion,[183] I grow even more sad.
Thinking again and again, I miss my father and mother.
When I recall the deeds of my kind parents, I feel sad.

Thoughts stirred, mood stirred, I'm moved toward the friend.
Recalling my friend, Tsebo, yearning only grows.
It's impossible to say how much I think of you.
Sole companion, joyful in spirit, you are like my heart.

Friend, may you be free from evil spirits,
May your life be undisturbed by illness.
May your youthful thoughts turn to dharma.
Our connection in previous lives in clear.

There's no need to be separate, I have no doubt.
By the power of Sarasvatī's compassion
And command of our lord guru, source of refuge,
Accompanied by the guardians, we are never parted.

Friend, all our aspirations across lifetimes
Provide the fortune to accomplish our aims.[184]

Namtrul Rinpoche | Letter 25

Preparing for her arrival, Namtrul Rinpoche welcomes Tāre Lhamo in a "song of joyous tidings."[185] Since this is the much anticipated moment for their union, he declares: "Today is an auspicious and fortunate time!"[186] In a celebratory tone, he invokes the dance of warriors, the convergence of blessings, and a tantric feast in which Tāre Lhamo is welcomed as Sarasvatī, the Indian goddess of learning and music. The central image for the song is the liquor served to welcome guests, typical of Tibetan weddings. This is homologized to the elixir distributed at a tantric feast and to the result of their own union, i.e., the "great substance symbolizing method and wisdom."[187] This liquor, and hence their union, is then endowed with numerous powers—from dispelling obstacles to engaging profound treasures. Namtrul Rinpoche gives a detailed account of the movements of the subtle body in the process of treasure revelation, making an explicit reference to the tantric rite of sexual union. The letter ends on an upbeat note, as Namtrul Rinpoche calls on each person to sing a happy song, given the presumption that their union will lead to the revelation of treasures and thereby bring great benefit to the Buddhist teachings and the Tibetan people.

OṂ SVASTI SIDDHI MAṄGALAṂ!

The time is today, a propitious star in the sky,
Planets rise and spread out in the evening expanse.
The propitious hour extends across the earth's breadth.

Protector, great emanation of all buddhas,
Soars to divine heights of the guardians of virtue
And stoops to the spirit level of demonic forces of evil.

Swift activity of the ocean of oath-bound protectors
Fulfills the aim of father Orgyan Padma,
Fulfills the wishes of mother Sarasvatī,
Fulfills, today, the great benefit of all the teachings and beings.

Friend, we two accomplish our aims today!
Kindness of wish-fulfilling three roots and guardians!

For this life and next, joy starts today!
Auspicious coincidence clicks into place today!
Words of truth to fulfill our aims are realized today!
The sun of bliss and joy shines today!

Faces of divine lamas smile and smile.
Dance of father heroes beats and beats.
Grand songs of mother heroines: *sha ra ra*.
Banners of the protectors swirl and swirl.
Music of the mandolin twangs and twangs.
Rainbow clouds in space gather and gather.
Rain atop the flowers jingle: *si li li*.

Converging blessings of father lamas of the three lineages,
Converging siddhis of the practice lineage yidams,[188]
Converging activities of mother ḍākinīs of the three abodes,
Converging sun and moon naturally in the azure sky,
Meeting the goddess of bliss-clarity, divine queen,
This is the joyous celebration of method and wisdom.
Converging a festival of dragon gem-holders and peacocks,
This is the display of reveling in the four joys of bliss-emptiness.
Converging on five-faceted peaks of the lofty snow mountains,
This is the prior aspiration and entrustment of Padma.
Converging in a splendid lotus grove along the turquoise valley,
This is the single intention, friend, to gather here,
Converging like the golden-eyed fish encountering water.

Above, the wishes of the virtuous gods are fulfilled.
Between, the intentions of sublime mighty spirits are fulfilled.
Below, the happiness of the Tibetan people is fulfilled.[189]
Happiness! Oh bliss! Oh joy! Gods and humans,
How could there be a happier time than today?
This is my song of joyous tidings!
Happy is the coincidence of auspicious joy,
Its import: words of truth to fulfill all aims.

In the festive gathering of mother ḍākinīs
And method heroes who display joyful reveling,

The supreme feast is arrayed, the pure basis of apparent existence.
Grand tantric substances of the great secret method
Are offered as a banquet of distillates: meat, liquor, and elixir,
Purified, transformed, and increased by mantra and samādhi.

The excellent place is the field of self-existing Zangdok Palri.
The excellent lord is the self-aware Padmākara.
The excellent dharma is the distillate of the ḍākinīs' mind.
The excellent maṇḍala is the rows of heroes and ḍākinīs.
The excellent time is the constant everlasting leisure.

I, the Lord of Secrets, the hero Padma,
And you, the mantra-born Shelkar Lhatso,
By the undeceiving coincidence of deeds and aspirations,
Today we have accomplished our happy goal!
Today we converge in one home and residence!
Coincidence clicks into place beyond meeting and parting.

In the first season of coincidence,
You, goddess Sarasvatī, assemble with an array of gods.
Supreme elixir mixed of thousands of grains and juice,
This great substance symbolizing method and wisdom
Is the liquor at the festival when you arrive here.
It is the liquor to inquire about your health.
It is the liquor to merrily enjoy this festival of delight.
It is the liquor for the vajra feast of great secret mantra.
It is the liquor of indestructible life and changeless form.
It is the liquor blessed by father gurus of the three lineages.
It is the liquor with the siddhi of the divine protector yidams.
It is the liquor with the activity of mother ḍākinīs of three sacred places.
It is the liquor with the power of divine dharmapālas and guardians.
It is the liquor that accomplishes the intention of the protector Padma.
It is the liquor that engages the profound and vast dharma treasures.
It is the liquor that soars to the lofty heights of virtuous gods.
It is the liquor that stoops to the level of unworthy evil spirits.

It is the liquor that accomplishes mind's desires without exception.
It is the liquor that clears away all kinds of adversity and stains.
It is the liquor of us two friends who have never parted.
It is the liquor without contradiction to the samaya vow.
It is the liquor that dispels obstructing conditions without exception.
It is the liquor that guides those with a connection to Palri.
It is the liquor that pacifies illness, evil spirits, obstacles, and the eight fears.
It is the liquor that expands life, merit, glory, and wealth.
It is the liquor that brings all saṃsāra and nirvāṇa, the cosmos, under one's sway.
It is the liquor that fiercely cuts the ten fields of enemies.
Tasting this liquor gives rise to a majestic form.
Consuming this liquor gives rise to melodious speech.
Drinking this liquor gives rise to bliss in the mind.
Partaking in this liquor enhances the qualities of realization.
Enjoying his liquor releases the three nāḍīs at the five cakras.
Tasting this liquor gives rise to the wisdom of bliss-emptiness.
The qualities of this liquor are indescribable.

Friend who meditates on the dharma of bliss-emptiness,
At your three nāḍīs and five cakra sites in the subtle body,
Are the maṇḍalas of the five families in *trikāya* form
And the twenty-four sacred places, completely arranged.

On the 21,000 hairs on your body,
Are the perfect 21,000 mother ḍākinīs.
On the 21,000 flowing prāṇa,
Spontaneously reside 100,000 clouds of mother heroines.

Also in the maṇḍala of the nāḍīs,
Are the fully perfect method aspect, the father heroes.
On the ground, the pure mind of enlightenment, the source of all,
Is perfect bliss-emptiness, beyond meeting and parting.

Smiling, the apparition of a girl in the sky,
With body hairs bristling in bliss-emptiness,

Exudes fragrance and sound from her lotus visage.
Smiling, she joyfully displays her nipples and organ.

The solar fire of caṇḍālī, method of bliss-emptiness,
Moves and melts the elixir at the moon, the essence.
Profound path in swift progression and its reversal,
This is the supreme great method of secret mantra.

Relying on A HAṂ, blazing and dripping,
This is the self-liberation of knots binding the mind in
fixation,
Which opens the initiation maṇḍala of great bliss,
Mounts the horse of prāṇa, possessing a powerful gait,
And turns the magic wheel of four modes of emptiness
and four joys of dharma,
Releasing the knots of the nāḍīs at the five cakras,
And inciting complete blissful joy through great passion.

When experiencing thirty-two joys and emptinesses,[190]
The treasure gate effortlessly opens within.
Hail to you, the beloved, sublime bliss-emptiness,
And to me, the playful vajra engaged in intercourse.

Cradled and tamed by the four joys of secret method,
One obtains the glorious youth of immortal life.
The heroes and ḍākinīs of the *nāḍī* elements delight!
The illusory physical body matures into the divine kāya of
bliss-emptiness.

Now, from this, in the midst of the heart of enlightenment,
Instantaneously, the command of Padma, never separated,
And every intention, activity and aspiration
By all the victorious ones of the three times,
Coalesces on a single hair-tip gate of us two friends.
May we have the power to accomplish these completely.

For as long as time and space remain,
Just so there are also limitless beings.

For that long, may we two friends remain without parting
In order to stir the depths of the three realms of saṃsāra.

In the succession of all our lifetimes,
According to the intention of Lord Orgyan Padma,
For all beings connected through whatever good or bad deeds,
May we have the power to lead them to the pure land Ngayab Palri.

Today is an auspicious and fortunate time!
Victory over adversity of the four māras in battle today!
The golden sun rises in the heavens.
The conch moon appears at mid-sky.
A rain of dharma falls to the earth.
Hoist the victory banner of dharma, the Buddha's teachings!
The sun of happiness shines for mother beings,
Pacifying strife, the damage of degenerate times!
Coincidence converges in the joy of dharma!
Now, each person sing a happy song!
Be quick! Gallop and race with your powerful horse.

This is my song of joyous tidings,
Composed without concealing what arose in my mind.

Precious friend, radiant essence of my heart,
Long life! I write in order to enhance your activities.
May you have auspicious good fortune and happiness![191]

Tāre Lhamo | Letter 30

As her penultimate letter,[192] this may have been composed after the couple had finally united at Nyenlung. Here Tāre Lhamo characterizes their convergence as a couple through images of abundance and growth in the natural world. She imagines herself as a swan who has found a fine dwelling place on a placid lake and as a vulture nesting in a rocky crag with its mate, invoking a sense of ease and enjoyment. The last line suggests that her verses were spoken aloud, vanishing as soon as uttered, while her final letter is an extended duet too long to include in translation. Perhaps the pretext of letter writing is dissolving as their correspondence comes to a close with her arrival at Nyenlung.

Ya! How lovely, look up at the vast open sky.
Above, the convergence of sun, moon, and stars,
Clouds of undesirable conditions strewn by the wind,
Friend, the contours of your form becomes clearer.

It's time to open the maṇḍala of channels and cakras;
The coincidence to join as a couple has clicked.

Between, the valleys have abundant good fortune:
Auspicious flowers bloom into a hundred petals;
The juniper bushes mature and flourish;
And the cuckoo's call is ever more melodious.

The forest becomes grand like a fortress,
A joyful stomping ground of the red tigress.
The crops, seeds sown in the past, are bountiful;
A wealth of food for the steadfast monkey.

Below, within the expanse of a grand lake,
The golden-eyed fish and jewels converge;
It's the coincidence to fulfill common aims.

On the surface of the water, golden birds,
Swan mother and swanlings are companions

Who reside peacefully on the still, clear lake.
It's the dwelling place for the swan, me, to stay,
Playing together on the lake, based on deeds and wishes.

Pursuing the summit of the white craggy peak,
The ancestral home of the bronze-breasted vulture.
The immutable peak is its worldly legacy
And the dwelling place for us two birds.
It's coincidence of our life and merit converging.

Please stay healthy and remain at ease.
Darling, I still think of you a hundred times a day.

Supplicating the swift-acting guardian,[193]
Relying on the Three Jewels as refuge,
Please remain stable as the vajra and at ease
As Jigdral Phuntsok, fearless good fortune,[194]
I, the glorious Devī Dekyi, goddess of joy,
And Pema Kundrol, the lotus liberating all, bring bliss.
Compatible friend, vine of the mind,
Now, today, in the first part of the morning,
The beautiful maiden and Yuyi Thögyancan,[195]
Sing and pluck the lute strings together.

Never tiring of following the friend,
The time for the sun to rise is not far away,
To accomplish the aims of the Lake-Born Guru,[196]
And heal the damage to the teachings and beings.
Hold in the heart the oath of mother ḍākinīs.

At this time, on the Turquoise Peak to the east,
Friend, let's make copious feast offerings together,
Ten thousand invocations to glorious ladies of mantra,
And thirteen extensive Spontaneous Accomplishment of Wishes.

By this, may our wishes be gradually fulfilled.
Words vanished as soon as spoken![197]

4. Travels and Teachings as a Couple

Union with Tāre Lhamo

The Iron Monkey Year (1980) begins the account of the couple's life together teaching and traveling throughout Golok and beyond. Despite being Namtrul Rinpoche's namthar, *Jewel Garland* presents them as joint protagonists for much of its narration, showcasing their collaboration in discovering and disseminating treasures. Tāre Lhamo and he did not wait long to begin their revelatory activities. That year, they ventured to Drongri Mukpo, the sacred mountain of Serta, to reveal a longevity ritual, intended to ensure the long life of those Buddhist teachers who had survived the Maoist period. Miracles accompanied the revelation, highlighting its cosmic significance. First the mountain was said to turn a crystal color and then, after they offered a seven-day gaṇacakra feast in thanksgiving, rainbow light reportedly filled the sky, visible near and far.

As Namtrul Rinpoche once described, Tāre Lhamo and he took turns revealing the symbolic script—the initial kernel of a treasure—and decoding it into textual form as a ritual or esoteric teaching.[1] In line with this, in their first collaboration after joining together, Namtrul Rinpoche offered a maṇḍala to Tāre Lhamo to request her to share a set of yellow scrolls with symbolic script on them, which she had previously discovered, and he transcribed a sādhana or liturgical cycle on that basis.[2] By taking turns revealing and decoding treasures, Namtrul Rinpoche and she were true partners in the revelatory process. This is no doubt why their revelations are gathered into a twelve-volume corpus bearing both of their names.

That same year, the couple visited Khenpo Jigme Phuntsok, who was one of the most influential Buddhist masters in eastern Tibet during the post-Mao era, to request the transmission for Apang Terchen's treasures. Tāre Lhamo had received this transmission directly from her father during childhood and, as his only direct descendant to survive the Maoist period, was the rightful holder of his lineage. But, in order to bestow that transmission alongside her, Namtrul Rinpoche also needed the transmission. Needless to say, Khenpo Jigme Phuntsok gladly agreed and authorized them to disseminate it widely.

Khenpo Jigme Phuntsok remained a celibate monk despite also being a tertön and later gained international renown for his efforts to revive monastic scholasticism through founding Larung Buddhist Academy in Serta.[3] With him and other surviving Buddhist visionaries in the region, Tāre Lhamo and Namtrul Rinpoche created a synergistic network of Nyingma masters who coordinated efforts to revitalize Buddhist teachings, rituals, and institutions in Golok and neighboring areas.[4]

Thereafter, Namtrul Rinpoche and Tāre Lhamo journeyed to Nyenpo Yutse, a mountain range and pilgrimage site in Jigdril County, and revealed a treasure at one of its sacred lakes in accordance with prophecies in their letters and elsewhere. Apparently, there was a slight glitch; they retrieved the treasure casket but not a small stūpa meant to accompany it. Nevertheless, miracles still attended the revelation, in this case, flowers blooming out of season.

Following the prophecies about their union and series of excerpted letters, *Jewel Garland* narrates their lives together as they began to teach and travel, propagating their own treasures alongside those of her father, Apang Terchen.

> For a short while, the two became deeply absorbed in wisdom expressed as a luminous miraculous display. Afterward, subsequent to absorption, as omniscient wisdom impartially shone forth like an apparition, they spoke at length about the positive qualities and shortcomings of the three times—past, present, and future.
>
> Then, to open wide the gateway to inaugurating auspicious coincidence and plentiful good fortune, the Dharma Master offered a golden maṇḍala and, in accordance with his request, the Supreme Khandro unsheathed the yellow scrolls of the dharma cycle of teachings dedicated to the noble queen Krodhī. And at the Khandro's request, the Great Tertön set down a sādhana cycle for the goddess Sarasvatī.
>
> From then on, as defenders of the teachings and beings, the Eminent Couple converged in one residence and together awak-

ened the deeds, aspiration, and coincidence to heal the extensive damage of degenerate times.[5]

On the tenth day of the tenth month of the Iron Monkey Year (1980), the couple and retinue turned their attention toward the treasure gate of golden Drongri Mukpo. In order to stabilize the lotus feet of all the holders of the teachings in the Land of Snow during that period of time,[6] they revealed symbolic script from a *zi*-stone casket at the navel of the protector Rāhula.[7] In accordance with that, they set down the sādhana of Mandāravā, associated with longevity. At that time, the great local guardian and upāsaka, Drongri Mukpo, turned the color of crystal, established as an appearance in common to all gathered there.

At that powerful site, where the mountain curves to the right in a crescent shape, they offered a seven-day gaṇacakra feast. After concluding the evening session, while enjoying the attainment, on the refined golden peak of the treasure site, Drongri Mukpo, spheres of rainbow light filled the whole sky, atmosphere, and ground as if the sun blazed with hundreds of thousands of dazzling light rays, a colorful offering lamp that shone forth in the sky for two days and nights without end. There were many wondrous auspicious signs like that, established as an appearance in common for hundreds of people as far away as Serta, Golok, and Dzamthang.

During the same year, in the presence of a cohort of lamas, with the Sublime Khenchen (Khenpo Jigme Phuntsok) foremost among them, the crown jewel wielding the saffron victory banner of monasticism, the Eminent Couple requested him to bestow the nectar of oral instructions that ripens and liberates for the entirety of the profound treasures of the Apang Terchen Orgyan Trinley Lingpa, who was in actuality the Lord of Secrets, a magical emanation of the three secrets of the victorious lord Padmākara. At that time, Khenchen Rinpoche said, "In the past, the precious lama and great tertön said to me: 'In the same way that I am now bestowing the empowerment on you, in the future, you should bestow it on others.' Although my vision is fading, you, the couple, are surely fortunate individuals and great beings who are emanations. From this time forward, you will accomplish great blessings for the benefit of the teachings and beings. Of this I am certain. Having completed the recitations, perfectly confer this empowerment." With great affection, he bestowed the initiation, reading authorization, and esoteric instructions as well as the subsequent teachings as if filling a vase to the brim. In this way, he entrusted them with the bequest.

At that time, a man called Nuzur Jamgön fell ill and stopped eating. On the brink of death, he came before the Eminent Couple. The master pierced him with a knife and made an incision up and down. As soon as he removed the knife, the wound spontaneously healed, and the man was freed from his illness for the time being.

Furthermore, from a prophecy of Khamtsang Tertön Pema Vajra:

> An emanation of Padma, a vidyādhara with the name Abhaya,
> And Yeshe Tsogyal in person, one holding the name of Tāre,
> Will release the nectar extract of treasures in the powerful Monkey Year;
> At the lake at Nyenpo Yutse, they will find a jewel casket.
> Their magnetizing activity will spread far and wide in every direction,
> And especially, by their profound secret, esoteric instructions,
> Five thousand disciples will attain liberation in this life.

In accordance with the meaning of that prophecy, on the tenth day of the tenth month of that zodiac year,[8] they traveled to the great treasure site of Nyenpo Yutse to extract a lake treasure there, including a crystal stūpa one cubit in height and a casket of five varieties of jewels sealed by the hand of the preceptor Padmasambhava. They extracted the jewel casket but did not receive the crystal stūpa due to circumstances of time and place, such as not completing the number of recitations for the gaṇacakra. Nonetheless, they offered a great feast of thanks to the treasure protector, the nāga king Dungda Bumpa. Although it was winter, the ground heated up, storm clouds slowly gathered, and a rain of flowers fell. A variety of flowers newly bloomed by the shore of the lake. Many such auspicious signs occurred.

Starting from that point, the gateway of auspicious coincidence

> and plentiful good fortune opened widely to propagate in all ten directions—from Markhok and Soruma to many districts—the esoteric instructions that ripen and liberate from the entirety of the profound treasures of Apang Terchen Orgyan Trinley Lingpa. Initially, they bestowed the extensive empowerment and reading transmission for the Secret Sādhana of the Guru,[9] on a group of worthy disciples, including Khamter Pema Chöying Rolpe Dorje. To the multitudes of faithful ones, they bestowed the empowerment for the Swift Path to the Realm of Great Bliss of the protector Amitābha.[10] Then the golden wheels on their feet turned toward Tsikhok.

A sense of optimism and auspiciousness pervades this depiction of the first year of their union. They revealed treasures at Drongri in Serta and Nyenpo Yutse in Jigdril and then, from Khenpo Jigme Phuntsok, together they received the transmission for Apang Terchen's treasure corpus in its entirety, which they disseminated locally in addition to their own treasures. Thus began the teaching career of this remarkable tantric couple.

Namtrul Rinpoche's Illness

Alongside this auspicious beginning to their revelatory career together, there were also obstacles. Namtrul Rinpoche had recurring bouts of illness throughout his life and, shortly after their union, he nearly died. Many of the great masters of the region tried to intervene without success. They said prayers, offered sacred objects, revealed medicinal rituals, and gave blessed medicinal pills to no avail. In the end, it was up to Tāre Lhamo to cure him just as his body began to grow cold. She performed a ritual called Averting the Call of the Ḍākinīs.[11] When Buddhist masters pass away, it is said that the ḍākinīs arrive to escort them, and the ritual attempts to interrupt the process. As Namtrul Rinpoche recounts, he was being escorted away by the ḍākinīs along a rainbow path made of silk, when Tāre Lhamo wielded a longevity arrow and broke the silk cord. Her success in performing this ritual is marked by miraculous signs: rainbow light, a mist of fragrance, and eagle feathers falling like snow.

> On one occasion, the Master was quite ill, yet he was steadfast in his commitment to accumulate the requisite number of recitations for the profound treasures of Apang Terchen Orgyan Trinley Lingpa

and stayed in retreat. At this time, Payul Chagme Rinpoche came before the Eminent Couple and said, "In the profound and vast, changeless and spontaneous temple at Samye, the victorious lord, the Great Orgyan, entrusted us with medical rituals to clear away sickness among the heart sons of the oral transmission. So, there is a way to abruptly clear the basis of your illness." Thereafter, five medical rituals to clear away sickness descended as mind treasures. Saying, "At Yarlung Crystal Cave, I retrieved a treasure allotment for you," he offered him a crystal casket as well as a rosary of jewels and made a supplication for him to remain in this life for a long time.

Khenchen Rinpoche Jigme Phuntsok Jungne the emanated manifestation of the three secrets of the victorious lord Padmākara, who illuminates the teachings in degenerate times, sent a statue of the protector of boundless life, Amitāyus,[12] along with a letter specifying the requisites to stabilize his lotus feet for a long time as the defender of the teachings and beings. In order to clear away obstacles to the Master's physical health, the eminent Lama Rigdzin Nyima set down the *Far-Reaching Laughter of the Hero who Conquered Jang*,[13] and Khandro Rinpoche, who is Yeshe Tsogyal in person, set down the sādhana of the glorious Vajrakumāra.[14]

Then, the precious Dharma Master returned home because of his illness. Villagers and disciples, such as Lama Peche, wondered if they would ever meet with him after that. Out of doubt, they wept as they escorted him back. The Supreme Dharma Master said, "There's no need for you to be sad. I can assure you that there is nothing wrong with me. We two have arrived here to perform the empowerment for the Great Compassionate One Holding a White Lotus."[15] As he said this, gleaming white snow fell like an expanse of flower petals. Everyone was in a state of amazement.

Next, they went to the pleasure grove of Serta and without deception approached the king of dharma, the great tertön Rigdzin Sang-ngak Lingpa, also known as Sera Yangtrul Rinpoche. They received and practiced the ripening and liberating nectar festival of all of his profound treasures. Moreover, from midair without any support, the precious great tertön received a treasure casket and many medicinal pills, saying to the Eminent Dharma Couple, "Previously Orgyan Padma made an entrustment to clear

> away your illness, and I retrieved it." He gave him these and cared for him with inestimable kindness.
>
> On the first day of the first month of the Iron Bird Year (1981), the Supreme Dharma Master said, "For the tenth day of this month, I don't know what to do about this sickness."[16]
>
> At that time, Khandro Rinpoche asked, "In that case, should the two of us invite either Sera Yangtrul Rinpoche or the Wish-Fulfilling Jewel, Khenpo Jigme Phuntsok?"
>
> He replied, "Since there are no negative causes, we should be able to clear up the conditions for my illness by ourselves. If the two of us are careful, then I don't think there will be any problem."
>
> When the tenth arrived, with a gathering of monks and disciples, the Supreme Khandro offered an extensive and profound gaṇacakra, reciting the liturgy for Averting the Call of the Ḍākinīs. The Master was quite ill, and his whole body grew freezing cold. When he was no longer able to speak, the Supreme Khandro became restless. While calling out the Master's name, she waved a longevity arrow three times, and slowly he came back to consciousness.
>
> When he had just regained the ability to speak and move, he recounted, "Many ḍākinīs welcomed me with various instruments and melodies along a silk cord and a rainbow path dangling in the sky. You waved the arrow with silk ribbons and cut the rainbow path and silk cord. Though the ḍākinīs were not pleased, since returning, I am now free of injury." At that time, the down feathers of a white eagle fell like snow on the whole house, outside and inside. A mist of fragrance descended. A dome of rainbow light formed. Many such auspicious signs occurred.

It seems that only a living ḍākinī can avert the call of celestial ḍākinīs. This dramatic episode showcases Tāre Lhamo's ritual prowess and shows how local masters in the region supported one another. This can also be seen in the many prophecies they bestowed confirming the couple's union and the benefit to come from their travels and teachings together.

Prophecies from Local Masters

As Namtrul Rinpoche's health improved, local Nyingma masters delivered further prophecies to authorize his union with Tāre Lhamo and conducted more longevity prayers on his behalf. In addition, Khenpo Jigme Phuntsok reinterpreted a cryptic prophecy meant for her brother, Wangchen Nyima, to refer to Namtrul Rinpoche, showing the adaptability in lineage formation with respect to specific sets of teachings. Pema Tumpo (better known as Kusum Lingpa) also played an early role in supporting the couple by confirming their emanation status.

In the early 1980s, rumors circulated that Tāre Lhamo was a tertön. *Jewel Garland* reports that Dudjom Lingpa's grandson, Tulku Dampa, and great-grandson, Tamdin Wangyal, alerted the couple and encouraged their revelatory activities.[17] Also important was their contact with the 41st Sakya Trizin, who was recognized in youth as the reincarnation of Apang Terchen despite being from a different tradition of Tibetan Buddhism. The Sakya Trizin, former head of the Sakya lineage who lives in Dehradun, India,[18] stayed in close touch with the couple and encouraged their propagation of her father's treasures through phone conversations and letters.

> Then, as the Master's health improved, Khenchen Rinpoche Jigme Phuntsok Jungne the source of teachings of the early translations, the glorious Orgyan, the king of dharma, taking human form in degenerate times and directing his attention toward creating Larung Buddhist Academy of the Five Sciences in Serta, accepted them as disciples and gave them numerous dharma teachings that ripen and liberate. He said, "In the midst of past gatherings, Dzongter Kunzang Nyima delivered this prophecy:
>
> > The powerful monkey youth
> > Adorned with the nectar of fruit and grains,
> > Carefree on a conch-white mountain
> > Must seize power with a fire lasso.
> > When the tigress finds her natural spot,
> > She should know that it is a strong lasso.
>
> With reference to the 'the powerful monkey youth,' I thought, 'Isn't that Wangchen Nyima?' But it is you."[19]
>
> In order to clear away the Master's physical obstacles, Khenchen Rinpoche gave him a bell belong to Terchen Lerab Lingpa that various genuine tertöns, such as Dudzaka Choktrul, Gurong Gyalse, and Chokgyur Dechen Lingpa, had used as the support for practicing the *Rinchen Terdzö*.[20] Before the whole assembly, he recited this longevity prayer:

Fearless in existence and peace with the *good fortune* of
renunciation and realization,[21]
Appearing in person as the spiritual friend with the intention to tame beings,
Supreme guide, glorious teacher, utmost sublime one,
I supplicate Amitāyus, the essence of boundless life, for
your life and prosperity.

Whatever activities you perform, they shine forth like rays
of the sun and moon,
Causing the merit of beings to mature as nectar for the
divine path
And likewise the water lily of the Buddha's teachings to
bloom.
May you dispel the darkness of damage from the five
degenerations.[22]

Then he said, "Tāre Lhamo and I should dispel the obstacles to your life," and so they made extensive aspiration prayers.

Afterward, Khenchen Rinpoche said, "Up until now, there has been a seal of secrecy by strict command around the Crimson Blood Kīla practice by Nyak La.[23] But because you two have arrived, I will give the empowerment." Saying so, he expelled obstacles into a cavity and made extensive praises.

Next, when they traveled up to the county's highlands office, Tulku Dampa Rinpoche and Rigse Tamdin Wangyal came together before the Eminent Couple, saying, "A rumor is currently circulating that this Khandro is secretly a tertön, so this has become the topic of discussion. Even if it was this way in the past, because of the times, it has not been easy. Now that you two have come together, all the treasure prophecies indicate the various ways that you can be of extensive benefit to the teachings and beings."

That being the case, the two continued, "In order to clear away your physical obstacles, we will certainly propitiate the guardians, endowed with the eyes of wisdom, of our ancestral line and family of tertöns."[24] They encouraged them in their aspirations and extensive activity.

Similarly, they met the tertön Pema Tumpo who, in order to clear away the Master's physical obstacles, performed a propitiation to the guardians and set down the *Dharma Cycle of the Ḍākinīs*.[25]

Moreover, he said, "When I first met you, the couple, I saw you, in actuality, as Nubchen Namkhai Nyingpo and the victorious lady Yeshe Tsogyal." Displaying tremendous respect, he delivered a prophecy that the master was at the final birth of a succession of sublime beings such as the mahāsiddha Dombupa;[26] the Sakya Trichen, the throne holder of the Sakya; and the omniscient Longchenpa.

In an interval during a set of teachings, when a craftsman named Gechö who occasionally worked at some other place, went to his work site, the Master said, "Today I saw that the craftsman in my family lost a sleeve of lamb skin."

Returning in the evening, he asked, "How did I lose the sleeve of a lamb skin?"

The Master replied, "This morning at the river crossing, you fell and dropped it. It's still there." In accordance with that, the craftsman found what he was looking for.

Then, from the treasure prophecies of Pema Garwang Tsal:

From the south, an emanation of Nam-Nying[27]
Will arise to restore the treasure teachings.

And:

A manifestation of the victorious lady, Vārāhī,[28] named Tāre,
Whoever is connected to her closes the gates to birth in lower realms.

From the treasure prophecy of Do-ngak Tenpe Nyima that invokes the supreme ḍākinīs:

When the timely guest appears during the Ox (Year),
Coming full circle, the pleasure grove of the teachings will bloom.
At that time, converging with an emanation of Ngari Paṇchen,
By the power of deeds, aspiration, and coincidence,
They will open the vast gates to the profound, secret dharma.

And Orgyan Trinley Lingpa prophesized:

> One day the heart son of Padma with the name Gāga[29]
> Will hold, preserve, and spread profound treasures,
> Benefiting beings extensively in India, Tibet, and China.

And:

> The mantra-born one who is an emanation of Tsogyal,
> If able to free herself from the fiery obstacles of circumstances,
> Will send forth benefit and welfare to all beings without bias.

From a prophecy by Rigdzin Pema Lingpa:

> At the place, Do Nying, the profound treasure
> (The Great Compassionate One with White Lotus and Rosary),[30]
> Once revealed by one named Dorje (Pawo Chöying Dorje),[31]
> It will be gloriously practiced by one named Mati (Pema Drime Lodrö).[32]

There are many such treasure prophecies, according to which the Eminent Dharma Couple came together based on deeds, aspirations, and coincidence.

Many sublime beings, such as Sakya Gongma Rinpoche,[33] repeatedly gave them encouragement orally or by letter that the time had come to propagate in all directions the profound treasures of Orgyan Trinley Lingpa, the father and teacher of the Supreme Khandro, so that they would not wane and to actualize the aspiration, through these activities, to situate those with a connection to the couple at Nyayab Palri in the pure land of Padmasambhava.

The support of other Buddhist masters, through prayer and prophecy, was important for their emerging role as figures of regional renown, whose status as tertöns was just beginning to become public. Given the ancient pedigree claimed, treasure revelations have often been controversial in Tibet, and tertöns establish their legitimacy in part through the confirmation of other masters. The ground for their regional renown had now been laid.

Home at Nyenlung

Namtrul Rinpoche and Tāre Lhamo worked together with Lama Rigdzin Nyima to rebuild Nyenlung Monastery. Over the years, it transformed from a modest hermitage to a full-fledged monastery with a monastic college and retreat centers for specific sets of advanced tantric practices. The rebuilding process took place across several decades, initially based on the contributions of funds and labor by the local community around Nyenlung, especially the Risarma clan. First came the main assembly hall and a few auxiliary temples, then later the couple's own residence, a meditation hall and school, the monastic college and two retreat centers, and a small outdoor pavilion for public teachings. A new wave of building took place in the 2000s as a sizeable number of Han Chinese disciples gathered at Nyenlung each year and donated generously. Today, there are numerous stūpas and temples, a guest house, and new assembly hall with a capacity to hold several thousand for large-scale rituals and teachings.

The couple was also instrumental in the rebuilding of Tsimda Gompa, the monastery founded by Tāre Lhamo's father and populated by clerics from her own Pongyu clan. Tāre Lhamo was responsible for the construction of the main assembly hall dedicated to Vajrasattva, a retreat center on the monastery grounds, and stūpas to memorialize her mother and son.[34] Had she not left Markhok to join Namtrul Rinpoche at Nyenlung, by birthright Tāre Lhamo would have been the head of Tsimda Gompa, since her three brothers had passed away, but instead this honor went to her relative Jamyang Nyima. Nevertheless, the couple remained the principal teachers there, with their own small residence onsite, and visited regularly throughout the 1980s and 1990s to give teachings.

The couple also provided financial assistance and spiritual guidance to at least ten other monasteries in the region,[35] though *Jewel Garland* seems more focused on their ritual activities. They transmitted several liturgies regularly, such as the Great Compassionate One with White Lotus and Rosary, dedicated to the bodhistattva Avalokiteśvara. We learn of the ritual programs they established at Nyenlung and elsewhere as well as the treasures they continued to reveal and the other Nyingma masters in the region with whom they collaborated.

> Next, the Eminent Couple returned to their own monastery and stayed a while. They newly established various sādhanas from the *Vajrakīla Innermost Wrathful One*,[36] a treasure cycle of Terchen

Lerab Lingpa. Gradually, they established various new dharma gatherings including an annual commemoration, a large celebration on the tenth day of the month, a month-long Vajrasattva practice, the sādhana of the Great Compassionate One with White Lotus and Rosary, and a summer retreat. They also built many supports such as eight stūpas, a Vajrasattva temple, and small and large Kālacakra maṇḍalas.

In the Wood Rat Year (1984), when the Eminent Couple departed for Serta, the road suddenly flooded. Many rocks and boulders abruptly rolled down the hillside, and their vehicle could not pass. At that time, the Supreme Dharma Master composed a song of experience and exclaimed, "Is it appropriate to obstruct the presence of an adept?" After that, the vehicles were able to go around without any harm or difficulty whatsoever, and they were easily able to continue with their travels.

Next, the Eminent Couple had an audience with the omniscient mahāsiddha Thubden Trinley Palzangpo (the Fourth Dodrupchen), who had returned for the first time to his own region.[37] They supplicated with fierce devotion, and thus the precious mahāsiddha granted them a profound empowerment of Yeshe Tsogyal as well as an extensive introduction to the complete view, meditation, action, and result of the luminous Great Perfection, the pinnacle of the nine vehicles, self-evident without bias. As a result, the treasure gate of the qualities of experience and realization burst forth from vast space, and the mind of teacher and students mingled as one.

Unexpectedly, based on past deeds and aspirations, the Eminent Dharma Couple met together with the Möngyur scioness, Kachö Wangmo.[38] She granted them teachings that ripen and liberate, such as those of the enlightened Palmo.[39]

Because the time had come for the aspirational entrustment of the victorious lord, Padmākara, they extracted a treasure casket, bearing a lion ḍākinī face, from the site, the golden protector Drongri, and set down the sādhana of Dudul Dragmo, the fierce female demon-tamer. In that zodiac year, at Tsimda Gompa in Golok, they granted the empowerment and reading transmission to the lamas and clerics of two monasteries. On that occasion, various auspicious signs occurred, such as the medicinal elixir and five ritual substances boiled of their own accord.

Their meeting with the Fourth Dodrupchen, Thubden Trinley Palzangpo, was significant. The Fourth Dodrupchen was among the great Dzogchen masters to flee into exile, where he settled in Sikkim. Since 1984, he has regularly returned to Golok to give teachings and, on that first visit, gave the couple precious oral instructions on Dzogchen, or the Great Perfection. Dodrupchen Monastery is just down the road from Nyenlung and served as an important source of inspiration for Tāre Lhamo early in life and for the couple in the post-Mao era.

Bestowing Empowerments

A key turning point in their teaching career together occurred in 1985, when the couple presided over a large-scale ritual gathering at Tsimda Gompa to bestow the treasures of Apang Terchen. *Jewel Garland* reports that clerics came from over fifty monasteries in the region to attend. Whether hyperbole or not, the grand scale of the occasion is evident. It is also noteworthy that their first major teachings took place at her father's monastery and focused on bestowing the transmission for his treasure corpus. In this way, the couple's early regional renown depended on Tāre Lhamo's stature as the daughter and direct lineage heir of Apang Terchen.

From there they traveled eastward to Jigdril County and onward to Ngawa, the prefecture neighboring Golok, before returning to Padma County for a public revelation of a nine-pointed vajra at the Gesar site they had identified at Tashi Gomang earlier that same year.

> In the Wood Ox Year (1985), on the twenty-fifth day of the third month, at the sacred site of Tashi Gomang,[40] they offered an extensive gaṇacakra. At the sacred mountain of the Great Lion (Gesar of Ling), sovereign of the world, a catalogue of its contents descended, and they declared it a treasure site. To all the lamas and monks of that area, they bestowed a great rain of nectar that ripens and liberates.
>
> Then they returned to Tsimda Gompa. To the lamas and monks from more than fifty different monasteries, they bestowed the extensive empowerments and reading authorizations in full for the profound treasures of Apang Terchen Orgyan Trinley Lingpa and their own revelations. To the general public, they opened the vast

gate of the inexhaustible gift of dharma, including the sādhana for the Swift Path to the Realm of Great Bliss.

Furthermore, at the encouragement of the Dharma Lord and Lady, 300 novice monastics and 4,000 lay upāsakas were newly established. They made a lengthy ethical exhortation to stop, as much as possible, any activities not in accord with the dharma, such as using pesticides, explosives, and snares to harm the lives of creatures, or gambling and drinking alcohol.

In addition, they encouraged virtuous conduct by protecting life up to and including insects, regularly doing prostrations, and putting out daily water offerings. They also encouraged reconciliations to be made through the pristine dharma in any conflict of interest between monasteries and the common people. Finally, they encouraged everyone to keep the vast expanse of grasslands beautiful like the pristine teachings of the buddha.

On the third day of the seventh month, they visited Soru Village in Qinghai, where they newly established the sādhana of the Great Compassionate One Holding a White Lotus and bestowed various dharma teachings that ripen and liberate in each valley. Successively, at the various monasteries and villages of Ngawa, they gave ripening empowerments to all the clerics and laity, made many dharma connections, and extensively promoted the performance of virtuous activities.

Thereafter, on the twenty-fifth day of the ninth month, they returned to the great sacred site Tashi Gomang. At the site of Gesar, king of dralas, in the midst of a crowd of many hundreds of people, they received as treasure a nine-pointed vajra made of various types of precious substances, called "the vajra which binds by oath the gods and demons." Then, returning home, they established the sādhana of the Great Compassionate One Holding a White Lotus at more than ten monasteries.

The mid-1980s was a crucial time in their teaching career together as they established a regional sphere of influence. During this time, they became esteemed teachers and spiritual guides to the local lay population and clerics at numerous monasteries in Golok, where they taught regularly, established liturgical programs, sponsored rituals, and funded building projects.

Authorization as Tertöns

After their public debut at Tsimda Gompa, they were authorized as tertöns by Khenpo Jigme Phuntsok and were further encouraged to teach by the Tenth Paṇchen Lama, a major figure in the Geluk tradition, second only in stature to the Dalai Lama. In 1986, the great Khenpo offered a Kālacakra empowerment to a large assembly at Larung Buddhist Academy and called them aside to bestow the treasures of Lerab Lingpa, his own previous incarnation. On this occasion, he confirmed their status as "genuine regents of Orgyan Padma," meaning those authorized to reveal the teachings of Padmasambhava as treasures. Following that, on his historic visit to Serta, the Tenth Paṇchen Lama spent time with the couple and encouraged their activities in bestowing empowerments and teachings widely.

> In the fourth month of the Fire Tiger Year (1986), the Eminent Couple traveled again to Serta to the gathering place of thousands of scholars and adepts, Larung Gar.[41] From the second buddha of the degenerate era, the Wish-Fulfilling Jewel Khenpo (Khenpo Jigme Phuntsok), they received the great, glorious Kālacakra empowerment. On that occasion, Khenpo Rinpoche specially requested their presence at his residence and bestowed the empowerment of Guru Terjung Gyalpo from the profound treasures of the great tertön Lerab Lingpa.[42] At the conclusion, he installed them on a throne and presented them with an image of Guru Terjung Gyalpo, ornamental attire and assorted sundries, as well as various secret mantric substances like meat and liquor. In addition, he gave them the following command: "In the past, Jamyang Khyentse Wangpo invested Chokgyur Dechen Lingpa as a genuine tertön. In the same way, I also authorize you, the couple, as the genuine regents of Orgyan Padma. Henceforth you should write down many treasure teachings."
>
> On the tenth day of the Hare Month, the omniscient Paṇchen Nangwa Thaye turned his golden face to our land and gave an audience.[43] Delighted, he took the hands of the Eminent Dharma Couple and pronounced, "We have never been separated over many lifetimes. You two must give as many empowerments and instructions to others as possible. Despite knowing great illness, I foresee that you have a responsibility to guide those connected to you to

Ngayab Palri."[44] Over the course of just one hour, the Paṇchen Lama engaged them in detailed and extensive conversation.

Next, they traveled to Taktse Samdrup Chökor Ling and bestowed various dharma teachings that ripen and liberate on all the assembled lamas and monks. At that time, at the door of the protector shrine, sacred substance suddenly fell from the sky as a welcome onto the neck of the Supreme Dharma Master. Many witnessed such wonders.

In the eighth month, the daughter of the mahāsiddha Jampa Chödzin, named Zönchuk, offered them a symbolic casket in the shape of a heart on the occasion of their meeting. From that, they set down the dharma cycle of the *Nine Expanses of Crescent Moons*.[45]

Next they traveled to Do Shukjung,[46] where they opened wide the gate to the inexhaustible gift of dharma for all the clerics and laity in accordance with the respective spiritual capacity of each, thereby establishing the path that ripens and liberates. At a soul site of Mayum Tenma,[47] they extracted three from among seven fragments of a jeweled casket and other substances. From this, they set down sādhanas for the Medicine Buddha and the Goddess of Coincidence.[48]

Moreover, from a treasure prophecy of Rigdzin Lerab Dorje:

The messenger of glorious Padma's activity
Must open its auspicious mouth
To enjoy the nectar from the resplendent lotus
Of the secret mother, Yeshe Özer, Wisdom Light,
Who now, for benefit and merit, is named Tāre.

The mind's knot of eternity, an iron hook of blessings,
If invoked through the method of secret mantra,
While displaying the good fortune of the two systems,
Is the medicine of dharma study and practice that ripens
  and liberates;
Its thunder will reverberate throughout the three worlds.

In accordance with the meaning of this prophecy, they newly established the sādhana of Ḍākinī Secret Wisdom[49] at that monastery. While staying there for seven months committed to

> practice, the omniscient one of the degenerate era, Khenpo Rinpoche Jigme Phuntsok Jungne, visited to discuss with them the way to bring about great benefit to the teachings and beings by traveling to Mount Wutai Shan in China together in the year of the Fire Rabbit.
>
> Next, the Eminent Couple visited a number of monasteries such as Dzurung Trakor where they constructed a new assembly hall and established such sādhanas as Red Tārā and the Great Compassionate One with White Lotus and Rosary. Furthermore, in the same zodiac year, for the longevity of the Supreme Khandro, they established a great demon-taming stūpa and a series of eight stūpas slightly smaller than that. They also had clay images made in the form of the peerless teacher, the King of the Śakyas, and more.

This passage offers the reader the only glimpse of the extensive retreats that Tāre Lhamo and Namtrul Rinpoche routinely performed. In fact, they engaged in six months of retreat each year.[50] So while *Jewel Garland* focuses on their public activities—giving teachings, establishing ritual programs, bestowing empowerments, traveling on pilgrimage, constructing and blessing new buildings, revealing treasures, and meeting with other dignitaries— at least half of each year was dedicated to their private lives and meditation practice.

Pilgrimage to Wutai Shan

In 1987, Tāre Lhamo and Namtrul Rinpoche joined Khenpo Jigme Phuntsok on his historic pilgrimage to Wutai Shan. Wutai Shan is a site associated with Mañjuśrī, the bodhisattva of wisdom, in Shanxi Province in central China. At least 10,000 Tibetans accompanied the great Khenpo and engaged in teachings and ritual activities at the site. Yet *Jewel Garland* focuses on the activities of Tāre Lhamo and Namtrul Rinpoche, who brought along their own retinue of disciples and revealed their own treasures at Wutai Shan. The couple had several shared visions of Chinese maidens who served as their guides or gave them the symbolic script for treasures and also of a goddess who appeared in the form of a cuckoo bird to convey esoteric teachings.

This pilgrimage marked the first occasion of their teachings beyond Golok and its vicinity, enhancing their stature and sphere of influence.

Once again, Khenpo Jigme Phuntsok (here Khenchen Rinpoche and the Supreme Khenchen) encouraged them to teach and travel more widely. On this basis, they stopped along the return trip home at sacred sites in Amdo, such as Lake Kokonor and Drakar Tredzong, to make feast offerings and bestow the transmission for their new revelations, especially the sādhana of Sarasvatī, the goddess of learning and music.

Their visit to Drakar Tredzong became the instance for a light-hearted sectarian exchange, given that this Nyingma pilgrimage site with sacred caves associated with Padmasambhava and Yeshe Tsogyal has a nearby Geluk Monastery along the road. As the couple and their retinue departed, a fierce rainstorm broke out, and the Geluk monks teased Namtrul Rinpoche, saying that if he were a great siddha, he should be able to alter the weather. Stereotypically, the Geluk have been closely associated with monastic scholasticism and the Nyingma more with tantric practice. Rising to the occasion, reportedly Namtrul Rinpoche cleared his mind and the clouds in the sky simultaneously dispersed. He cautioned their group to cross the river before evening, when the rains would return.

Thereafter, proceeding south and homeward, they traveled to the base of Amnye Machen, outside Tawu, the prefecture seat of Golok, to perform a feast at this sacred mountain range. This is the site where they would later build a Gesar temple, one of the six state-recognized temples to Gesar of Ling in Golok.[51] The couple traced their past lives together to the time of Gesar and one full volume of their treasure corpus is dedicated to the Gesar epic. Next, they continued southward to give teachings at Tongchap Gompa in Gabde County, eventually touring several of the monasteries in Padma Country before returning home to Nyenlung.

> In the Fire Hare Year (1987), on the twenty-fifth day of the third month, the Eminent Dharma Couple traveled to the great sacred site of Wutai Shan.[52] When encountering a stūpa called Janak Shengan, they had a vision of a Chinese maiden dressed in red who introduced the Eminent Dharma Couple to much that was ancient, including the history of the stūpa, and then vanished. They said that she seemed like an apparition of the Chinese princess Kongjo.
>
> In the meantime, at Wutai Shan, there were tens of thousands of Tibetans staying with Khenchen Rinpoche in their midst. As a collective, they propagated extensive good works, like making

sacred objects, offering feasts, and making aspirations for virtuous activity.

At a monastery called Yandrosi, the goddess Ngawang Tsochung taught the dharma to the Eminent Dharma Couple in the guise of a cuckoo bird to the amazement of their retinue. Also, one day they ventured to the stone staircase called Phosatin. While resting along the way, a young Chinese maiden with the syllable HRING on her forehead appeared. She wrote many symbolic letters on the palm of the master's hand and then vanished. From that symbolic script, they set down the sādhana cycle of Sarasvatī along with its empowerment. They bestowed the initiation to all the lamas and monks who came from all over to that place.

Then, the Supreme Khenchen pronounced, "Now the pair of you should travel extensively to such places as Lake Kokonor, Drakar Tredzong, and the snow mountain Machen."[53] In accordance with this, the Eminent Couple and a retinue of monks first visited Lake Kokonor. On the twenty-fifth day of the fourth month, they offered an extensive gaṇacakra at the lakeshore. Many wondrous signs appeared on that occasion: the whole lake filled with rainbow-color light rays and the sound of various musical instruments reverberated.

On the third day of the fifth month, they traveled to the sacred site, Drakar Tredzong, where they made extensive aspirations for a connection to the place. From a site on the glorious mount called the Indestructible Cave of the Monkey Fortress, they received a powerful red casket as treasure and set down many profound teachings including a sādhana cycle of Yeshe Tsogyal. At Tredzong Monastery, the assembly of monks including Alak Chuja rendered service to them impeccably.

Then, as the Eminent Dharma Couple was about to depart for the county seat of Shingho in Qinghai,[54] a fierce rainstorm broke out. The valley floor filled with water, making it impossible to be traverse the Hang-nge river. The lamas and monks of Tredzong Monastery said teasingly, "If you Nyingma have the power to stop rain, we can see you off this morning."

The master replied, "Oh, that's easy!" Merely by focusing his mind, the sky became perfectly clear, and the river diminished. That morning, on the way back to the county seat of Shingho, after traversing the river, the master said, "You should try to reach home by five o'clock. At that point, I will dispatch the rains." In accordance with his statement, at five o'clock, heavy rains once again descended, and there was no longer any way to clear the swelling river.

On the tenth day of the fifth Tibetan month, the Eminent Couple and retinue traveled to Machen in Golok Prefecture to the Gesar mountain of Pema Bumdzong,[55] where they offered an extensive gaṇacakra and set down several profound teachings. To several fortunate disciples, they conferred the empowerment of the goddess Sarasvatī. On the twenty-third day, they traveled to Tongchap Gompa in Gabde County.[56] There they bestowed various dharma teachings that ripen and liberate to the assembly of lamas and monks and newly established the sādhana of the Great Compassionate One Holding a White Lotus.

On the tenth day of the sixth month, at several monasteries in Markhok, such as Dogongma,[57] they bestowed empowerments and reading authorizations, including for the Medicine Buddha and Sarasvatī. Then their golden faces turned toward home. On the twenty-fifth day of the ninth month, while practicing the Guru Terjung Gyalpo, they received a casket with empowered treasure to clear away illness. From the tenth day of the tenth month, to the lamas and clerics at glorious Nyenlung Thekchen Chökor Ling, they gave dharma instructions on the *Way of the Bodhisattva* and the *Thirty-Seven Practices of a Bodhisattva*.[58]

Through this tour and others that followed, the couple extended the reach of their teachings incrementally northward into Amdo in Qinghai Province and southward into Kham in Sichuan Province.

Travels and Teachings

During the late 1980s and early 1990s, Namtrul Rinpoche and Tāre Lhamo continued to travel and teach in ever-widening circles. To the south, they visited Dartsedo—on the border between ethnically Tibetan and Chinese areas in Sichuan Province—to attend a conference, touring monasteries in Kandze Prefecture of Kham on their return. To the north in Qinghai Province, they taught to thousands gathered in the Nyingma enclave in

Rebkong, converting peripheral communities to normative Buddhist practice by forbidding the "red offering" of animal sacrifice. Later, to the west, they made an extensive pilgrimage to Lhasa and sacred sites in Central Tibet with a retinue of disciples.

Nearer to home, they continued to teach at monasteries in Golok, especially Padma and Jigdril Counties as well as Dzamthang in Ngawa Prefecture, establishing a pattern for their regional teaching tours that continued for the rest of their lives. During one of those tours, in 1990, they met Dola Chökyi Nyima, the son of Dujdom Rinpoche who was the reincarnation of Dudjom Lingpa and served as the head of the Nyingma lineage in exile until his passing in 1987. From Dola Chökyi Nyima, they received the transmission of Dudjom Rinpoche's treasure corpus, were authorized as lineage holders, and encouraged to propagate his teachings widely. The following year, Tāre Lhamo gained international recognition for recognizing the reincarnation of Dudjom Rinpoche in Dola Chökyi Nyima's own family.[59] From that point forward, they propagated the treasures of Dudjom Rinpoche alongside their own and those of Apang Terchen.

In *Jewel Garland*, this pivotal period in their teaching career as a couple begins with Namtrul Rinpoche again offering Tāre Lhamo a maṇḍala to request her to spread the sādhana of Tārā, the female bodhisattva of compassion. Thereafter, she established liturgical performances dedicated to Tārā at various monasteries in the region, including a rigorous three-month practice intensive.

> In the Earth Dragon Year (1988), on the tenth day of the third month, according to the prophecies of the deities and lamas, His Eminence offered a white dharma conch with a clockwise coil and a maṇḍala of various jewels, beseeching the Supreme Khandro to establish the sādhana of the victorious mother Tārā throughout Amdo and Kham. Accordingly, she established a one-hundred day Tārā practice at various monasteries.
>
> For the sake of virtue, they exhorted most of the districts to construct approximately 1,500 stūpas following the example of glorious Nyenlung Thekchen Chökor Ling. In addition, they newly constructed a temple and established a performance from their own treasure revelations from the life of the Great Lion (Gesar), sovereign of the world, regarding the horse race and the golden fortress.[60] In order to heal the earth, they buried one hundred treasure vases in various sacred places.

During the seventh month, while in Dartsedo attending a conference, they made dharma connections with a few lamas, tulkus, and others from Kandze Autonomous Prefecture. And on the tenth day, they initiated dharma connections with the local populace from the area, such as Nadran and Tawu.[61] On the twenty-fifth, they traveled to Kyilung Drashul Monastery,[62] where they conferred an empowerment and reading authorization on the assembly of lamas and monks and a day-long empowerment for the local populace, turning the wheel of dharma regarding the Swift Path and other topics.

From there, they traveled to Tsimda and Wangda monasteries.[63] To the assembly of lamas and monks, they performed the empowerment and reading authorization for the Eight Command Deities, the Great Sādhana of the Sugatas. And to the general populace, they granted dharma instructions on the ritual for rousing bodhicitta and the *Thirty-Seven Practices of a Bodhisattva*. Based on connections with them, the Eminent Couple exhorted them to build 300 stūpas. Immediately afterward, they traveled to Serkhar, where they gave the initiation and reading authorization for the Great Compassionate One Holding a White Lotus and established the sādhana at the monastery. To the local populace, they presented the gift of dharma and made extensive exhortations for them to practice virtue.

In the Earth Snake Year (1989), on the tenth day of the third month, during the consecration of a stūpa at Serta Larung, as he expounded on the teachings on both sūtra and tantra, Khenpo Rinpoche was seated on a throne in the section for saffron-robed monastics. The Supreme Dharma Master was seated on a throne in the section for white-robed ones with matted-hair (tantrikas), and Khandro Rinpoche was seated at the head of the assembly of nuns. When the flowers for the consecration were tossed, the circumstances and good fortune coincided for the swift arrival of the reincarnation of the omniscient Paṇchen Rinpoche.[64]

From the fourth day of the seventh month, at the monasteries of Payul Tarthang and Dong Dzong,[65] to the assembly of lamas and monks, they performed the empowerment and reading authorization for the Great Compassionate One Holding a White Lotus and established the sādhana there. To all the laity, both male and female, they bestowed the empowerment for the Swift Path to the

Realm of Great Bliss and extensively promoted the performance of virtuous activities.

At Wangda and Böpa monasteries, they established an annual practice of the Swift Path to the Realm of Great Bliss and a hundred-day Tārā practice. They newly constructed a stūpa on the meadow facing the teaching throne. On the eighth day of the eighth month, they consecrated representations of the body, speech, and mind and bestowed all sorts of dharma instructions that ripen and liberate to all the clerics and laity.

From the twentieth day, at Utsa Gompa in Markhok, they gave various dharma instructions that ripen and liberate to the assembly of lamas and monks as well as taught and made dharma connections with all the local populace. From the twenty-third, at such places as Dumda and Getse Tradong,[66] they bestowed a variety of dharma instructions that ripen and liberate on all the clerics and laity.

On the tenth day of the fifth lunar month of the Iron Horse Year (1990), the noble son Dola Chökyi Nyima bestowed on the Eminent Couple all of the profound treasures of Dudjom Rinpoche Jigdral Yeshe Dorje including the initiation, reading transmission, esoteric instructions, and auxiliary teachings as if filling a vase to the brim. He requested them to propagate these profound teachings throughout Amdo and Kham and entrusted them as accomplished masters.

In the twenty-second of the fifth month, the construction of a commemorative stūpa at his birth place in Wuzi at the site called Sang-ngak Gakyil Valley had been completed. From afar, the Eminent Couple tossed flowers as its consecration, which actually fell on top of the terraces and dome of the stūpa. Many such auspicious signs occurred.[67]

Next, to a gathering of monks and laity at various monasteries, they bestowed ethical advice and teachings in order to forge a dharma connection, including the initiation and reading authorization for the Great Compassionate One Holding a White Lotus.

On the eighth day of the seventh lunar month, for the assembled lamas and monks of Abzö Gompa, Palri Thekchen Shedrup Pelgye Ling, they performed the initiation and reading authorization of the Great Compassionate One Holding a White Lotus and the Phurba that Subdues Demonic Forces.[68] They newly established the tenth day practice of Padma Öbar[69] and set forth for the first time a system of study and practice there. To the local population, they disseminated the gift of dharma far and wide.

Moreover, when the Eminent Couple first arrived at Abzö Gompa, they were welcomed by a procession that looked like a golden rosary. On the occasion of their reception with various musical instruments, the Supreme Dharma Lord had the following vision. At the head of the procession, a stūpa appeared in the middle of a golden eight-petalled lotus flower. The symbolic text of EVAṂ also appeared there, indicating that the occasion was right to build a stūpa at that site so that great benefit for the teachings and beings would come about. According to this vision, a stūpa was later constructed at the site.[70] Then they traveled to the village of Drasar, where they bestowed dharma teachings that ripen and liberate.

On the twenty-seventh day, they were invited to a hermitage in Rebkong called Yu Ngog. They were welcomed with horses and told that a red offering would be performed as "an ancient custom of the area." However, they could not accept this since it would be inauspicious to agitate the local goddess, even though it was explained, "Various saints such as Maṇi Lama Pema Gyedor Kyabgön Rinpoche have also visited and not prevented the red offering."

The Eminent Couple bestowed the initiation and reading authorization for the peaceful and wrathful deities to the lamas and monks. When the time came for the goddess' life force initiation, according to skillful means, they requested several individuals to hold a support flag. As they tossed rice to bless the supports, the goddess descended. The support flag waved and fluttered. More than ten men were unable to hold it. Everyone was amazed and shed tears of devotion. In the evening, the local people made an oath to end the tradition of performing the red offering.

Although they were invited to visit people's homes throughout the area, they did not have time to remain there. For the whole countryside, they uttered auspicious prayers for rousing the unsurpassed enlightened intent to benefit others and, at the same time, tossed rice as a blessing. At that moment, consecration flowers actually fell on top of the houses, tents, and horse trails, remaining there for a few days. Many such wondrous signs occurred.

On the occasion of visiting at the Olza clan, where previously

> there had never been a monastery or dharma tradition, the Eminent Couple newly established a temple and images, as well as the tenth-day practice of Padma Öbar from the Longsal tradition of Katok, naming the new monastery Thubten Palgyeling, the place to propagate the Buddha's teachings. To the assembled populace from the four Hor clans in the surrounding six districts, they gave an initiation and extensive dharma instructions.
>
> At that time, although thousands of nomads from Golok and Rebkong made offerings to them, they maintained equipoise and did not accept. At the monasteries of Terton Chögar, Shingtri, and Rongpo,[71] they opened the door to the inexhaustible gift of dharma for the assembled monks and laity, more than 17,000 in number. Near the slaughterhouse there, to set an example and propagate virtue across the grasslands, they ransomed the lives and liberated hundreds of thousands of animals.
>
> From the seventh day of the ninth month, at the great dharma center of Tashi Gomang, they bestowed at length the initiation, reading authorization, and esoteric instructions for the profound treasures of Dudjom Rinpoche Jigdral Yeshe Dorje to more than a thousand lamas and monks.

Liberating lives, called *tsethar*, is a longstanding Tibetan practice. Traditionally, it involves paying the purchase price for livestock destined to be slaughtered. One or more yaks or sheep are thereby freed from a terrible death and marked with a red ribbon to indicate its special status, rendering it taboo to sell or slaughter. This practice has become popular today among Han Chinese disciples of Tibetan teachers, taking the form of releasing fish into lakes.[72]

Along these lines, ethical advice has been a noteworthy aspect of the revitalization of Tibetan culture in Buddhist terms. *Jewel Garland* makes reference to Namtrul Rinpoche and Tāre Lhamo asking nomads to forgo the use of pesticides, explosives, and snares during their public teachings, and here shows them convincing a community near Rebkong to abandon animal sacrifice and later liberating animals near the site of a former slaughterhouse. Khenpo Jigme Phuntsok was a leading proponent of tsethar and, in a speech in 2000 attended by thousands from the surrounding area, he asked nomads to give up selling their livestock for slaughter. Many took vows on the spot and others later committed to abandon the practice for a period of time. Since 2008, Larung Buddhist Academy has become a hub for ethical reform with cleric-scholars there propagating a new set of ten Buddhist virtues.[73]

Danger at Shukjung

On the grasslands of Golok, the danger of hailstorms and flooding from the Do, Ser, and Mar rivers has always posed a periodic threat to travelers, livestock, crops, and low-lying monasteries. Prophecies and ritual interventions like prayers or offerings were sometimes sought out by local Tibetans and performed by Buddhist masters to mitigate these natural hazards. Indeed, Apang Terchen had constructed Tsimda Monastery in 1925 on the basis of a prophecy that a nāga spirit on the Mar River needed to be tamed.[74] On an occasion in 1991, a prophecy warned that Shukjung Monastery was in danger of flooding unless an emanation of Rigdzin Gödem intervened to protect it. Namtrul Rinpoche counted this well-known tertön among his past lives, so representatives of Shukjung approached the couple for help. Shukjung Monastery sits along the Do River; it is relatively small, yet due to its proximity to Nyenlung and Dodrupchen, the couple visited often.

When advice was sought, Namtrul Rinpoche and Tāre Lhamo suggested specific rituals to be performed, including the Gesar of Ling performance from their own treasure corpus. As the monastic performers were dispatched, more danger ensued and, in one voice, the couple warned the troupe not to get distracted and gave them blessed cords as protection. Namtrul Rinpoche made further offerings and aspirations to the protectors. In the end, the troupe encountered a hailstorm but survived unscathed, though their clothing was soaked. The next year, despite heavy rains and flooding, Shukjung Monastery did not get damaged. The tale concludes that this was "solely due to the compassionate activity of the Master himself."

Somewhere along the way, Tāre Lhamo's contribution gets lost. Indeed, there is a subtle tension in *Jewel Garland* since it is ostensibly Namtrul Rinpoche's "story of liberation," and yet much of its narration in the 1980s and 1990s covers activities performed alongside Tāre Lhamo. For the most part, the couple serves as joint protagonists, however, when it comes to miracles, author Pema Ösal Thaye prefers to credit Namtrul Rinpoche, even when the couple act in tandem.[75]

Here is the account of Shukjung Monastery along the Do River:

In the Iron Sheep Year (1991), at Do Shukjung Monastery, there was a prophecy as follows: "In a round cavity in the ground at Shuk, the water will be destructive on account of the king. An emanation of Gödem will offer protection." The moment of this prophecy had come. On the sixteenth day of the second lunar month, representatives of the monastery arrived before the Eminent Couple and requested a prophecy regarding the best course of action. They prophesized that various rituals pertaining to the buddha Akṣobhya and especially the Gesar of Ling performance from their own treasure corpus, if performed, have the ability to reverse those conditions.

Thereafter, approximately fifty lamas and monastics from glorious Nyenlung Thekchen Chökhor Ling, as well as Choktrul Rinpoche Rigdzin Longyang,[76] set out to perform in accordance with the invitation to Shukjung Monastery. At that time, the Dharma Lord and Lady warned, "Along the way there, you should not get distracted even for a moment from the inseparability of your own mind with that of the teacher." They tied protection cords on all the people and horses and entrusted them to the three roots and protectors. Later, the Supreme Dharma Lord made a tea offering, saying that presently there would be problems with the weather and further enjoining the protectors for aid and making aspirations.

At that time, as they were passing through a place called Rula Valley, suddenly black clouds gathered and a hailstorm erupted. Lightning struck near the people and horses. Some of the performers such as Drupchen Lagya and Yagshul wailed, thinking that the lightning and hail would destroy them. Though their garments and costumes were drenched, no harm whatsoever came to them. They arrived at Do Shukjung in good spirits and completed the performance in its entirety.

The following year, there was a flood, but the monastery was not badly damaged. This was attributed to the prophecy above that an emanation of Gödem would protect them. Certainly, this came about solely due to the compassionate activity of the Master himself.

The focus on Namtrul Rinpoche in this final statement, despite the active role that Tāre Lhamo played in the episode overall, may well be because it occurs in his own liberation story. This makes all the more remarkable the moments in which Tāre Lhamo comes to the fore in *Jewel Garland*: the inclusion of excerpts from a dozen of her letters, the numerous prophecies about their union, his maṇḍala offerings to request her teachings, the healing ritual she performed to save his life, rumors about her being a tertön, and her promotion of liturgies dedicated to the female bodhisattva Tārā. Since tantric partners usually play a minor role, if they appear at all in the life stories of Buddhist masters, this clearly signals Tāre Lhamo's elevated stature in the religious community that the couple led together.

Back at Nyenlung

In the early 1990s, Namtrul Rinpoche and Tāre Lhamo held their first large-scale teaching at Nyenlung Monastery. Its full name is Nyenlung Thekchen Chökor Ling, which literally means Melodious Valley, Dharma Gathering Place of the Great Vehicle. Lamas and monastics in the region gathered there for the transmission of the treasures of Apang Terchen and Dudjom Rinpoche. To a smaller group later the same year, they bestowed a set of Dzogchen teachings from Apang Terchen's corpus, the *Six Dharmas of the Profound Path*,[77] which the couple only gave to close disciples who had completed the preliminary practices. In typical fashion, *Jewel Garland* reports the wondrous signs that occurred on such auspicious occasions. As before, miracles by Namtrul Rinpoche are peppered through the account of their teachings and revelations together.

> From the sixteenth day of the third lunar month, at glorious Nyenlung Thekchen Chökor Ling, to the lamas and monks of approximately thirteen monasteries, they bestowed the initiation and reading authorization for sections of teachings from the profound treasures of Apang Terchen Orgyan Trinley Lingpa and Dudjom Rinpoche Jigdral Yeshe Dorje of Kham.
>
> Then, on the tenth day of the seventh lunar month, they offered a summer retreat for the saṅgha and, accompanying that, a celebratory feast gathering. On that occasion, all of the feast substances melted into light and transformed into elixir. Next, on the tenth day of the eighth lunar month, they performed an initiation

on behalf of Nyarong Chagdud Tulku. At that time, there were wondrous signs of various kinds, such as the initiation substances melted into elixir tinged with *sindūra* and eagle feathers fell from the sky.

During the tenth lunar month, they gave teachings on the *Six Dharmas of the Profound Path* to a gathering of approximately twenty lamas and monastics from a few different monasteries. Over the course of the instructions, during the Display of Awareness Initiation,[78] the wandering thoughts of the assembled monastics and disciples were banished into space and their minds merged with luminous naked awareness. During the Display of Cutting-Through Initiation,[79] the sky cleared and, during the Display of Direct-Crossing Initiation,[80] the sky and earth in its entirety was suffused with rainbow light. Many such marvels occurred. Also that year, they completed the construction of a protector shrine and its images and established the continuity of protector practice there.

In addition, as a remedy for illness—such as that caused by malevolent spirits—the Master himself drew symbolic letters and markings. Merely by wearing them, one is liberated from illness. For example, the mother, father and uncle of a young woman named Pemo died from an illness akin to mad cow's disease. Now she herself and her child had become ill and were close to dying. The Dharma Lord drew a protection circle marked with a vajra on their stomachs. In the morning, due solely to that design, they were free from illness.

Furthermore, in the region of Golok, there was a woman who had been blind from the age of nine. Due to his signs of accomplishment, when the Master himself showed her a dyed piece of cloth three times, asking if she could see, instantaneously she recovered her sight. In addition, he was able to freely enter houses without relying on doors or windows, and he was able to cook elixir in a dry skull to offer to more than thirty disciples. These are many such great deeds of the Supreme Adept and Lord.

On the twentieth day of the fourth lunar month of the Water Monkey Year (1992), they were invited to Yashul District. In accordance with this, they performed the empowerment for the Swift Path and made various exhortations to virtue. On the thirtieth day, they offered a feast at Dröphug Khandro Duling.[81] On that

> occasion, the Supreme Dharma Lord spontaneously chanted a self-arisen vajra song and later set down the initial symbolic letters for the sādhana of the Radiant Azure Ḍākinī.[82]
>
> Next, they performed the consecration for a newly constructed assembly hall at Tsimda Gompa. To the assembled monks and laity at various monasteries—such as Takthok, Khargong, and Kyilung—they gave the empowerment for the Swift Path and made extensive exhortations to virtue. In a similar manner, they were invited to monasteries such as Taklung Gön Kadak Trödral Ling in Khangsar and Ösal Thekchok Ling in Minthang.[83] To the assembled lamas and monastics there, they performed empowerments and reading authorizations, including the Root Sādhana of the Vidyādharas,[84] and consecrated their assembly halls. They made extensive dharma connections with the communities in those places among others in Golok,[85] such as at Mura Monastery, where they bestowed initiations and made many dharma connections.
>
> At the shore of Shimtso Lake at the great treasure site of Nyenpo Yutse, they offered an extensive gaṇacakra feast and withdrew a treasure casket for the *Radiant Azure Ḍākinī*. They performed other such virtuous deeds, which blazed forth brightly.

As they traveled, *Jewel Garland* suggests that the couple made "dharma connections" and "place connections" along the way.[86] When asked how such connections were made, Namtrul Rinpoche stated that dharma connections are made through a request for teachings. The more advanced the teaching, the closer the connection. Place connections, on the other hand, occurred through pilgrimage and ritual activities at a sacred site. Thus, through their teaching and ritual activities, Tāre Lhamo and Namtrul Rinpoche had a formative role in reintegrating networks of Tibetan people and places in Buddhist terms. Given that the years leading up to and including the Cultural Revolution unleashed massive disruption, in the decades that followed, healing that damage involved, in part, reestablishing connections within Tibetan society and to its sacred landscape.

Pilgrimage to Lhasa

In 1992, Namtrul Rinpoche and Tāre Lhamo went on a pilgrimage tour with a retinue to Central Tibet. On that tour, they visited sacred sites from the imperial period and advent of Buddhism in Tibet, such as the Jokhang Temple, housing the precious Jowo Śākyamuni brought to Tibet by the Chinese bride of the emperor Songtsen Gampo, and Samye Monastery, the first Buddhist monastery constructed by the emperor Trisong Detsen in the configuration of a Buddhist maṇḍala. According to the lore surrounding this period, the gods and demons of Tibet obstructed the building of Samye until the Indian tantric master Padmasambhava, upon the emperor's invitation, ritually tamed them at nearby Hepo Hill and bound them by oath to protect the dharma. Namtrul Rinpoche reenacts this moment when the couple visited the site and Tāre Lhamo was suddenly put under a spell by a malevolent spirit.

At Samye, in a vision of Padmasambhava, they received their tertön names, Orgyan Jigme Namkha Lingpa and Ḍāki Tāre Dechen Gyalmo, and thereafter revealed a ritual cycle dedicated to Hayagrīva, the horse-headed tantric deity. When performing its sādhana at the Hayagrīva temple there, it is said that those assembled heard the neigh of Hayagrīva himself. Later when visiting Chimpu, the famous hermitage above Samye, they revealed more treasures, performed an extensive gaṇacakra feast, and gave teachings to those assembled. In line with its emphasis on miracles by Namtrul Rinpoche, *Jewel Garland* reports that he left his footprint in rock.

For the period of their pilgrimage, the protagonist of *Jewel Garland* shifts from the "eminent couple" to the "couple with entourage." On that trip, they made a special connection with the sacred mountain range and local protector Nyenchen Thangla. Colorful clouds gathered around its peaks when they visited and seemed to escort them along the road to Lhasa. As so many other Tibetan pilgrims across the centuries, Namtrul Rinpoche and Tāre Lhamo made offerings at the Jokhang Temple, the Potala Palace, and the three great Geluk monasteries, Drepung, Sera, and Ganden. As a particularly potent way to gain merit, some pilgrims sponsor a fresh coat of gold leaf that is placed on the Jowo Śākyamuni and other statues. The couple followed suit and also held a feast offering in the courtyard of the Jokhang Temple with their retinue and other pilgrims from eastern Tibet. Apparently, quite a crowd gathered, and miraculously the feast offerings multiplied to feed them all. In addition, they set down a treasure dedicated to Padmasambhava at the site.

Their travels also took them to sacred sites associated with Nyingma progenitors, such as Gangri Thökar, the former hermitage of Longchenpa, and Tsogyal Latso, the reputed birthplace of Yeshe Tsogyal and location of a nunnery. At those sites, they revealed treasures and bestowed empowerments on the lamas and monastics residing there. The couple made a particularly strong connection to the nuns at Tsogyal Latso and continued to send financial support to them over the years. On this tour, they also visited sites to the west in Tsang, including Tashi Lhunpo, the monastery of the Paṇchen Lamas and Sakya, the seat of the Sakya Trizin.

> On the twenty-second day of the eighth lunar month, the Couple with Entourage turned their attention toward Lhasa and the Potala Palace in Central Tibet.[87] En route, on the twenty-fifth, they visited Jangyul.[88] Since, in a previous life, the Supreme Dharma Lord had been the prince of Jang, Yulha Thogyur, he spontaneously uttered many folk songs from memory as well as offerings and praises to the guardians of that land, expressing a range of moods, happy and sad. Gradually, they came before Nyenchen Thangla with an assortment of crimson and orange clouds spread about its mountain peaks, which seemed to accompany their car along the many bends in the road like an escort. Glistening snow fell like flower petals of various shapes. Many such auspicious signs occurred.
>
> Before the deity Damshö,[89] the Supreme Dharma Lord made a tea offering and said to the gathered disciples, "From here forward Thangla will not need to escort us." After that, the crimson clouds returned to the slopes of Thangla and remained, a spectacle to behold. As the reason for Nyenchen Thangla's joyful countenance upon their arrival, it is said that this land deity was the designated guardian for the northern treasures of Rigdzin Gödem and the Supreme Dharma Lord is the emanation of that great vidyādhara.
>
> On the second day of the ninth lunar month, the Couple with Entourage made their pilgrimage to the wish-fulfilling jewel, the Lhasa Jowo; the Potala Palace; and Drepung, Sera, and Ganden monasteries. They offered donations and made great aspirations for the benefit of the teachings and beings. In particular, they offered gold to cover the bodies of the Jowo Śākyamuni and Avalokiteśvara statue with five naturally arisen features.[90] With just a little gold, the entire statues were covered. All were amazed.
>
> On the tenth day, they made a guru feast offering before the Lhasa Jowo together with many thousands of the faithful on

pilgrimage from various areas in Do Kham. Through the power of mastery, the feast offerings increased as an inexhaustible sky treasury, offered to the whole crowd. Not only that, the butter lamps, blessed as cloud banks of Samantabhadra offerings, multiplied. This was perceived in common by all. Accompanied by many auspicious signs, they set down the sādhana of Great Orgyan, the Sphere of Secret Completion.[91] For this teaching, they appointed as trustees Dodrak Rigdzin Chenpo and Choktrul Lozang Norbu.

On the twelfth day, at Gangri Thökar, according to a vision of the Great Omniscient One (Longchenpa), they set down the *Heart Essence of Samantabhadra: Instructions Introducing One's Own Nature as Luminosity* from the *Radiant Azure Ḍākinī*.[92] On this basis, primordial awareness—the nature of the three kāyas, the great luminous emptiness beyond expression—manifested within: the boundless merging with the great perfection beyond conventional mind. They performed a guru empowerment and reading authorization for the assembled lamas and monastics residing there, such as Shuksep Rinpoche, and offered a supreme feast of the Queen of Great Bliss from the *Longchen Nyingtik*.[93] Flowers fell to consecrate the representations of body, speech, and mind, augmenting their extensive virtuous activities.

Next, they traveled to the shore of Tsogyal Latso in Drakda. Together the local community came to welcome them and invited them to the Tsogyal temple. Inconceivable signs of auspiciousness and good fortune occurred inspiring faith, including the coming forth of an elixir referred to as "Tsogyal's breast milk." Together with the lamas and monastics of that place, they performed an extensive Yeshe Tsogyal practice over more than seven days. During the display of accomplishment, the eyes of the Yeshe Tsogyal statue rolled, and a maiden named Yeshe Tso presented a crystal stone and sindūra powder. These signs of accomplishment visibly manifested.

At Chakri,[94] they contributed to the restoration of a temple and its images. Here the command seal for the *Radiant Azure Ḍākinī* released instantaneously, and they bestowed on the lamas and monastics there the empowerment that ripens. Rainbow light filled the sky and formed a dome above them. At Jomo Yuri, they forged a new trail called "the path leading to the arena for empowerment." In that area, the crops had been damaged in the past by blight, frost, and hail, but from that time onward they enjoyed timely rains and the cattle and crops flourished. Many such auspicious signs occurred, and their many kindnesses were remembered. In addition, in that place, they performed a fire pūjā and ten million burnt offerings. To the whole community there, they gave the empowerment and reading authorization for the Mahāguru, Sole Refuge, and extensive teachings on the two systems.[95]

At Tsogyal Latso, they made ablutions and smoke offerings to the lake. Many spontaneous vajra songs were sung. Then, at the Yamāntaka cave at Yangdzong in the region of Drak, they offered an extensive feast. With great devotion, all the monastics and laity of that place, reluctant to see them go, escorted them on horseback.

Next, the Eminent Couple turned their attention to Samye. Along the marked path to Chimpu, in the direction of Draktsen,[96] there were dark orange clouds that spread out like shooting stars as if to greet them, said to be Draktsen's own welcome. Right away, the lamas and monks of that area invited them to the southern chapel of Hayagrīva at the unchanging and spontaneously accomplished Samye Temple, fortuitously rendering them service and honor.

On that occasion, Choktrul Rinpoche Ngawang Gyatso and the assembled monastics stated, "Although we have built the white stūpa at Samye many times, it falls apart over and over again. If anything can be done, please offer a prophecy."

The Supreme Dharma Lord replied, "Even though in the past Orgyan Padma bound the gods and demons by oath, a few have escaped." The Eminent Couple went to the top of Hepo Hill above Samye with the intention to bind the gods and demons by oath, but when making offerings at the shrine there, a malevolent spirit suddenly struck the Supreme Khandro. Everyone was terrified, not knowing what to do. Just at that moment, the sublime Master himself arose as a glorious chief magnetizing apparent phenomenon. Performing a vajra dance, he sang this spontaneous song to bind the gods and demons by oath:

HŪṂ! Listen here, assembly of haughty gods and demons,
Why won't you abide by our own promise, crooked ones?

In the past, here at Glorious Samye, vast and profound,
The great guru Padmasambhava, in wrathful form,
Made you take an oath by command, remember?
Since then, the vidyādhara gurus of the three lineages
Have subdued you with mudrā seals, no?
At present, I, the regent of Orgyan Padma,
With the blazing and powerful vajra syllable HŪṂ,
Utter this command and solemn oath for you to hear:

These days, in the spreading gloom of five degenerations,
Gradually the teachings and their holders are in decline.
As the dominion of the supreme vehicle deteriorates,
Please help increase the jewel of Buddha's teachings!
Assembly of gods and demons, abide by your promise!
If not, transgressing your vow, wisdom emanations
In the form of wrathful hordes will proliferate,
Like atoms; don't think they won't demolish you.
Abide by the command, keep your samaya vow!
VAJRA SAMAYA!

As he uttered this solemn oath, Khandro Rinpoche awoke as if from sleep and was released from the spell. A seal binding the gods and demons by oath was placed above the gate at Samye, and after that the construction of the white stūpa with a thousand smaller ones around it proceeded, free of obstruction.

Remaining there, in accordance with supplications made with fierce devotion by all the lamas and monastics gathered, the Eminent Couple bestowed the empowerment that ripens for the *Radiant Azure Ḍākinī* and the Seven Line Supplication and its activities to all who gathered, like constellations in the sky, from various regions in the resplendent Yushal Barwa chapel on the second floor of Samye. On that occasion, everyone remarked that they thought this was no different than when in the past the great master Padmākara bestowed the good fortune of the profound secret elixir of teachings on the gathered assembly. Eyes streaming with tears of faith, those present made many such comments.

Furthermore, with fortunate disciples, they offered a great feast. While setting down some profound treasures, a vision of the Great Orgyan appeared and crowned them with the names, Orgyan

Jigme Namkha Lingpa and Ḍāki Tāre Dechen Gyalmo. Later, when setting down the ritual cycle, the *Play of the Great Lord and Supreme Horse-Headed One*, in the Hayagrīva temple at Samye and performing the sādhana of Hayagrīva, there were many wondrous signs, such as the resounding neigh of glorious Hayagrīva.

On the twenty-sixth day, while making a pilgrimage to Samye Chimpu, a bird flew toward them and landed before the Lord and Lady of Dharma. It conveyed greetings from the guru Orgyan, repeating itself three times, and then few away. All were amazed. Then they ventured to Drakmar Ke'u Tsang,[97] Along the way, while riding a horse, the Dharma Lord said, "If I can, I should put my footprint on this boulder." As if it were dough, he placed his left footprint clearly on the boulder. Remaining there, everyone took a look and made aspirations. The Supreme Dharma Lord said, "It's not appropriate to tell anyone that I placed my foot on rock; I was just playing. What's so wondrous about making a footprint on rock? As a sign of accomplishment, its purpose is to uproot fixation." Although swearing them to secrecy, there was an old lama staying at the site, who upon seeing the footprint generated great faith and spread the news everywhere like the wind.

Then, at Drakmar Ke'u Tsang, they offered an extensive gaṇacakra feast and set down instructions on the introduction to the nature of mind as clear light and the Abbreviated Sādhana of the Eight Pronouncements of the Sugatas.[98] To all the monks and pilgrims assembled there, they bestowed the gift of dharma, both ordinary and extraordinary. Then, at the Flower Cave at the great secret site Palri,[99] they had a vision of the great vidyādhara Jigme Lingpa and set down the Good Vase for the Four Abhiṣekas: A Guru Yoga. Once again returning to Samye, the assembly of lamas and monks residing there invited the Supreme Dharma Lord to sit on the fearless lion throne. Red light shined out from his forehead and suffused the environment, as witnessed by those with pure karma.

Thereafter, while fording the Tsangpo River,[100] the Eminent Couple were underway in the water when three splashes of water were offered in their direction. In amazement, their followers asked, "Who did that?" The Supreme Dharma Lord responded, "That is the female nāga Gangkar Drolma making offerings to all of us." On the new moon of that month, while offering a great feast before the Orgyan Look-Alike statue at Yoru Tradruk,[101] the Supreme Dharma Lord uttered this spontaneous song:

Kye! Essence of all sources of refuge,
Guru for the Snow Land of Tibet,
Victorious lord, Lake-Born Vajra,[102]
Supreme consort, Yeshe Tsogyal,
And the ocean of vidyādharas,
Learned masters and adepts,

With devotion, I supplicate you:
In this and all my future lives,
Accept me and never be separate,
So that I may effortlessly and spontaneously
Bring great benefit to the teachings and beings.

When this illusory body is no longer,
May we manifest in Zangdok Palri
And come before the self-cognizant guru,
So that your blessings and siddhi
May liberate all at once those beings
With a connection in all the six realms.

In this very practice session:
May I see my own primordial face,
And in the self-manifest wisdom wheel,
Self-liberate saṃsāra and nirvāṇa as nondual,
Self-expressive awareness wisdom,
Naturally actualized in its own place.

Through the power of aspiration and bodhicitta
Of the only father and guru, and the blessings
And compassion of the Three Jewels,
May these wishes be fulfilled!

While uttering this supplication with fervent devotion, the face of the Great Orgyan statue changed color and the statue's eyes rolled. In addition, the feast substances increased manifold; all were amazed.

During the second day of the eleventh lunar month, they went to Tashi Lhunpo in Tsang. Coming before the reliquary of the omniscient Paṇchen Lama, they made offerings and vast aspirations. In addition, they spontaneously made keen aspirations for his swift reincarnation.[103] Because the Dharma Lord and Lady were individuals with spontaneous mastery over the invocation of buddhas residing in the ultimate sphere and the descent of blessings, the entire reliquary shook, and the statue's eyes rolled. There were many such wondrous signs. Thereafter at Dechen Phodrang,[104] as a consecration, flowers fell on the statues, which rose up and rolled their eyes. Various signs of accomplishment occurred, which propel even some logicians on the path of faith.

Next, gradually, they made visits and offerings in Sakya and Gyantse, including the Palkhor Stūpa. They quickly visited the seat of Sakya Gongma Rinpoche, so that an auspicious connection could be established. They made an extensive offering of gifts and robes there and then returned to Lhasa. At that time, there was a big snowstorm, and everyone said they had never seen snow with this kind of bluish tinge in Lhasa before, regarding it as a marvel.

In this way, in the Lhasa area, they distributed gifts and funds at an array of monasteries, made offerings at all the temples, recoated holy images with gold leaf, and accomplished millions of mantra recitations at their many gaṇacakra feasts, expanding their enlightened activities like a great lake during the summer rains.

On the way home, they visited the snowy range of the great local guardian, Nyenchen Thangla, and expressed their gratitude in extensive praises. Over the slopes of Thangla, within a dome of rainbow light, was a varied spectacle—youths with turbans riding on lions, flowers blooming, white horses, and geese—witnessed by all in the vehicles of their entourage, much to their amazement.

When they reached the place known as Tengla, they went to a high ridge where the Eminent Couple made offerings to the local guardian. As a result, it became as warm as a sunny day in summer and flowers burst forth, extolled by all. As described, wherever the Eminent Couple visited together, countless visions, prophecies, and signs of accomplishment accompanied them. It is said, "One should hide one's own qualities / And proclaim the qualities of others." As in the life stories of the great masters of yore, their qualities cannot be captured in writing due to the high value placed on

> hidden adepts and efforts made by them to conceal their qualities as much as possible.
>
> Thereafter, they arrived in Jangyul. The Supreme Khandro spontaneously uttered many songs and bardic verse at Tramoling to commemorate her previous life as Ne'u Chung.[105]

Jangyul plays a role in the Gesar epic as one of the neighboring regions to the Kingdom of Ling, which Gesar conquers. Namtrul Rinpoche is identified with the prince of Jang, a so-called "converted hero" who joined Gesar as an ally. For the time of Gesar, Tāre Lhamo is most closely identified with Ne-u Chung, one of the prominent maidens of Ling, though she takes on other identifications in their correspondence, illustrating the fluid nature of emanation status among the Nyingma in eastern Tibet.

Further Teachings

From 1993, *Jewel Garland* records just two more years of their activities. Its narration ends in 1995, and it was published in 1997. From here, its account is slim with only a few highlights for each year, including bestowing teachings and initiations to prominent teachers such as Khenpo Munsel. The presumption is that the couple continued traveling and teaching in line with previous years. Indeed, Namtrul Rinpoche told me that for the period from 1996 until Tāre Lhamo's passing in 2002, the two of them continued to tour the same monasteries in Golok and neighboring areas, giving teachings and empowerments as before. In addition, in 1996, they began to host an annual dharma gathering at Nyenlung during the auspicious month of Sagadawa. This gathering brought together hundreds, and later thousands, of their disciples, both Tibetan and Han Chinese, for ten days of rituals and esoteric teachings. After Tāre Lhamo's passing, Namtrul Rinpoche continued to tour the region and host the annual dharma gathering until his own passing in 2011. Today, his son Tulku Laksam carries on their lineage of teachings, visiting many of the same monasteries throughout the region and hosting the annual dharma gathering at Nyenlung.

> On the second day of the third lunar month in the Water Bird Year (1993), the Supreme Khandro took the main responsibility for newly establishing the sādhana of the noble queen Tārā throughout the monasteries of Amdo and Kham, with Tsimda Gompa as the principal among them.

On the twenty-sixth day, they offered a profound gaṇacakra feast at the holy place, Lingri Pema Bumdzong. On that occasion, the sky, earth and everything in between turned the color of vaiḍūrya and was filled with rainbow light. Various such wondrous signs occurred. Next they visited the village of Mekor, where they bestowed various dharma teachings that ripen and liberate and established a new center for monastics.

On the fifteenth day, for Khenpo Munsel, an adept of the profound and secret Dzogchen, they performed the initiation for the Radiant Azure Ḍākinī and gave the instructions and reading authorization for the *Heart Essence of Samantabhadra*. Greatly pleased, Khenpo Rinpoche said, "In our renowned lineages, there is not even the slightest difference. Who is the master of your renowned lineage?" The dharma lord replied, "It was spoken by the lord of the victorious ones, the great Orgyan." Thus they engaged in a lengthy discussion. Thoroughly pleased, Khenpo Rinpoche said, "You, the couple, should hold the lineage of teaching and propagating the secret esoteric instructions of the profound and secret Dzogchen for as long as possible."

Furthermore, they conferred numerous dharma teachings that ripen and liberate to the lord of realization, the sublime Lama Garcho and Khenpo Yeshe among many other lamas and tulkus. Their minds merged as if one. From the second day of the fourth lunar month, they consecrated a stūpa at Marong, performed an initiation and reading authorization suitable for the assembled monks and laity, and established the sādhana of the Compassionate One Holding a White Lotus. Next, a great rain of dharma to ripen and liberate fell at Getse Gompa and elsewhere. When they viewed the site for the construction of a new stūpa in Padma County, the glory and prosperity of good fortune spread.

From the thirtieth day of the eleventh month, at glorious Nyenlung Thekchen Chökor Ling, they gave instructions on the *Six Dharmas of the Profound Path of the Great Perfection* to an assembly from numerous districts like an ocean.[106] At that time, heaps of grains newly blossomed into greenery as if it were summertime. Such things appeared to all in common. During the construction of the retreat facility for the Three Roots, a rain of *arura* descended on the meditation hall and vulture feathers fell. Many such wondrous signs occurred.

On the thirteenth day of the seventh month in the wood dog year (1994), someone called Geshe Rabgye placed a statue of Yeshe Tsogyal in a small crystal case and offered it to the Eminent Couple. The Master himself removed it from the crystal case and tossed flowers on it as a consecration. Later, when he tried to replace it in the small case, the image had grown in size so that it no longer fit. Everyone was amazed.

On the eighth day of the twelfth lunar month, according to a prophecy by the Eminent Couple that performing numerous supplications and offerings to the twelve Tenma goddesses and praises to the ḍākas and ḍākinīs would give rise to great benefit for the teachings and beings, the lamas and monastics at Glorious Nyenlung Thekchen Chökor Ling accomplished more than 300,000 such offerings. On the fifteenth day, they conducted an extensive smoke and *lungta* offering. While praising the ḍākas and ḍākinīs, conch-colored snow fell like lotus flower petals and rainbows created a canopy in the sky.

In the Wood Sow Year (1995), while preparing for the great tenth day commemoration, the calcite powder for drawing out lines could not be located. The Supreme Dharma Lord said to the monks Drodön and Döndrub, "I'll make a select tea offering and you two go to the steep side of Gyabri and find some calcite."[107] Accordingly, they left and located a treasure cache of calcite. "Now take as much as you wish; you never know later if there will be any left." After that, the place was reputed to no longer have any calcite.

On the eighth day of the Dragon Month in the Wood Sow Year, to aid in spreading far and wide all their profound treasures generally and their teachings on the profound secret Dzogchen in particular, the Eminent Couple invoked their treasure protectors: the two mountains behind the monastery, Döndrub Norbu Wangyal and Yangcan Chödrön, the son and daughter of Amnye Machen, as well as the mountain in front, Tsungpa Dungi Lathöcan. Rainbow light formed a dome in the sky and thunder gently rumbled. Many such auspicious signs occurred.

On the tenth day, they gave extensive instructions on the *Six Dharmas of the Profound Path of the Great Perfection* to a great gathering of more than 200 fortunate students, Tibetan and Chinese, congregated from sixteen provinces in China.[108] Previously,

> on retreats at Wutai Shan and elsewhere in China, more than 300 students joined them and committed themselves to practice.

This concludes the narration of the couple's travels and teachings together. In its final note, their instructions on Dzogchen, or the Great Perfection, to both Tibetan and Chinese close disciples is emphasized. After Tāre Lhamo's passing, the number of Chinese disciples coming to Nyenlung Monastery swelled. By at least 2006, all twenty-two provinces of China were represented at the annual dharma gathering at Nyenlung.

Treasure Sites

Jewel Garland ends with a summary of their treasure sites, spanning from Golok to Central Tibet. Their treasure revelations are credited with no less than healing the damage of degenerate times and, indeed, were central to their activities reinvigorating Buddhist teachings, practices, and institutions in Tibetan regions during the post-Mao era. This is what Tāre Lhamo and Namtrul Rinpoche imagined in their correspondence and lived out in their two decades of traveling and teaching together as part of a synergistic network of Nyingma teachers in Golok. Their accomplishments were remarkable: rebuilding and leading Nyenlung and Tsimda monasteries, supporting at least ten other monasteries through financial contributions and spiritual guidance, revealing treasures that were compiled into a twelve-volume corpus, traveling and teaching throughout Golok and beyond on annual teaching tours, building a Gesar temple and founding a performance troupe to stage a section of the epic from their own revelations, establishing ritual programs at monasteries in the region, reconnecting people and places through pilgrimages and ritual occasions, and establishing an annual dharma gathering at Nyenlung attended by thousands of disciples.

> As described, these two Eminent Protectors of Beings revealed various treasure caches at all the major and minor sacred sites, thereby healing the damage of degenerate times. Touring various monasteries without bias, they bestowed the elixir of the essential instructions that ripen and liberate as much as requested. While instructing fortunate disciples according to the level of their maturity on the path, at the same time, they planted the seed of liberation in the mental continuum of numerous beings, equal in

number to the sands of the Ganges, who encountered them in person and heard their speech.

From Rigdzin Taksham Dorje:

> The protector of beings, Jigme, regent of Padma,
> If able at thirty-four to meet with one named Tāre,
> Will open the sky treasury gate of profound treasures,
> And lead those connected to Ngayab Palri.

Accordingly, the speech of this enlightened pair, inseparable in intent and symbol, is contained in more than ten volumes of various profound teachings, like a ripened fruit, chief among them the dharma cycle, *Nine Expanses of Crescent Moons.*

Their treasure sites include: Samye Chimpu, Gangri Thökar, Amnye Machen, Drakar Dredzong, Drongri Mukpo, Nyenpo Yutse, Dröphuk Khandrö Duling, Tashi Gomang in the Mar valley, Yangdzong in the Drak region, Pema Bumdzong at Shukjung, Lake Kokonor, Tsogyal Latso in Drakda, and the sacred site, Doyi Nyingpo.

The protectors of their treasures include: Senge Dongcan, Nöchin Tse'u Marpo, Nyenchen Thangla, Sechung Döndrup Norbu Wangyal, Tsangpa Dungila Thöcan, Lugyal Dungla Bumpa, Zamar Khyungzhon Tsal, Dorje Racigma, guardian of mantra, Palden Makzor Gyalmo, Yudril Dorje Zugle, Mantsun Dorje Ziledrön, the seven Yeshe Lhamo, and Machen Semo Yangcan Chödrön.

These guardians of treasures, with their judicious gaze, prevent decline and promote the wide dissemination of their profound dharma, and their disciples who are lineage holders of their teachings appear like constellations of stars in the sky.

As defenders of the teachings and beings, they establish those who are connected in Ngayab Palri, as is abundantly clear in all the adamantine prophecies.

From this account of their travels and teachings, the reader gets a vivid sense for the collaboration between Tāre Lhamo and Namtrul Rinpoche, discovering and disseminating their treasures together over two decades. Given how rare it is to see a visionary couple, teaching side by side on elevated teaching thrones, their lives and letters are a testament to how a tantric partnership took shape in contemporary Tibet and contributed to the revitalization of Buddhist teachings, practices, and institutions in the post-Mao era through the revelation of treasures.

5. Visions of Tāre Lhamo

The Time is Ripe

Two of Tāre Lhamo's visions are included at the end of *Spiraling Vine of Faith*. They occurred during the 1980s, providing encouragement from the ḍākinīs as she launched her teaching career with Namtrul Rinpoche. In the first vision in 1985, the couple are dressed in ritual garb as if preparing to bestow a tantric initiation. In unison, they invoke a series of signs indicating that the time is ripe for them to discover and disseminate treasures. A celestial ḍākinī appears to confirm their destiny, identifying Tāre Lhamo with the goddesses Tārā and Sarasvatī and correlating Namtrul Rinpoche's with masters of yore, while making cryptic reference to others in their midst who will support their activities. At one point the ḍākinī has them look into a mirror, a type of divination technique, and they see a large tree laden with fruit and crowned by a radiant prajñā sword. Tāre Lhamo interpreted the sight as a sign to propagate her father's teachings. It is not surprising that this was the year the couple held their first large-scale ritual gathering at Tsimda Gompa.

> At daybreak of the first day of the first month in the Wood Ox Year (1985), in a vision, the Supreme Khandro delighted in a vast open area with a grassy valley ornamented by flowers. Beside the gate to a large mountain of precious iron, which she did not recognize, Namtrul Rinpoche offered various garments, radiant in the five-colored lights, while holding a bell and vajra in his hands. Meanwhile, the Khandro herself wore a crown and green robe, dressed in a dance costume including a brocade apron covering. The two of them appeared to speak in one voice:

Ah ho!
A sign to propagate the undamaged teachings of Buddha,
A sign to open the manifold gates of profound treasures,
A sign to sustain the practice of great secret mantra,
A sign in body to support the longevity of masters,
A sign in speech to sing unceasing celestial melodies,
A sign in mind to practice unwavering samādhi,
A sign to awaken karma, aspiration and entrustment,
A sign to reverse the chaos of degenerate times,
A sign to establish the welfare of all beings,
A sign to pacify conditions of plague and strife,
A sign to turn the dharma wheel of four joys,
A sign to practice the Anuyoga of bliss-emptiness,
A sign to guide those karmically connected to pure realms,
A sign to unite method and wisdom,
A sign to transform concept into bliss-emptiness,
A sign to spread the dharma of Atiyoga,
A sign to unite the primordial expanse with spontaneity,
A sign to maintain the ground, unfabricated luminosity,
A sign to scatter the mist of duality,
A sign to display whatever arises as wisdom.
A la la ho! E ya ya!

While they performed various dances, inside the gate to the iron mountain, a white ḍākinī wearing bone ornaments also performed a dance. Holding a silk-strewn arrow in her right hand and a mirror in the left, she spoke thus:

E bo ya!
I come from Palri to the southwest.
I am the messenger of Lord Orgyan Padma,
Called the mother Tingchung Zile Mendrön.

Listen here, noble couple!
This year, at the time of Sagadawa,
It is time to propagate in the region of Do Kham
The profound treasures, medicine to dispel the damage of
degeneration,
Of the lord Pawo Chöying Dorje (Apang Terchen),
The activity of the lords of three families distilled into one.

Don't mistake the pith certificate, the symbolic text.
At the glorious mountain named Yuldha
Are uncorrupted sites of early translation teachings,
One hundred and thirty-eight to be counted.
The reincarnation of that lord is Āyu by name.[1]
Through the power of his intense resolve,
The sun of profound treasures will spread to India and
Nepal.

In the land of Rebkong to the north,
The pair, named after lord Prajñāvajra,
Creates the favorable conditions
To spread the profound nectar of dharma.

In the magnetizing pleasure grove of Serjong,
The true emanation, the lord Nanam Pawo,
Spreads the profound nectar of the eminent Abhekarma.
In the snowy land, he radiates the teachings like the sun.
Whoever encounters him, he guides to Zangdok Palri.

The activity of glorious Nuden Dorje, named Padmavajra,
In the sheep year, will perform deeds for the teachings.

Also at Gakyil Chöling in Wangtöd,
The emanation of lord Longchen named Nyima,
Whoever encounters him will benefit
And be guided to the vidyādhara realms.

At the place, Shukjung Sang-ngak Chöling,
An emanation of mothers Tārā and Sarasvatī,
Will appear with the name, the twice-born Lodzin Wang.
Whoever encounters her will be guided to ḍākinī realms.
By the very ḍākinī who bears that name,
The lives of the twelve heroes are prolonged.

Also, in the center at Yarlung Wangdrong,
The mind emanation of the glorious Lotus-Born Vajra
In the manner of a madman with erratic behavior,
At this time, by one named Maṅga in the earth sow year,
The strife of spirits and demons is reversed.

The coupling of method and wisdom
Will protect the benefit of beings.
This I saw in the mirror's surface
By means of symbols. E ma ho!

When she showed the mirror to both of them, on the surface of the mirror arose a tree with abundant leaves and fruit in the middle of a turquoise lake at the base of a white mountain. On top of it, there was a sword blazing with blue light, the light rays of which radiated out and pervaded in all directions.

At that moment, the ḍākinī spoke:

I am the display of wisdom dharmadhātu,
Coursing in the unborn sphere of dharmakāya.
May the two of you remain in good health.

Once that was said, the Supreme Khandro awakened from sleep. Relying on this prophecy, at a gathering of monastics from more than fifty monasteries at Tsimda in Golok, she and Namtrul Rinpoche bestowed the extensive transmission for the profound oceanic treasures of Apang Terchen Orgyan Trinley Lingpa in their entirety.

Liberation

In the second vision, Tāre Lhamo's liberation occurs with the aid of ḍākinīs. The vision arose during a gaṇacakra feast that extended over several days at Nyenlung Monastery. Initially, Tāre Lhamo recognized on the hill behind the monastery, called Gyabri, a site where the nineteenth-century master Patrul Rinpoche had practiced. From there, a gate opened into the splendor of a pure land comprised of precious jewels and rainbow light. There she encountered a ḍākinī who took her on a tour of the pure land's four directions, inhabited by ḍākinīs in a standard maṇḍala configuration: vajra to the east, ratna to the south, padma to the west, and karma to the north. In the center of the maṇḍala was the pure realm, Oḍḍiyāna Dhumathala, presided over by Vajravārāhī, the female tantric deity, red and wearing bone ornaments, here inseparable from Yeshe Tsogyal. The ḍākinīs were having their own gaṇacakra feast and invited her to join. Yeshe Tsogyal reminded Tāre Lhamo that they are one and the same being and transmitted the nature of mind. Tasting the feast substances and hearing the instructions, Tāre Lhamo attained liberation. Yeshe Tsogyal then pointed out various sites at Nyenlung where treasures awaited revelation and, in the process, sanctifying Nyenlung as a special place blessed by the presence of Padmasambhava, Yeshe Tsogyal, and other seminal Nyingma figures.

> On the twenty-fifth day of the eleventh month of the earth dragon year (1989), when offering an extensive gaṇacakra feast to the ḍākinīs, a vision of radiant light appeared.
>
> On the side of Gyabri at glorious Nyenlung Thekchen Chökor Ling, the Supreme Khandro saw a site where Dza Patrul Rinpoche Orgyan Jigme Chökyi Wangpo had previously stayed. It was a grassy meadow in the shape of a crescent. Since the great gate at that site was open, she went inside. From near the gate, she saw a pure realm.
>
> The ground of this land was composed everywhere of precious jewels and ornamented by a variety of flowers. Manifold kinds of jewel trees bore an abundance of leaves and fruit, fully ripened. In the sky, there appeared a dome canopy of rainbow light extending across the whole area, beautified by tiny crystalline spheres. A sweet aroma permeated the air giving rise to an experience of bliss without dissipating. Various birds sang melodious tunes conveying the Mahāyāna teachings.
>
> Looking at the array of this pure land that lacked nothing, she noticed a woman there, gracious and beautiful, ornamented with a white scarf and jewels, who smiled and spoke thus:
>
> > E e! You, woman of worthy mantra-born stock,
> > What undertaking brought you to this place?
> > Tell me your heart's aspirations in full,
> > And I will surely accomplish them.
> > Keep that in mind!
>
> Hearing that, the Supreme Khandro replied:
>
> > Kye! Beautiful and enchanting goddess,
> > Regarding the layout of this wondrous place,
> > Called Nyenlung Thekchen Chöling,
> > Which I have taken as my permanent home,

Since I would like to see the sights in detail,
With great delight, I request you to be my guide.

The ḍākinī replied: "If you would like to see this land, I can guide you. I am the protector of this place, named Tingchung Yuyi Drönma, an emanation of glorious Vajravārāhī. Now, let's go—the two of us." The two flew off into the sky like birds and landed on a hilltop similar in color to coral.

Beholding the many bejeweled lands to the furthest limits of visibility, the girl said, "Ya! Look now. That land to the east is the vajra ḍākinī land." There, in the peaceful eastern dharma palace complex, the eminent queen White Tārā resides surrounded by countless white ḍākinīs. Various sorts of white food and drink were heaped like a mountain and collected like an ocean, while the countless ḍākinīs celebrated a gaṇacakra feast.

Next, when she gazed to the south, there was the ratna ḍākinī pure land. In the extensive southern palace of enjoyment, the bejeweled Norgyun Lhamo was surrounded by a retinue of countless yellow ḍākinīs, who celebrated a gaṇacakra feast of various sorts of yellow food and drink.

Next she traveled west to the pure land of the padma ḍākinī. In the mighty western lotus palace, the magnetizing Kurukulle was surrounded by countless red ḍākinīs, who celebrated a gaṇacakra feast of various sorts of red food and drink.

Next she traveled north to the land of the karma ḍākinī. In the wrathful northern assembly hall of activity, the ḍākinī Thing Öbarma was surrounded by countless green ḍākinīs, who celebrated a gaṇacakra feast of various sorts of green substances of means and knowledge.

Then, at the central mountain was the pure land of Oḍḍiyāna Dhumathala. In the mighty crescent palace, the glorious Vajravārāhī was the paramount lady among myriad ḍākinīs and, indivisible from her, the noble queen Yeshe Tsogyal was dazzling red in color and naked wearing bone ornaments. In her right hand she held a ḍamaru, and in her left a hooked knife rested on her hip. She wore a jewel crown and stood with both feet alike in striding posture. She resided there, surrounded by a retinue of countless ḍākinīs of the five families.

In her presence, the Supreme Khandro prostrated reverently with her three gates of body, speech, and mind. The Paramount Lady spoke thus:

> Kye! My heart daughter, you and I are no different.
> How wondrous you came here, mantra-born ḍākinī.
> This place is Akaniṣṭha Dhumathala,
> I am Yeshe Tsogyal, the delight of Padma.
> Today is the worthy occasion when the ḍākinīs gather.
> Enjoy the gaṇacakra feast of supreme substances.
> A la la ho!

The five sections of ḍākinīs offered the Supreme Khandro the substances of method and wisdom. At the moment of ingesting them, the knots of her nāḍī elements were freed, and the nondual wisdom of bliss-emptiness blazed. In addition, the Paramount Lady held in her hand a six-facetted self-arisen crystal stone, proclaiming:

> This flawless naturally arisen crystal stone
> Is luminous essence within the empty nature.
> By this introduction to emptiness-luminosity
> Through sign, rest effortlessly beyond concept
> In the ground of primordial uncontrived awareness.
> Within the state of nonfixation like the sky,
> No distraction and no meditation. A Ā PHAṬ!

Wholly at ease, the Supreme Khandro became thoroughly immersed in the state of innate luminosity transcending mind—free of conceptual elaborations.

Once again, the Paramount Lady among the ḍākinīs spoke:

> Kye! Women of mantrin stock, Tāre Devī,
> You and a method companion, named Abhaya,
> Will converge to perform activities of the Lotus-Born Guru
> At the maṇḍala of three stacked crescents.
>
> The daytime vulture's nest to the right of here
> Is the supreme site of Lord Mañjugoṣa.
> There on the changeless rock face are self-arisen letters,
> Forming the mantras: ARAPACANA and HRĪḤ.

A self-arisen image of Sarasvatī protrudes
Alongside a stone covered with sindūra,
A meteoric iron sword and golden vajra.
There are thirty-two timely treasure caches.

Then the hill to the left is the supreme site of Vajrapāṇi,
A delightful grove of juniper called Yarlung Lodrak.
There are various material treasures in the changeless rock.
Also, HŪṂ, the seed syllable of Vajrapāṇi,

Appears there and the glorious vajra hand- and footprints
Of Nam-Nying, Tsogyal, Chokyang, and Paldor.[2]
One day, a supreme being named Vajra
Will reveal a treasure cache of seven sādhanas.

The supreme site of the seven white brahmins,
At the peak of a lofty mountain in a vast thicket of trees,
In the rock are the armor and three weapons of Yulha,
Hidden also are a ring of Ne'u Chung and necklace of Tsogyal.

There are various treasure caches of self-arisen crystal stones
And springs with white and red "father VAṂ" medicinal plants.
Though present, seventeen self-arisens have yet to manifest.
In the end, a tantrika named Padma will bring them forth.

At Senge Namdzong, a garuḍa's nest on the shady side of a hill,
Toward the top, there is a meditation cave of Vārāhī.
There are five caskets of substances and a self-arisen vase
To consecrate the implements for the *Gathered Intent of the Ḍākinīs*.

If the vital point of coincidence falls into place well,
You two, the eminent couple, need to reveal these.
The mountain, behind and central to Nyenlung, the supreme site,
Has been blessed (respectively) by Avalokiteśvara and Vajravārāhī.

Atop a three-storied palace is the Cakrasaṃvara couple.
In the middle level, the great mighty one, Hayagrīva,
On the lower level, the noble queen Vajravārāhī,
Along with countless vidyādharas, vīras, and ḍākinīs.

What's more, the maṇḍala of the twenty-four sacred places
Concludes at this site, the dome of Drakri, where
Twenty-five caskets of precious substances remain.

In the future, the tertöns Dharma, Ratna, Vajra, Padma
 and Sūrya
Will reveal as the glory of the teachings and beings:
The seven dharma cycles of the ḍākinīs and, in particular,
The profound esoteric instructions on the *Three Inner
 Tantras*.[3]

At this site hand- and footprints
Of the Guru, Tsogyal, Nam-nying and Vima,[4]
Remain plus self-arisen divine forms,
Like the hearts of the five classes of ḍākinīs.

At this place, if you circumambulate one time,
You gain the benefit of reciting SIDDHI 700 million times.[5]
If you enter and perform the sādhana properly,
Realization increases, and you will have visions of intrinsic
 awareness.

At this site, if you establish the offering, praises and lungta,
The Sampe Döndrup will pacify all shortcomings.[6]
If you perform the gaṇacakra feast, breaches will be
 amended,
And your lifespan will increase through the realization
 of wisdom.
It is certain that in the next life you will go to the land
 of khecarīs.

At this place, the thirteen lord and subjects
And the twenty-five emanations of ḍākinīs of the five families
Emerged successively. This is clear from the certificate.
The time for all to gather at this site will be the sow year.

Though the benefits of this place are beyond speech,
Even this short summary should be kept secret.

Keep this in mind! Eminent gathering of ḍākinīs,
"You" and "I" are merely conceptual labels;
There is only one basis in actuality.

In the vast expanse of dharmakāya,
Within the innate state transcending mind,
A Ā!

After uttering this, the ḍākinī transformed into a red bindu drop and dissolved into the heart center of Khandro Rinpoche, who remained thoroughly immersed in the vast expanse of emptiness-luminosity—unimpeded and free of conceptual elaboration. These accounts were taken from her dharma cycle of visionary experience.

6. Final Letter by Namtrul Rinpoche

Namtrul Rinpoche | Letter 30

As a lament and addendum to the correspondence, Namtrul Rinpoche wrote a final letter to Tāre Lhamo on the anniversary of her passing. The letter expresses his grief in vivid terms, depicting him wailing in anguish and emitting a cascade of tears. The truth of impermanence is invoked in a series of images, including the sun setting over the western peaks and flowers crushed by hail and frost. Instead of symbolizing the fertility of spring, the sunshine and flowers now conjure the onset of winter and the fleeting nature of worldly happiness. In response to his grief, Tāre Lhamo appears in the sky in ḍākinī fashion in order to console him. Harkening to the two truths of relative impermanence and ultimate nonduality, her visionary apparition reminds Namtrul Rinpoche of their inseparability across lifetimes. This letter provides a tender ending to their correspondence.

> On the twelfth day of the second month, the water sheep
>   year (2003),
> On the anniversary of my constant companion Khandro's
>   passing,
> During the commemorative feast offerings to the ḍākinīs,
> When thoughts arise of your loving speech at the time
>   of death,
> Unable to hold back, I utter these sorrowful words
>   of lamentation:
>
> Kye kye! Orgyan Vajradhara, essence of all buddhas
> And bodhisattvas of the three times, distilled into one,
> Mother Tsogyal, lady among the gathering of countless ḍākinīs,

The assembly of the three roots, heroes, ḍākinīs, and
dharmapālas,
Immediately think of me with compassion and unwavering
samaya.

Kye ma! By the power of intention, aspirations, and vows
Of the Orgyan couple, Namkai Nyingpo and Shelkar Tso,
And our many lives of shared deeds, aspirations, and
coincidence,
The time has come for coincidence to unfold naturally on
its own.

Constant companion, Tsogyal in the guise of a woman,
Mantra-born, endowed with special qualities, Tāre Khandro,
Having joined in the union of method and wisdom,
bliss-emptiness,
Among the twenty-five (disciples of Padmasambhava),
Holding in heart the great benefit of the teachings and beings,
You set down the profound treasures in shapes like jewels;
Your enlightened activity pervades the vast earth.

While enjoying the glories and joys of the two systems,[1]
Due to the meager merit of beings in degenerate times,
The curse of barbarians harboring perverted aspirations,
And my own feeble fortune and store of merit,
Your human form departed to formless dharmadhātu.
As a natural defect of saṃsāra, what is compounded falls apart.

Reflecting on the circumstances, my grief swells,
Wondering why now and not later, in despair.
My constant companion, the Wish-Fulfilling Jewel, departed,
Leaving the old, ailing Namtrul, behind.

In our retreat hut, pleasure grove of the vidyādhara's great bliss,[2]
There's no occasion to awaken the mind seeking to end anguish,
There's no chance to be nurtured by your loving affection,
Now that suddenly you rest in the peaceful space of dharmatā.

The maṇḍala of the sun rises, spreading its light rays;
Without remaining long, it chases the western peaks.
This is like a teacher showing impermanence.

On highland meadows in summer, the honeyed flowers bloom;
In winter, they're crushed suddenly by hail and frost.
This is like a teacher showing impermanence.

As honored guests among our circle of disciples,
In years past; but this year, I'm left alone by myself.
This too is like the teacher showing impermanence.

The illusory conditioned body, like a rainbow in the sky,
When the time comes, mind and its receptacle part ways.
This is like the teacher showing impermanence.

When leaves and fruit grow on trees, when flowers bloom,
When the cuckoo sings its sweet melody and thunder claps,
When light rays of the sun and moon spread across the sky,

I recall the loving affection of my constant companion.
Constant companion, Tsogyal in person, gone to peace.
With regard to all this, is it a dream? Or is it real?

From the murky depths of anguish and sorrow,
Expressing my gloom, tears cascade in a constant stream.
Distraught with grief, audibly wailing: alas!
Unable to bear the situation, my personal flaws burst forth.
Without fabrication of any sort, I almost lost consciousness.

At that moment, in the vast, dazzling azure sky,
Amidst a dome made of radiant rays of rainbow-colored light,
Accompanied by the enchanting sound of lute music,
At the center of a co-emergent gathering of ḍākinīs,

Hail, the beloved bestowing the wisdom of bliss-emptiness!
My constant companion, the precious Wish-Fulfilling Jewel,

Smiling with pleasure and passion, joyfully flashing sidelong glances,
Dancing beautifully with grace and suppleness,
Delivered this advice in a pleasing, melodious voice:

"Kye ho! Eternally kind guru and lord,
My precious, sole, constant companion across lives,
Your Eminence, the Supreme Incarnation and Wish-Fulfilling Jewel,
I cannot bear to be separated from you even for an instant.

Although the intimacy of our bond and affection cannot be reversed,
The nature of illusory phenomena is impermanent.
Kind one, who has intentionally not departed from this life,
When the time for past karma to ripen comes, what is there to do?
You remain nurtured by my affection. Here is a support for mind:
Constant companion, we have not been separated even for an instant.

Rinpoche, don't let your mind grow weary with sorrow.
Train in recognizing all apparent phenomena as illusion.
Vajra awareness, the stable and steady consummated nature,
Is not separate from the mind of me, Tāre.

Now residing in the sphere of luminous dharmakāya,
A manifest form, complete in the circle of wisdom,
This is the play of wisdom, ceaseless and self-radiant,
You're never apart from me, the ḍākinī giving rise to bliss.

Now residing in the nowhere of Akaniṣṭha heaven,
A manifest form in the sphere of saṃbhogakāya,
Visible potency of wisdom, all-knowing and all-pervading,
Constant companion, you're never apart from me, the mantra-born one.

Now the dance of mudrā, like the moon in water,
The glory of dharma and beings arises
With respect to their level of training and devotion,
A manifest form, pervading all of the six realms.

Even when separated in the manner of relative appearances,
In the definitive truth, fundamentally, we've never been separated.
From your indestructible, original mind beyond measure,
I didn't go anywhere. There is nowhere else for me to go.

Within primordial dharmakāya, changeless great bliss,
Visualize all sights and sounds as the body of the wisdom
ḍākinī;
Recite all sounds as the mantra of the ḍākinīs of great bliss;
Within the sole dharmatā, whatever thoughts arise,
Spontaneously realize them to be great nondual wisdom.
Within the unfabricated, self-arising, unimpeded, naked nature,
Leave it as is! This is the union of method and wisdom,
bliss-emptiness.

A la la ho! Awareness in its own character.
E ma ho ya! The kindness of the glorious guru.
Within the wisdom of equality, abide in bliss.
Carefree and unrestrained, dwell joyfully.
In an effortless, self-arising state, rest free and easy.

Until enlightenment, there is no separation even for an instant.
Until the impure karmic manifestations of beings are
exhausted,
For that long, we two, method and wisdom, as inseparable,
Effortlessly accomplishing the benefit of the teachings and beings.

When the three realms of saṃsāra are emptied, our wishes
fulfilled,
The darkness of impure duality is awakened on its own to reveal
Apparent phenomena of saṃsāra and nirvāṇa already perfected,
The ground of existence purified into the great equality. A la la!
Dear, dear, you and I are nondual, one taste."

With affection, we touched foreheads.
Then she dissolved into light, transforming
Into a red bindu, which melted into my heart.

In a state free of thoughts, pure, unobstructed awareness,
Wisdom arose unadorned, beyond speech or expression.
In that way, for a little while, the manifest aspect
Of appearance, thoughts of despair, slipped from my mind.

Although not necessary to record in writing, now or later,
In the coincidence of being exhorted by the Supreme Khandro,
I, the old yogin, impetuous in activity, Namtrul Jigme,
Wrote whatever he heard under the care of Khandro.

May all beings be liberated into the vast expanse, the ground
of being![3]

Sources in Translation

THIS BOOK PRESENTS the original source materials, translated into English for the first time, that I analyzed in my monograph, *Love Letters from Golok: A Tantric Couple in Modern Tibet*. In translating the letters and life stories of Khandro Tāre Lhamo and Namtrul Rinpoche here, I made certain choices about what materials to include and in what order to arrange them. The heart of this book is forty-two of their fifty-six letters, more than two thirds of the correspondence. These selections showcase the diverse poetic and song styles that Namtrul Rinpoche and Tāre Lhamo employed, illustrating the evolution and multifaceted nature of their tantric partnership. While prophecies and past life recollections permeate the correspondence as a whole, for the most part, I leave out letters comprised of long cryptic prophecies about the location of their treasures, since these are less likely to be relevant to English readers.[1] Instead, the letters selected for translation balance the human and visionary aspects of their courtship and correspondence and highlight the range of ways this couple expressed their mutual compatibility.

Before and after the correspondence, I have placed their life stories, *Jewel Garland: The Liberation of Namtrul Jigme Phuntsok* and *Spiraling Vine of Faith: The Liberation of Khandro Tāre Lhamo*. These provide the lived context for their tantric partnership: their coming of age during the Maoist period (in their respective accounts) and their shared teaching career during the post-Mao era as recounted in *Jewel Garland*.[2] This arrangement mirrors the structure of *Jewel Garland*, which excerpts a selection of letters and places them in between Namtrul Rinpoche's youth and his travels and teachings with Tāre Lhamo later in life. However, here I begin with Tāre Lhamo's youth as recounted in *Spiraling Vine of Faith* and include many more letters than found in *Jewel Garland*. In order to avoid duplicating long passages, when most or all of a letter is excerpted, I refer the reader to the letter's translation within the section on their correspondence. When the excerpted passage is short, I include it within my translation of *Jewel Garland*. In parallel fashion, *Spiraling Vine of Faith* excerpts sections from the (auto)biographies of two of Tāre Lhamo's female antecedents, Yeshe Tsogyal and Sera Khandro. While I include the former, being just a few stanzas in length, I omit the latter since it is more extensive and already available in translation in separate publications by Christina Monson and Sarah Jacoby.[3]

In terms of the arrangement of the letters, I also make some adjustments. As published in Tibetan, their letters are grouped into two collections, *Adamantine Garland: The Collected Letters by the Lord of Refuge, Namtrul Jigme Phuntsok, to the Supreme Khandro Tāre Lhamo* (his letters to her) and *Garland of Lotuses: The Collected Letters by the Mantra-Born One, Khandro Tāre Lhamo, to the Supreme Namtrul Jigme Phuntsok* (her letters to him).[4] So in referring to specific letters, I use the number in their respective collections, e.g., her Letter 3 (KTL 3) or his Letter 3 (NJP 3). Rather than mirror their organization into separate collections, here I interweave their letters to give the reader a sense for the back and forth of their exchanges. Note that the ordering is tentative and complicated by several factors: first that only a handful of letters are dated and second that the letters were sometimes sent in batches given the two-day journey by horseback separating them.[5] Since Namtrul Rinpoche and Tāre Lhamo sent their letters surreptitiously by messenger, oral messages and gifts were also conveyed, and these are irretrievable aspects of their exchanges except where referenced directly in their letters.

The outline below indicates the organization of the original source material and the interventions I made in the ordering to enhance the chronological flow of the narrative for the reader.

Tibetan Source Materials

Source One: *Cloud Offerings to Delight the Vidyādharas and Ḍākinīs: The Liberation of Namtrul Jigme Phuntsok and Khandro Tāre Lhamo* (paperback volume with both of their biographies)

- *Jewel Garland: The Liberation of Namtrul Jigme Phuntsok* (JG 1–104)
- *Spiraling Vine of Faith: The Liberation of Khandro Tāre Lhamo* (SVF 105–160)

Source Two: Single Volume Addendum to *The Profound Treasure Corpus of Orgyan Jigme Namkha Lingpa and Ḍākinī Tāre Dechen Gyalmo* (facsimile edition containing their correspondence in its entirety)

- *Adamantine Garland: The Collected Letters by the Lord of Refuge, Namtrul Jigme Phuntsok, to the Supreme Khandro Tāre Lhamo* (NJP 1–29: 1–73.3)
- *Garland of Lotuses: The Collected Letters by the Mantra-Born One, Khandro Tāre Lhamo, to the Supreme Namtrul Jigme Phuntsok* (KTL 1–31: 75–180.4)
- Final letter by Namtrul Rinpoche on anniversary of Tāre Lhamo's passing (NJP 30: 181.1–188.4)

Arrangement of Translations

1. Early Life of Tāre Lhamo (*Spiraling Vine of Faith*, Part I): Tāre Lhamo's previous lives, training in youth, and miracle tales during the years leading up to and including the Cultural Revolution (SVF 105–147.5). In my translation, I omit the opening verses of praise, her father's garland of past lives, and an excerpted autobiography of Sera Khandro.

2. Early Life of Namtrul Rinpoche (*Jewel Garland*, Part I): Namtrul Rinpoche's training in youth, practice during the period of the Cultural Revolution, and prophecies about his impending union with Tāre Lhamo (JG 1–47.6). Opening verses of praise are not included. Excerpted letters are referenced, and shorter excerpts are included.

3. Letters of Tāre Lhamo and Namtrul Rinpoche (Selected Letters from *Adamantine Garland* and *Garland of Lotuses*): A selection of forty-two letters exchanged between Namtrul Rinpoche and Tāre Lhamo between 1978 and 1980; these are integrated into a tentative ordering, and the corresponding page numbers in their respective collections can be found in notes.

4. Travels and Teachings as a Couple (*Jewel Garland*, Part II): Travels and teachings of Namtrul Rinpoche and Tāre Lhamo (JG 47.6–104). One arcane visionary sequence is omitted.

5. Visons of Tāre Lhamo (*Spiraling Vine of Faith*, Part II): Visions of Tāre Lhamo (SVF 147.6–160); omitting the afterword and colophon by author Pema Ösal Thaye.

6. Final Letter by Namtrul Rinpoche (following *Adamantine Garland* and *Garland of Lotuses*): This is a letter that Namtrul Rinpoche wrote on the anniversary of Tāre Lhamo's passing.

This arrangement of source materials in translation allows the reader to encounter the lives and letters of Namtrul Rinpoche and Tāre Lhamo in chronological fashion. It also removes certain redundancies and tangents that, while expected by readers of Tibetan texts, might impede the narrative flow for English readers.

For the sake of accessibility to a broad audience, I add subheadings and brief contextual overviews for each of the distinct periods of their lives and otherwise attempt to keep the scholarly apparatus to a minimum. All spellings of Tibetan names are phoneticized and, when relevant, foreign terms and names are discussed in the notes, where the transliteration for text titles can also be found. Brackets are not used for added pronouns or explanatory supplements that are clear from the Tibetan, i.e., rendering "three gates" (*sgo gsum*) as "three gates of body, speech, and mind." So, in my translation of *Jewel Garland*, while Tibetan syntax can omit pronouns when the subject is understood, I use "they" without brackets as the default pronoun, given the joint nature of their activities. Otherwise, the stated protagonist in the Tibetan is the "Eminent Couple," also referred to as the "Dharma Lord and Lady."[6] Pema Ösal Thaye is consistent in indicating when the deeds narrated are attributed to one or the other of them alone by using epithets such as the "Master himself" or the "Dharma Lord" for Namtrul Rinpoche and the "Supreme Khandro" or "Khandro Rinpoche" for Tāre Lhamo.[7] Parentheses are used to indicate an interpretative gloss of a passage, such as identifying a person or place, in which the meaning would otherwise not be clear.

With respect to the letters, I have attempted to capture the diversity of literary styles and the liveliness of their language in the use of erotic innuendoes, colloquial expressions, and amorous verses. Where possible in my translations, I parallel the meter and keep the syllable count as close to the original as possible. Tibetan is more condensed in verse than English, so this can be challenging, and it sometimes means dropping the translation of a syllable that in the Tibetan may have served as meter filler. An example is "turquoise dragon" for "turquoise dragon of the south," where the direction "south" does not add to the meaning for English readers and increases the relative syllable count significantly. For the sake of clarification, I provide an explanatory note before each letter to discuss its place in the unfolding of their courtship and mention any stylistic considerations. For a catalogue of the correspondence, I would refer the reader to *Love Letters from Golok* where I also discuss the dating of letters and provide more details about the historical and literary context of their correspondence.

Notes

Foreword

1. Yum mkha' bde chen rgyal mo. This is a liturgy dedicated to Yeshe Tsogyal, the eighth-century Tibetan disciple and consort of Padmasambhava.
2. For more information about the Tibetan tradition of recognizing tulkus (Tib: *sprul sku*, Skt. *nirmāṇakāya*), see *Incarnation: The History and Mysticism of the Tulku Tradition of Tibet* (Thondup 2011). On the phenomenon of treasure revelation, see *The Hidden Teachings of Tibet* (Thondup 1997).
3. Her second husband, otherwise known as Namtrul Rinpoche, should not be confused with Khenpo Jigme Phuntsok (1933–2004), founder of Larung Buddhist Academy in Serta.
4. The Do (Rdo) and Mar (Smar) valleys are part of the greater region of Golok.

Introduction: A Visonary Buddhist Couple

1. His full name is Namtrul Jigme Phuntsok. Here I use his abbreviated local name to avoid any confusion with Khenpo Jigme Phuntsok (1933–2004), the monastic founder of Larung Buddhist Academy, also known as Larung Gar, in Serta.
2. Note that their correspondence is divided into two collections by author: *Adamantine Garland: The Collected Letters by the Lord of Refuge, Namtrul Jigme Phuntsok, to the Supreme Khandro Tāre Lhamo* (*Skyabs rje rin po che nam sprul 'jigs med phun tshogs kyis mkha' 'gro rin po che tā re de vī mchog la phul ba'i zhu 'phrin phyag yig rnams phyogs bsdus rdo rje'i phreng ba*) and *Garland of Lotuses: The Collected Letters by the Mantra-Born One, Khandro Tāre Lhamo, to the Supreme Namtrul Jigme Phuntsok* (*Sngags skyes mkha' 'gro rin po che tā re de vīs nam sprul rin po che 'jigs med phun tshogs mchog la phul ba'i zhu 'phrin phyag yig rnams phyogs bsdus pad ma'i phreng ba*). For this reason, the ordering of the letters in this book is tentative, and I refer to individual letters by their sequence in each respective collection. So their initial letters would be her Letter 1 (abbreviated in the notes as KTL 1) and his Letter 1 (abbreviated NJP 1). Page numbers are from the facsimile edition addendum to their

treasure corpus; see the appendix Sources in Translation for more details. The excerpts from their correspondence in this paragraph come from NJP 1: 6.2, NJP 6:17.5–6, and KTL 7: 83.4–5.

3. For surveys of the tradition of treasure revelation (*gter ma*), see Gyatso 1993, Thondup 1997, Doctor 2005, and Gayley 2008.
4. Most treasure teachings are traced to Padmasambhava, though other figures from the imperial period have also served as their source; see Gyatso 1993: 98 note 2 and Doctor 2005: 198 note 14. Kapstein 2000 and Hirshberg 2016 discusses the historical and mythical role of Padmasambhava during this period.
5. Tantric deities in embrace are referred to as *yabyum*. Conceived in heterosexual terms, the *yab* refers to the male partner and *yum* to the female.
6. An important exception is *vajrācārya* priests in Nepal as discussed in Gellner 1992.
7. See Jacoby 2014a: 299 and Gayley 2016: 296n81.
8. See Donatello Rossi 2008.
9. See Jacoby 2014a, especially chapter 5, regarding the years they lived together toward the end of his life. This couple is an important antecedent for Tāre Lhamo and Namtrul Rinpoche as she was recognized early in life as the reincarnation of Sera Khandro. Later in life, Namtrul Rinpoche claimed Drime Özer as a past life, but this has not yet been widely accepted.
10. In their life stories translated in this book, *Spiraling Vine of Faith* (*Dad pa'i 'khri shing*) depicts Tāre Lhamo's youth, early training, and miracles during the years leading up to and including the Cultural Revolution. Her life together with Namtrul Rinpoche is found in his life story, *Jewel Garland* (*Nor bu'i do shal*). These were published together in Pad ma 'od gsal mtha' yas 1997. A derivative account, *Jewel Lantern of Blessings* (*Byin rlabs nor bu'i gron me*), which likewise interweaves their life stories, places the narrative of their joint career into the section on Tāre Lhamo's life. See A bu dkar lo 2001.
11. See Thondup 1997: 82–84 and 106–107 regarding the role of sexuality in treasure revelation.
12. KTL 14: 98.2–3 and KTL 22: 133.5.
13. As a mnemonic aid, treasures can also be material objects puportedly retrieved from the landscape, such as rocks marked with seed syllables or caskets containing yellow scrolls bearing the numinous *ḍākinī* script. Classification schemes within the treasure tradition distinguish between "mind treasures" (*dgongs gter*) and "earth treasures" (*sa gter*) in this regard, yet as Gyatso 1986 suggests those material objects or symbolic scripts discovered as earth treasures nonetheless serve as a mnemonic device to access the memory of former teachings in the mind. See Thondup 1997: 106–107 for a discussion of this process and Doctor 2005 for a more extensive typology of treasures.
14. NJP 1: 6.5–6.
15. This is not the "healthy attachment" described in modern psychology, which is deemed necessary for early child development. In Buddhist doctrine, attachment has a negative association with ego-clinging (*bdag 'dzin*) and the negative

emotions that derive from self-preoccupation, called *kleśas* or afflictions (*nyon mongs*).

16. See Rock 1956 and Pirie 2005. In a local history, *Annals of Golok History*, the clan federations of Golok are depicted as successfully resisting domination and incursions from outside forces, even as they were also caught up in their own disputes over territory (Don grub dbang rgyal and Nor sde 1992: 33). The sacred mountain Drongri to the south in Serta is associated with the Washul clan of that area; see Jacoby 2014: 113–20.
17. Padma County is within the boundaries of present-day Golok Prefecture in Qinghai Province, while Serta to the south in Sichuan Province has a shared cultural and religious milieu.
18. See Germano 1998.
19. His full name is Apang Terchen Orgyan Trinley Lingpa (1895–1945), also known as Pawo Chöying Dorje.
20. His full name is Dudjom Rinpoche Jigdral Yeshe Dorje (1904–1987). He was one of three recognized reincarnations of Dudjom Lingpa, along with two of Dudjom Linpga's own grandsons, Dzongter Kunzang Nyima (1904–1958) and Sönam Detsun (1910–1958). Tāre Lhamo was a joint emanation of Sera Khandro (female, 1882–1940) and Tra Gelong (male, 1866–1937). As a complication to this identification, Sera Khandro passed away in 1940 and Tāre Lhamo was born in 1938. A third association was added later in life: Lushul Khenpo Könchok Drönme, a respected cleric-scholar from Dodrupchen Monastery.
21. Her age here is by Tibetan reckoning, which counts age by the year one is entering into, so this would be her ninth year, rather than the international standard which counts the year by the one just completed.
22. There were three recognized incarnations of the Third Dodrupchen: Yarlung Tenpe Nyima, Rigdzin Jalu Dorje, and Thubten Trinley Palzangpo. English-language readers will be most familiar with the latter, who currently lives in Sikkim.
23. Tulku Milo is the local abbreviation of his name, Mingyur Dorje (1934–1959), and he was also known as Pema Ösal Nyingpo.
24. This place is also known as Lunghob.
25. Tāre Lhamo's son did not reach the age of ten; he died at the outset of the Cultural Revolution.
26. The domains of knowledge or traditional "sciences" (*rig gnas*) are broken into two categories: major (grammar, logic, medicine, visual arts, and Buddhist philosophy) and minor (poetics, composition, drama, astrology, and synonymy).
27. Monastics were forcibly defrocked and encouraged to marry during the years leading up to and including the Cultural Revolution.
28. Their official biographies are translated in this book, namely *Jewel Garland: The Liberation of Namtrul Jigme Phuntsok* (*Nam sprul 'jigs med phun tshogs kyi rnam thar nor bu'i do shal*; hereafter JG) and *Spiraling Vine of Faith: The Liberation of Khandro Tāre Lhamo* (*Mkha' 'gro tā re lha mo'i rnam thar dad pa'i 'khri shing*; hereafter SVF) in Pad ma 'od gsal mtha' yas 1997.

29. The seminal study on the genre of namthar is Gyatso 1998. In namthar, liberation may be gained by virtue of arduous practice along the Buddhist path or attributed as a birthright for those considered to be emanations of tantric deities or reincarnations of great masters.
30. On the divinization of female identity and agency in *Spiraling Vine of Faith*, see chapter 1 in Gayley 2016. On the ḍākinī as a multivalent female symbol, see Simmer-Brown 2001.
31. These works were published together in *Cloud Offerings to Delight the Vidyādharas and Ḍākinīs: The Liberation of Namtrul Jigme Phuntsok and Khandro Tāre Lhamo* (*Skyabs rje nam sprul rin po che 'jigs med phun tshogs dang mkha' 'gro tā re lha mo mchog gi rnam thar rig 'dzin mkha' 'gro dgyes pa'i mchod sprin*, Pad ma 'od gsal mtha' yas 1997) through the County Office of the Bureau for Cultural Research in Serta. Pema Ösal Thaye works for the Bureau of the Culture, History, Education and Health (*Rig gnas lo rgyus tshan slob 'phrod rten mthun tshogs su u yon ltan khang*). As previously mentioned, I use Namtrul Rinpoche throughout this book rather than the full version of his name, Namtrul Jigme Phuntsok, to avoid confusion with Khenpo Jigme Phuntsok, the monastic founder of Larung Buddhist Academy in Serta.
32. Due to the idealization of these accounts and the Buddhist framework in which they are situated, elsewhere I refer to their life stories as *hagiography* to comment on the style of narration of these specific works. Since this term may be less familiar to a general audience, here I use *biography* instead. Elsewhere I discuss miracles during this period as a distinctive way to to narrate cultural trauma; see chapter 2 in Gayley 2016.
33. Her three brothers were Gyurme Dorje (b. 1928), Wangchen Nyima (b. 1931), and Thubten Chökyi Nyima (b. 1939?). The first child of her parents died in birth. During this period, her teachers Rigdzin Jalu Dorje died in prison and Dzongter Kunzang Nyima of natural causes.
34. See Tshul khrims blo gros 2002 and A bu dkar lo 2003.
35. He shares an identity with Tāre Lhamo as the reincarnation of Tra Gelong. Interview with Aku Chöying, May 2006.
36. I discuss the selectivity process in conditions of self-censorship in Gayley 2016: 78–83.
37. SVF 140. 15–141.9.
38. The title of this work is *The Wonder of Divine Music: A Condensed Account of the Liberation of the Supreme Khandro Tāre Lhamo Rinpoche, the Daughter of Apang Terchen* (*A paṃ gter chen gyi sras mo mkha' 'gro tā re lha mo mchog gi rnam par thar ba mdo tsam brjod pa ngo mtshar lha yi rol mo*) by Rig 'dzin dar rgyas in 2017.
39. See Tshul khrims blo gros 2002 and A bu dkar lo 2003.
40. The list includes: Rigdzin Sang-ngak Lingpa (Sera Yangtrul), Khenpo Jigme Phuntshok, Dodrupchen Thubten Trinley Palzangpo, Lama Rigdzin Nyima, Khenpo Munsel, Payul Karma Chagme, among others. The full list is given in SVF 144.11–145.5 and found in the translation below.

41. *The Indestructible Knot: A Long Life Sādhana* (*Tshe bsgrub rdo rje'i rgya mdud*).
42. Interview with Rigdzin Dargye, May 2007.
43. For a discussion of dating in the correspondence, see Gayley 2016: 317n7.
44. I discuss the epistolary features of their courtship at more length in my article, "The Love Letters of a Buddhist Tantric Couple: Reflections on Poetic Style and Epistolary Intimacy" (2017).
45. The Tibetan for these phrases is: *mdo med rgan mo*, *dman phran*, and *smyon pa*. See DiValerio 2015 on enactments of "holy madness" as a form of tantric antinomianism.
46. See the appendix Sources in Translation for further discussion of the selection criterion and gayley 2016: 279–86 on the numbering of letters.
47. On this view, see Siegel 1978: 17 and Vaudeville 1962: 32.
48. As Per Kvaerne puts it, this is "presenting Sophia in the form of a whore" (1977: 60). By contrast, the four women portrayed as realized yoginīs and mahāsiddhas in their own right in Abhayadattaśrī's lives of the eighty-four siddhas come from merchant or royal families. See Robinson 1979.
49. See Jacoby 2014a: 252–53.Biernacki 2007 has contested this depiction with respect to late medieval Indian texts.
50. For example, one might think of the revered Sangyum, Khandro Tsering Chödrön (1929–2011), the consort of Jamyang Khyentse Chökyi Lodrö (1893–1959), who lived her days in the Tsuklakhang by the old palace in Gangtok, Sikkim. For a historical lens on the consort relationship and its complexities, as Tibetan Buddhism moves beyond Asia, see my article, "Revisiting the Secret Consort (*gsang yum*) in Tibetan Buddhism" (Gayley 2018).
51. The Tibetan for these is: *snying sdug*, *snying gi nor bu*, *brtse grogs*, and *snying grogs*. These epithets are part of a common repertoire of epithets for lovers, whereby "friend" (*grogs*) can connote an amorous liaison. See Tshe tan zhabs drung 2007, vol. 9: 192.
52. Sociologist Anthony Giddens (1992) discusses the importance of creating a shared narrative and sense of mutal compatibility as key aspects of romantic love. See my discussion in Gayley 2016: 150–55.
53. On the Gesar epic, see the Translator's Introduction to *The Epic of Gesar of Ling* (Lama Chönam et al. 2015). As with other tertöns from eastern Tibet, the couple identified themselves with figures in the Gesar epic, in this case, from neighboring kingdoms that Gesar ultimately conquers: Namtrul Rinpoche with Yulha Thogyur, the prince of Jang (to the east) and Tāre Lhamo with Metok Lhadze, the lady of Mön (to the south), though in youth she was also identified with one of the maidens of Ling, named Ne'u Chung.
54. The Tibetan for these is respectively: *'bral med grogs* and *sngon ma'i bkod thang*.
55. The Tibetan is: *rten 'brel*.
56. The Tibetan for these is respectively: *brtse ba* and *'dod chags*. Jacoby 2014a: 262–79.
57. For example, KTL 7, NJP 9, NJP 11, and KTL 26. The Tibetan terms are: *brtse gdung*, *byams brtse*, and *mdun ma'i brtse gdung*.

58. For example, KTL 2, NJP 3, and KTL 5.
59. NJP 15: 43.2–3.
60. The Tibetan is: *thos pa'i ri mo*. KTL 18: 123.5 and 124.2.
61. The Tibetan is: *'dod pa'i sgyu rtsal*.
62. NJP 3: 9.5, KTL 8: 85.4, NJP 22: 56.2–3, KTL 24: 137.5, and NJP 25: 65.4. In her Letter 8, she fashions him as the vase used in tantric initiations and her the feather-ornamented lid, which when conjoined produces the elixir (*bdud rtsi*, *amṛta*) contained within. And in her Letter 24, ḍāki is shorthand for ḍākinī and references her own anticipated pleasure with Namtrul Rinpoche.
63. KTL 5: 81.6–82.1.
64. See Gayley 2016, especially chapter 3.
65. The Tibetan term is: *chags gtam*.
66. This can be found in KTL 15: 103.3–6 and is described below.
67. NJP 25: 59.3–67.3.
68. NJP 25: 65.4–5. The Tibetan reads: *rtsol med kyi gter sgo ngang gis 'byed*.
69. NJP 25: 65.5.
70. For further discussion of this term, *skyabs rje yab yum*, see Gayley 2016: 213–17.
71. See Germano 1998. For an overview of cultural revitalization efforts in the post-Mao period, see Kolas and Thowsen 2005.
72. On the significance of Khenpo Jigme Phuntsok, see Germano 1998, Terronne 2010, and Gayley 2011.
73. See http://www.nyingma.com/artman/publish/dudjom_yangsis.shtml (published on February 12, 2007).
74. I discuss the masculinizing of thaumaturgy in *Jewel Garland* at more length in Gayley 2016: 217–221.
75. JG 89.5–91.3.
76. This miracle is reported during a visit to Samye Chimphu, the hermitage above Samye. JG 92.4–5.
77. JG 91.6.
78. JG 91.10–14.
79. JG 91.14–17.
80. Interview with Namtrul Rinpoche, July 2006.
81. See Gayley 2016: 244–52.
82. JG 68.6–9. The temple dedicated to Gesar is called *Ling Mountain Fortress of One Hundred Thousand Lotuses* (*Gling ri pad ma 'bum rdzong*), today one of six state-recognized Gesar temples in Golok.
83. See epilogue of Gayley 2016.
84. See epilogue of Gayley 2016.
85. For discussions of the growing Han Chinese interest in and patronage of Tibetan Buddhism, see Osburg 2013 and Yü 2014.
86. Her name is Kunzang Drolma. When I last saw her in May 2014, she still lived in Namtrul Rinpoche's quarters at Nyenlung, presiding over it as a memorial shrine.

87. When a new, larger assembly hall was built in 2007, the main throne was made wide enough for two and, when unused, it holds a photograph of the couple on it.
88. This is a two-page print-out, composed by Namtrul Rinpoche and which he shared with me, providing a brief account of Tāre Lhamo's passing and final remarks to gathered disciples. *Nam sprul 'Jigs med phun tshogs*, n.p. This quote can be found on 2.11–14.
89. I received permission from Tulku Laksam to publish the names of both reincarnations, although the Sakya Trizin did not confirm the latter identification when I met him in 2015, presumably due to his granddaughter's young age.
90. The others are his own nephew, Jigme Wangdrak Dorje and a local siddha named Tulku Wulo. Namtrul Rinpoche serves as his activity emanation—a late identification that occurred well after he and Tāre Lhamo had joined together as a couple.

Chapter 1: Early Life of Tāre Lhamo

1. On sex change in Mahāyāna sūtras, see Paul 1985, chapter 5.
2. This is a gloss of Gaṅgādevī's role not found in the *Prajñāpāramitā* literature. Likely a Tibetan intervention, it mirrors Yeshe Tsogyal's role in treasure lore as the compiler of Padmasambhava's teachings, recording them for posterity and hiding them throughout the Tibetan and Himalayan landscape as treasures.
3. We know little about Yeshe Tsogyal as a historical figure, but she looms large in Tibetan ritual, myth, and iconography; see Gyatso 2006.
4. The best-known biography of Yeshe Tsogyal was revealed by Taksham Nuden Dorje a thousand years after she is reported to have lived. It has been translated as *Mother of Knowledge* (Tarthang Tulku 1983), *Sky Dancer* (Dowman, 1996), and *Lady of the Lotus-Born* (Padmakara Translation Committee, 1999).
5. The excerpted portion comes from the sixth chapter of *Bod kyi jo mo ye shes mtsho rgyal gyi mdzad tshul rnam par thar pa gab pa mngon byung rgyud mngas dri za'i glu phreng* (134.3–136.3).
6. For example, the recently discovered biography revealed by Kunga Drime in the fourteenth century focuses on Yeshe Tsogyal's inner journey and visionary experience. See the *Life and Visions of Yeshé Tsogyal: The Autobiography of the Great Wisdom Queen*, translated by Chönyi Drolma (2017).
7. Tāre Lhamo's garland of past lives contains both male and female figures, including: Yeshe Tsogyal of the imperial era; Ne'u Chung at the time of the legendary king Gesar; the female siddha Lakṣmīṇkarā in medieval India; a "conch-bearer" named Vajradeva to the north; a learned man named Sīla in eastern Tibet; two other figures who are difficult to place geographically, Palkyi Lodrö and Shedrub Tenpai Nyima; and finally the female tertön Sera Khandro, referred to by the name, Sukha (the Sanskrit for *bde ba* in Dewe Dorje). The male figures are less easily identifiable than the female ones.

8. The story of Lakṣmīṇkarā is available in translation in *Buddha's Lions: The Lives of the Eighty-Four Siddhas* (Robinson 1979).
9. Tra Gelong is referred to in *Spiraling Vine of Faith* as Tsultrim Lodrö but is also known by Tsultrim Dargye.
10. The *Excellent Path of Devotion: The Abbreviated Autobiography of Sera Khandro*, is available two recent translations, Monson 2013 and Jacoby 2014b. The portion excerpted in *Spiraling Vine of Faith* includes most of the work, *Ku su lu'i nyams byung gi gnas tshul mdor bsdus rdo rje'i spun gyis dris lan mos pa'i lam bzang* (104.3–128.5 in Se ra mkha' 'gro 1978), omitting the opening verses and colophon. For a study of Sera Khandro's life and longer autobiography, see Jacoby 2014a.
11. See Jacoby 2010 for an astute analysis of Sera Khandro's laments of the female body.
12. An additional name, Kunzang Dekyong Chönyi Wangmo, is used to introduce the extended excerpt of Sera Khandro's short autobiography.
13. "Orgyan" (O rgyan) is a well-know epithet of Padmasambhava, referring to his purported land of origin in Northwest India, called Oḍḍiyāna.
14. The Lady of Karchen refers to Yeshe Tsogyal.
15. In a well-known biography of Padmasambhava, the *Copper Island Biography of Padmasambhava* (abbreviated *Zanglingma*, *Zangs gling ma*) revealed by Nyangral Nyima Özer, this kingdom is located in Oḍḍiyāna. See Kunsang 2004: 39.
16. Excerpt of the *Excellent Path of Devotion: The Abbreviated Autobiography of Sera Khandro* is omitted here. See translations in Monson 2013 and Jacoby 2014b.
17. her brothers were Gyurme Dorje (b. 1928), Wangchen Nyima (b. 1931), and Thubten Chökyi Nyima (b. circa 1939).
18. On the ḍākinī, see Willis 1987, Herrmann-Pfandt 1990, Shaw 1994, Campbell 1996, Gyatso 1998, and Simmer-Brown 2001.
19. This comment repeats a misogynist trope in Buddhist literature that belittles the capacities of ordinary women; here it appears to be a strategy to elevate Tāre Lhamo as extraordinary from birth.
20. The Nyingtik Yabshi or Heart Essence in Four Sections (*Snying thig ya bzhi*) is a seminal treasure collection containing Dzokchen or "Great Perfection" (rdzogs chen) teachings specific to the Nyingma tradition.
21. This is a euphomistic way to indicate her father's passing.
22. *The Wonder of Divine Music: A Condensed Account of the Liberation of the Supreme Khandro Tāre Lhamo Rinpoche, the Daughter of Apang Terchen* (*A paṃ gter chen gyi sras mo mkha' 'gro tā re lha mo mchog gi rnam par thar ba mdo tsam brjod pa ngo mtshar lha yi rol mo*) is the newest and as yet unpublished namthar of Tāre Lhamo by Khenpo Rigdzin Dargye, a cleric-scholar originally from Tsimda Monastery but now the disciplinarian at Larung Buddhist Academy in Serta. I first received an untitled draft from the author in 2014 and subsequently the completed version in 2017. This 2017 version will be referred to hereafter in the notes as WDM. The stories recounted below can

be found on WDM 237.17–238.8 and 278.13–18 of this published work (Rig 'dzin dar rgyas 2017).

23. There were three recognized incarnations of the Third Dodrupchen: Yarlung Tenpai Nyima, Rigdzin Jalu Dorje, and Thubten Trinley Palzangpo, who currently lives in Sikkim.
24. WDM 186.15–16. The Tibetan reads: *rje btsun ā rya tā re dngos mi'i sha tshugs su byon pa.*
25. For a typology of treasures, see Doctor 2005.
26. WDM 191.6–192.6.
27. This likely refers to a teaching from the Longchen Nyingtik or Heart Essence of the Vast Expanse (*Klong chen snying thig*) cycle of teachings revealed by Jigme Lingpa, referred to as the "Two Sections of the Heart Essence" (*Snying thig dum gnyis*).
28. *Khandro Gongdu* (*Mkha' 'gro dgongs 'dus*).
29. The text states Dodrupchen Rinpoche here, but I have used Lingtrul Rinpoche for the sake of consistency, since the account above gives Lingtrul Rinpoche as the figure who magically introduced her to the site by pouring tsampa into a crystal glass.
30. Dralas (*dgra bla*) are a type of indigenous spirit, sometimes translated as "war god" and particularly associated with the Gesar epic.
31. These accounts can be found in WDM 189.7–190.3 and 190.15–191.5.
32. For a genealogy of the Dudjom lineage, see my "Who's Who in the Dudjom Lineage" (http://about.tbrc.org/whos-who-in-the-dudjom-lineage/).
33. These are the uncle and cousin, respectively, to Dzongter Kunzang Nyima.
34. Some monasteries in Golok were allowed to reopen in 1962, only to be closed again in 1966 with the onset of the Cultural Revolution. Don grub dbang rgyal and Nor sde 1992: 106.
35. This included the elderly Namkhai Jigme and Dorje Dradul, uncles to Kunzang Nyima, and Kunzang Nyima himself plus Sönam Detsen and two other cousins. Two out of three of Kunzang Nyima's own sons died; while the youngest, Pema Thegchok Gyaltsen, survived. See my "Who's Who in the Dudjom Lineage" (http://about.tbrc.org/whos-who-in-the-dudjom-lineage/).
36. Doli Nyima was the son of Sönam Detsen and Sera Khandro's daughter, Chöying Drolma (alt. Chöying Drönma). It is likely that they had a liaison together. Sometime in the 1960s he was arrested, and Tāre Lhamo found a way to send him a letter to secure his release. He disappeared thereafter, and I was told that Tāre Lhamo often dreamt of him.
37. I discuss this narrative strategy in the context of cultural trauma at length in chapter 2 of Gayley 2016, including the choice to frame the period as the result of collective karma.
38. Her writings and revelations during this period have been compiled with those jointly revealed with Namtrul Rinpoche later in life in their treasure corpus, *O rgyan 'jigs med nam mkha' gling pa dang dākki tāre bde chen rgyal mo rnam gnyis kyi zab gter chos*, a facsimile edition in twelve volumes. There is also a

paperback version in 14 volumes, published together with Apang Terchen's corpus of treasures, which includes their correspondence and more recent writings by Namtrul Rinpoche: *Khyab bdag gter chen bla ma ' ja' lus pa dpal mnyam med nam mkha' gling pa rin po che dang mkha' 'gro rin po che tā re lha mo zung gi zab gter nam mkha' mdzod kyi chos sde* (2013).

39. WDM 5223.5–14 and 224.5–8.
40. WDM: 224.8–17. The Tibetan reads: *thams cad sprul gzhi sgrol ma ljang mo gcig las med pa*. On praises to the twenty-one Tārās, see Willson 1986.
41. This is likely Pema Tsewang (b. 1927), the son of Garra Gyalse Padma Namgyal (A bu dkar lo et al 2000: 246–9).
42. This is Ngari Paṇchen's name, rendered as Pema Wangyal in this line.
43. Ngari Paṇchen is a well-known sixteenth-century Nyingma master and tertön. For a biographical sketch of this figure, visit: https://treasuryoflives.org/biographies/view/Ngari-Panchen-Pema-Wangyal/3006.
44. This passage uses the term *Indranīla* (Tib: *In tra ne le*), also known as *nīlamaṇi* in Sanskrit, referring to sapphire.
45. Swift walking (*rkang mgyogs*) is considered one of the ordinary siddhis or accomplishments resulting from advanced tantric practice.
46. WDM230.11–231.1. The 2017 version makes the mantra's appearance on her garment more explicit than the 2014 draft.
47. Deng Xiaoping promoted the "reform and opening" (*gaige kaifang*) of China at the Third Plenum of the Eleventh National Congress in 1978.
48. The Tibetan term for "renewed propagation" (*yang dar*) literally means "to spread once again." It is a neologism for the revitalization of the Buddhism in the post-Mao period (roughly 1980 forward) that places the events of recent history within a broader Buddhist framework, echoing the early and later propagations (*snga dar, phyi dar*) of Buddhism in Tibet.
49. Khecarīs are another class of celestial female deities, alongside ḍākinīs.

Chapter 2: Early Life of Namtrul Rinpoche

1. The names Dundubhīśvara, Śikhin, Vipaśyin, and Kāśyapa refer to previous buddhas.
2. This is a tentative reconstruction into Sanskrit of *Khye'u skar ma'i 'od* in the Tibetan.
3. The long "ā" in dharma in this line and the next appears to be a spelling mistake so it is omitted here.
4. This is the Sanskrit for Chöying Dorje, one of the names for Apang Terchen, Tāre Lhamo's father. Later in life, after his union with Tāre Lhamo, Namtrul Rinpoche asserted his status as her father's "activity emanation" (*phrin las sprul ba*). Otherwise, the main incarnations of Apang Terchen are the 41st Sakya Trizin, Nawang Kunga, and Jigme Wangdrak Dorje, the nephew of Apang Terchen enthroned in youth and lives at Abzö Monastery in Jigdril.

5. This refers to Rigdzin Gödem, the tertön who revealed the so-called "northern treasures" (*byang gter*).
6. Tse refers to Namtrul Rinpoche's name in childhood, Tsedzin.
7. This refers to the pure land of Padmasambhava, also known as the Glorious Copper-Colored Mountain (Zangs mdog dpal ri) located on the subcontinent Cāmara of Buddhist cosmology.
8. *Ayu* is the Sanskrit for "life," translating *Tse* (*tshe*) from Tibetan, the first part of Tsedzin.
9. This was Namtrul Rinpoche's name in religion prior to his union with Tāre Lhamo. The longer version of his name then was: Pema Drime Ösal Lodrö Thaye.
10. This refers to the great tertön, Nyangral Nyima Özer, who revealed the *Assembly of Sugatas* (*Bde gshegs 'dus pa*).
11. Nyenlung Monastery lies on the road north out of Serta towards Padma County; this is the monastery that Namtrul Rinpoche and Tāre Lhamo rebuilt, with the help of Lama Rigdzin Nyima, as their main seat.
12. This refers to two ritual practices in the Katok tradition, namely the treasures of Rigdzin Dudul Dorje and Rigdzin Longsal Nyingpo.
13. This is the Tibetan transcription of the initial syllables of the mantra of Mañjuśrī, the bodhisattva of wisdom.
14. *Gangloma* (*Gang blo ma*) is the shorthand for a well-known praise to Mañjuśrī, titled Śrījñānaguṇaphala (*Dpal ye shes yon tan bzang po*).
15. *Mahāmokṣa Sūtra* (*Thar pa chen po'i mdo*).
16. For a study of the transmission of the *Bardo Thödrol* and its translations into English, see Cuevas 2003 and Lopez 1999, especially chapter 2.
17. *The Application of Mindfulness* (*Dran pa nyer bzhag*) refers to the *Smṛtyupasthāna Sūtra,* and the *Ascertaining the Three Vows* (*Sdom gsum rnam nges*) refers to a treatise on the three vows (*sdom gsum*) by Ngari Paṇchen Pema Wangyal.
18. Zhuchen Monastery, located in Serta, is a branch of Kathok Monastery.
19. Jamyang Chökyi Lodrö was the reincarnation of Jamyang Khyentse Wangpo at Dzongsar Monastery in the Dege region of Kham. An influential master of the early twentieth century, he spent his final years in Sikkim as the guest of the king.
20. *The Precious Treasury of Dharmadhātu* (*Chos dbyings rin po che'i mdzod*) is one of Klong chen pa's "seven treasuries" (*mdzod bdun*).
21. This is an expression of surprise or wonderment.
22. This is the fasting ritual (*bsnyung gnas*, alt. *smyung gnas*) founded by Gelongma Palmo in the tenth to eleventh century.
23. Shukjung is a small monastery east of Dodrupchen Monastery on the road to Dzamthang. In the previous generation, there was a famous ḍākinī associated with it.
24. Drongri Mukpo is the mountain deity who serves as the protector of Serta.

25. This figure may be the reincarnate lama of either Yukhok Thekchen Chökor Ling, a Nyingma monastery in Tawu County, or Yuthok Monastery, a Kagyu monastery just down the road from Dodrupchen Monastery.
26. The Tibetan term for collective karma is: *spyi mthun las*. The notion of collective karma appears to be modern, but not restricted to Tibet; it appeared in Buddhist discourse in colonial Southeast Asia and elsewhere. I discuss narrative strategies that foreground Tibetan agency in Buddhist terms in chapter 2 of Gayley 2016.
27. Namtrul Rinpoche mentioned in an interview in 2004 that, during these years, he meditated in valleys and hermitages throughout the area surrounding Nyenlung.
28. JG 21.10–22.1. A dzo is a yak and cow hybrid.
29. Reting is a Geluk Monastery outside of Lhasa.
30. There were four emanations of Apang Terchen, including the 41st Sakya Trizin, the longstanding head of the Sakya lineage in exile, who currently lives in Dehradun. The only one enthroned was Jigme Wangdrak Dorje, the nephew of Apang Terchen. The others are Tulku Wulo, the son of a Golok chieftain, and Namtrul Rinpoche as the activity emanation (A bu dkar lo et al 2000: 213).
31. In an interview, Namtrul Rinpoche emphasized that this Yeshe Tsogyal sādhana was identical to the one that Tāre Lhamo sent him with her first letter.
32. The aspirational empowerment (*smon lam dbang bskur*) and entrustment (*gtad rgya*) are more typically viewed as aspects of the concealment process, when Padmasambhava appointed one of his close disciples to reveal the treasure in a future lifetime, rather than constituent of the revelation of those treasures. See Thondup 1997.
33. There is a monastery in Kham called Khordong that had a tertön named Drophan Lingpa from the eighteenth century whose incarnation line appears to be based there.
34. The lines of these letters are all marked with the orthographic sign for terma, called tertsek (*gter tsheg*) consisting of two circles with a horizontal line between them, indicating the prophetic or visionary status of their content.
35. The system of nine *mewas* (*sme dgu*) in Tibetan astrology is a diagram, or "magic square" as Phillipe Cornu calls it, made up of nine smaller squares, which can be arranged into islands. For each year, there is a natal mewa, a body mewa, a mewa of vitality, a mewa of power, and a mewa of windhorse. See Cornu 2002: 106.
36. This is a shrine at Samye, referred to as Butsal Serkhang (*Bu tshal gser khang*), but here the spelling would render it Utsal Serkhang (*Dbu tshal gser khang*). In the *Clear Mirror of Royal Genealogy* (*Rgyal rabs gsal ba'i me long*), its construction is attributed to Gyelmotsun, Princess of Poyong (Taylor and Yuthok 1996, 241).
37. In this line, the flower likely refers to the flower tossed into a maṇḍala during a tantric initiation which determines one's affinity for one of the buddha fam-

ilies. Here the implication seems to be that they tossed their flower in the same direction.

38. According to treasure lore, this is the moment when Padmasambhava appointed one of his disciples to reveal a specific teaching in the future as a revelation.
39. A reconstruction into Sanskrit of *Ye shes blo gros*.
40. A reconstruction into Sanskrit of *Dpal lha mo*.
41. Not all of this letter is included in *Jewel Garland*. There are five excerpts: KTL 17: 116.1–6, 117.1–3, 118.1–5, 122.1–3, and 112.4–115.4.
42. This references an emanation of Namkhai Nyingpo, namely Namtrul Rinpoche himself.
43. Jangyul was a neighboring land to Ling in the Gesar epic. One of Namtrul Rinpoche's past life identities is as the Prince of Jang, a converted hero (*dpa' thul*) who joined Gesar in the conquest of his own land.
44. There is a difference in the last line between the letter as excerpted in *Jewel Garland* and as it appears in the facsimile edition. Instead of *'gro don*, the term *gdul zhing* is used, implying that their domain of conversion will consist of billions of lands. KTL 27: 145.5–6.
45. Nangsal Drönme (*Snang gsal sgron me*). Its revealer is the son of Garra Gyalse Pema Namgyal, associated with Banak Monastery in Padma.
46. This refers to Tsimda Gompa, the monastery that Apang Terchen founded in Markhok. There is no lake at the monastery itself, which is perched on a mesa above a river, but the prophecy could refer to a lake nearby.
47. Lotus Radiance (Padma Ö) is the name of the palace of Padmasambhava in his pure land of Zangdok Palri.
48. In this context, the Protector Guru couple (*mgon gu ru yab yum*) no doubt refers to Padmasambhava and Yeshe Tsogyal.
49. Abhaya is the Sanskrit for "fearless," which is rendered *jigme* (*'jigs med*) in Tibetan, part of the formal name, Namtrul Jigme Phuntsok, that Namtrul Rinpoche took after joining together with Khandro Tāre Lhamo.
50. The country of Jang, or Jangyul ('Jang yul), is said to lie in present-day Yunnan province. Mukpo (Smug po) is the clan to which Namtrul Rinpoche belongs.
51. Yulha Thogyur, the prince of Jang, is reference to one of Namtrul Rinpoche's past lives. The "Lord of Secrets" (*gsang bdag*) in the previous line refers to Vajrapāni.
52. The "five excellences" (*phun tshogs lnga*) describe the ideal setting for tantric teachings and include the perfect time, place, teacher, teachings, and disciples.
53. The three poisons of passion, aggression, and ignorance—depicted as a rooster, snake, and pig at the hub of Wheel of Existence (*srid pa'i 'khor lo*)—are regarded as the causal basis for suffering within the six realms of saṃsāra.
54. This excerpt spans KTL 17: 112.4–115.4.

Chapter 3: Letters of Tāre Lhamo and Namtrul Rinpoche

1. For a catalogue of their letters, see appendices to Gayley 2016.
2. This is likely a reference to Nyenpo Yutse (Gnyan po g.yu rtse), a sacred mountain range in Golok with two sacred lakes, Shimtso (Bye'u mtsho) and Ngöntso (Sngon mtsho), that served as important treasure locations for Namtrul Rinpoche and Tāre Lhamo.
3. This is Drakar Trezong (Brag dkar sprel rdzong), or White Cliff Monkey Fortress, a well-known pilgrimage site in northern Amdo with caves associated with Padmasambhava and Yeshe Tsogyal.
4. KTL 1: 76.1–78.1.
5. The Tibetan for these phrases is: *bde stong dbang mo*, *'dod pa'i sgyu rtsal*, and *dga' bzhi'i ye shes dbyings*.
6. This is a reference to the Nyingma school, which traces its scriptures to the time of the "early translations" (*snga 'gyur*) during the imperial period of the seventh to ninth centuries.
7. This describes Yeshe Tsogyal, referred to as the Princess of Karchen (Mkhar chen) and considered to be an emanation of Sarasvatī.
8. The certificate (*kha byang*) provides key information regarding a treasure, including its location and sometimes also its contents. The two knowledges (*mkhyen gnyis*) refers to the ability to see things in their multiplicity and their nature.
9. The Lotus Born (*mtsho skyes*) is an epithet for Padmasambhava.
10. Mutik Tsanpo was the son of Trisong Detsen, one of the great emperors of Tibet during the imperial period.
11. This is most likely a reference to the great Nyingma monastery in Central Tibet, founded by Terdak Lingpa.
12. NJP 1: 2.1–7.1.
13. A "song of marvels" (*kha mtshar glu*) is sung on celebratory occasions.
14. KTL 2: 78.2–6.
15. KTL 3: 78.6–79.2. The last line gestures to the *tendrel*, or "coincidence" (*rten 'brel*) for their own union to fall into place. Throughout my translations, I use "click into place" as a homophonic translation for the Tibetan *drik* (*'grigs*); when used with tendrel in their letters, this term refers to causes and conditions for their union and revelations coming together in an auspicious way.
16. The Tibetan terms are: *zab bcud* and *bstan 'gro'i rgud gso*.
17. NJP 2: 7.2–8.1.
18. The Tibetan for this is *lha* (*lha*), *nyen* (*gnyan*), and *lu* (*klu*).
19. In this context, the term for "friend" (*grogs*, *rogs*) can alternatively be translated as companion or consort.
20. KTL 4: 79.2–80.5.
21. The Tibetan is: *reg grol phyag rgya*.
22. The Tibetan is: *bde stong ye shes bskyed pa'i mchog gi grogs*.

23. Do Kham (Mdo khams) refers to eastern Tibet, encompassing Amdo and Kham.
24. *Zab bcud bde stong dga' bzhi'i gsang lam.*
25. Recall that Dewe Dorje is one of the names of Sera Khandro. Tāre Lhamo was recognized in childhood as the emanation of two masters of the previous generation, Tra Gelong (male) and Sera Khandro (female).
26. Māras are demonic forces, so this stanza suggests their aspiration to benefit any and all.
27. NJP 3: 8.1–12.4.
28. The Tibetan is: *zur mig g.yo.*
29. This line referencing yogic exercises, literally the "magic wheel" (*'phrul 'khor*), was a difficult one to translate. I omitted the final phrase, *rlung gis bshigs.*
30. The six elements (*khams drug*) refer to earth, water, fire, wind, space, and consciousness.
31. KTL 5: 80.5–82.2. This closing employs the Sanskrit, Sukha and Mati. Sukha translates the Tibetan for the first part of Sera Khandro's name, Dewe Dorje, and thus refers to Tāre Lhamo by one of her past lives. The second Mati translates the Tibetan name, Lodrö, which is the second part of Namtrul Rinpoche's name in religion prior to his union with Tāre Lhamo, Pema Lodrö or in its extended form, Pema Drime Ösal Lodrö Thaye.
32. The treasure certificate (*gter byang*) is a visionary guide to the location of a treasure, sometimes also containing a list of its contents. Receiving this is often the first step in the revelation process. See Gyatso 1986.
33. The Tibetan is: *snyigs ma'i ru 'dzing bzlog.*
34. KTL 6: 82.2–83.4.
35. The Tibetan is: *dpa' thul.*
36. The Tibetan is: *yid dwangs gsal shel gyi me long.*
37. The country of Jang, or Jangyul ('Jang yul), is said to lie in present-day Yunnan province. Mukpo (Smug po) is the clan to which Namtrul Rinpoche belongs.
38. Yulha Thogyur, the prince of Jang, is reference to one of Namtrul Rinpoche's past lives. The "Lord of Secrets" in (*gsang bdag*) the previous line refers to Vajrapāni.
39. These refer to the districts conquered by Gesar.
40. These are the creation (*bskyed*) and completion (*rdzogs*) stages of tantric practice.
41. Ngayab Palri (Rnga yab dpal ri) is the glorious mountain in Padmasambhava's pure land.
42. *Yangtik Thigle Serzhuma* (*Yang tig thig le gser zhun ma*).
43. These are specified as Nyingtik or "heart essence" (*snying thig*) cycles of Dzokchen teachings, but not the famous Nyingtik Yabzhi (*Snying thig ya bzhi*). Later reference is made to Yangtik cycles considered "even more essential" (*yang thig*).
44. This may be the sacred Bön site, Takrong Tsamkhang (Stag rong mtshams khang).

45. A ḍākinī abode associated with Oḍḍiyāna and the great Indian master Padmasambhava (Huber 2008: 103–104).
46. This may refer to Taksham Nuden Dorje, the revealer of the most widely-known version of Yeshe Tsogyal's life and the rebirth of her consort, Atsara Sale. In her Letter 9, Tāre Lhamo makes this correlation (KTL 9: 87.1).
47. Phurba (*phur pa*) can refer to a type of ritual dagger or the deity Vajrakīla who wields it.
48. Per Ringu Tulku, this is a cryptic way to refer to the dog year.
49. NJP 5: 13.6–17.5.
50. The Tibetan is: *byams brtse ldan*.
51. The Tibetan is: *gdol spyod smyon pa*.
52. The Tibetan for these phrases is respectively: *sems kyi rten*, *stong nyid lha mdzes*, and *thabs mchog gyur kun grol vajra*.
53. The Tibetan is: *thabs shes*.
54. "Tarpo" is Namtrul Rinpoche's nickname for Tāre Lhamo, taking the first syllable of "Tāre" and adding "po." His name in youth was Tzedzin, so he sometimes refers to himself as "Tse" and she uses "Tsebo" as a nickname for him.
55. The two benefits are the benefit of self and others. The twofold noble family implies worldly and transcendent potentials.
56. The term used here is "pool of nectar" (*bdud rtsi 'khyil ba*). Given the repetition of this formula of names, this may be an epithet linked to the Vajrapāni cycle called Drop of Nectar (*Bdud rtsi'i thig pa*).
57. NJP 6: 17.5–19.2.
58. KTL 7: 83.4–84.1.
59. The Tibetan is: *gtum mo*.
60. This may be a variation on other names given in the correspondence for Namtrul Rinpoche's past life during the time of King Gesar, primarily Yulha Thogyur and Yuyi Thortsug. Yuyi Lathöcan means "the one with the turquoise turban" (*G.yu yi la thod can*) as does Yuyi Thortsug (*G.yu yi thor gtsug*) and one other variant, Yuyi Thögyancan (*G.yu yi thod rgyan can*), found later in the correspondence.
61. Tibetans often associate certain features of the landscape or precious objects as a dwelling place for their "soul" (*bla*), in this case a "soul mountain" (*bla ri*).
62. Here I combine two lines which otherwise create an anomaly in the structure of the couplets.
63. KTL 8: 84.1–86.3.
64. According to Ringu Tulku, Dzalandar Peak originally means on the top of his head.
65. His use of "lowly one" (*dman phran*) to refer to himself reflects the humility appropriate to first person speech in Tibetan as well as his abject state in illness.
66. This prayer, *Sampa Lhundrup* (*Bsam pa lhun grub*), is a supplication to Padmasambhava.
67. The tigress refers to Tāre Lhamo, who was born in the tiger year.
68. NJP 7: 19.2–25.6.

69. The Tibetan is: *Nus ldan sprul pa'i myu gyu.*
70. I have interpretted this as Yutse, the "Turquoise Peak" where the text simply says "Yu" (*g.yu*) since at other moments in the correspondence they speak of a turquoise peak with a white cliff in the east, and Nyenpo Yutse in the eastern part of Golok is one of their important treasure sites.
71. KTL 9: 86.4–87.4.
72. Elsewhere, I render this name as Padma when it stands alone, since it is so often shorthand for Padmasambhava in their letters. Tibetans pronounce this Pema, so I use Pema in Tibetan compounds like Pema Ösal Thaye. Here I use Pema since it is shorthand for Namtrul Rinpoche's name in religion at the time, Pema Drime Lodrö.
73. Here the crown refers to the crest on the top of the peacock's head.
74. This image of ice represents peace as suggested to me by Ringu Tulku.
75. Ma can refer to the Ma River (Rma chu) which turns into the Yellow River in China or the region surrounding Amnye Machen (A myes rma chen), a sacred mountain range in Golok, through which the river flows.
76. This is an epithet for King Gesar, a.k.a. Norbu Dradul (Nor bu dgra 'dul).
77. These are the eighteen districts (*rdzong*) conquered and incorporated into Ling.
78. The expression "mother beings" (*ma 'gro*) is based on the longstanding Mahāyāna idea that all living beings have at one point been one's own parents through the endless successsion of rebirth.
79. KTL 10: 87.5–92.4.
80. The Tibetan term for "love song" is literally "songs of the mountain pass" (*la gzhas*), the locus of amorous encounters in nomadic areas of eastern Tibet. See Rossi 1992 and Anton-Luca 2002.
81. Namtrul Rinpoche told me that they only met once for a brief period during their correspondence, when he ventured to Markhok to visit Tāre Lhamo and meet her relatives. That meeting is still to come in the sequence of letters and is also depicted in their biographies. Yet it is likely that the two encountered each other in youth in the shared Nyingma milieu of Golok.
82. NJP 9: 26.4–28.6.
83. The Tibetan is: *yid dwangs gsal shel gyi pho brang.*
84. A tertsek (*gter tsheg*) consists of two circles stacked vertically with a horizontal line between them. A number of her letters are marked in this way. I indicate these in a list of the contents of their letters in the appendices to Gayley 2016.
85. Manene is a female protector and aunt figure in the Gesar epic.
86. Magyal Pomra is another name for Amnye Machen, the magnificent mountain range and protective deity in the northwest part of Golok.
87. The "descendants of the monkey" (*sprel tsha*) likely refers to the widespread myth of the origin of the Tibetan people through the union of a local demoness and a monkey, understood to be an emanation of Avalokiteśvara.
88. Palri is shorthand for Zangdok Palri, the Copper Colored Mountain, domain of Padmasambhava.
89. KTL 13: 93.4–94.6.

90. The term for "folly" here is: *rmongs*.
91. The Tibetan for these is respectively: *grogs gzhon nu* and *sngon las bskod thang*.
92. The Tibetan is: *chags gtam*.
93. In this line, the flower likely refers to the flower tossed into a maṇḍala during a tantric initiation which determines one's affinity for one of the buddha families. Here the implication seems to be that they tossed their flower in the same direction.
94. According to treasure lore, this is the moment when Padmasambhava appoints one of his disciple to reveal a specific teaching in the future as a revelation.
95. KTL 13: 94.6–97.2.
96. NJP 10: 32.5–33.6.
97. The Tibetan term is: *dran pa*.
98. An alternative for Yulha Thogyur, one of Namtrul Rinpoche's past lives.
99. This is the combination of two lines.
100. This is an epithet for Lake Kokonor in northern Amdo, based on a creation story that the lake drowned 10,000 when it came into being.
101. This may refer to Dangra Khyungdzong (*Dang rag khyung rdzong*), a sacred Bön site.
102. This is a typical way of describing the benefits of making a connection to a Buddhist teacher or lama; through that connection, the lama can then guide the disciple in the death process.
103. NJP 11: 34.1–37.5.
104. The throne and parasol can be a metaphor for the sun and moon; in this case it seems more plausibly to refer to the sun and its rays.
105. NJP 12: 37.5–39.1.
106. The Tibetan is: *skyo ba'i glu*.
107. The Tibetan is: *dga' bzhi'i ye shes*.
108. Creation (*bskyed*) and completion (*rdzogs*) are the two main phases of tantric practice.
109. KTL 14: 97.2–99.2.
110. The term "lowly me" in Tibetan is: *dman phran*.
111. The Tibetan for these is respectively: *skyid* and *bde*.
112. NJP 13: 39.2–41.2.
113. The Tibetan is: *rtag brtan*, pronounced "tak ten." With "stable and steady," I have attempted to reproduce the alliteration.
114. The Tibetan is: *'gyur med*.
115. NJP 14: 41.2–6.
116. NJP 15: 41.6–44.4.
117. These sections are demarcated as separate letters in the paperback version of their correspondence, whereas the original facsimile edition indicates section breaks within a single letter.
118. *Glu rdzong bkra shis sgo brgyad don 'grub bsam 'phel nor bu*.
119. Tsukna Rinchen refers to the king of the nāgas, a class of serpentine spirits who

occupy the watery lowlands. Note the arrangement of these consecutive verses according to an indigenous formulation of divine (*lha*), the mighty deities of the land (*gnyan*), here cast as war gods (*dgra bla*), and the nāgas or water spirits (*klu*).

120. Werma (*wer ma*) are an enlightened form of war god (*dgra bla*).
121. The tsan (*btsan*) are another fierce spirit.
122. Thank you to Lama Chönam for clarifying the colloquial expressions in this passage.
123. The eight worldly concerns are gain or loss, pleasure or pain, praise or blame, fame or censure.
124. The reference here is kleśa (*nyon mong*) which refers to affliction or negative emotion.
125. This refers to the two aspects, the freedoms and favors (*dal 'byor*), of a precious human birth.
126. This is another possible variation of Namtrul Rinpoche's identity as Yulha Thogyur.
127. This refers to Padmasambhava (a.k.a. Orgyan Padma), Śāntarakṣita, and the Tibetan emperor, Trisong Detsen.
128. The Ser, Do, Mar, and Ma (Gser, Rdo, Smar and Rma) are the four main rivers defining the Golok landscape.
129. The four are material goods, dharma, fearlessness, and loving kindness.
130. Recall that Yeshe Tsogyal is referred to as the Princess of Karchen.
131. KTL 15: 99.2–110.1.
132. The Tibetan for these is respectively: *brda byang* and *nor bu'i chun po.*
133. NJP 16: 44.4–6.
134. The Tibetan for these is respectively: *grogs snying gces*, *rogs rtse mthun*, and *snyings gi thig le*. Bindu (Tib: *thig le*) refers to the seminal male and female drops in the subtle body.
135. NJP 17: 44.6–45.5.
136. KTL 17: 116.1–6, 117.1–3, 118.1–5, 122.1–3, and 112.4–115.4.
137. KTL 17: 118.1–119.4.
138. Apart from this opening line, the whole letter is marked with tertsek, the orthographic feature indicating its status as treasure. Five passages are excerpted in *Jewel Garland.*
139. The "five excellences" (*phun tshogs lnga*) describe the ideal setting for tantric teachings and include the perfect time, place, teacher, teachings, and disciples.
140. This is Padmasambhava's pure land, variously referred to as the Glorious Copper-Colored Mountain (*Zangs mdog dpal ri*) and the Glorious Mountain of Cāmara (*Rna yab dpal ri*).
141. This is a reference to Apang Terchen's untimely death at the age of fifty in 1945.
142. Raudracakrin (Lcags 'khor lo can) is the twenty-fifth *kalkin* or Rigden king (*rigs ldan*) of Shambhala, prophesized in the Kālacakra tantra to preside victorious over an apocalyptic battle with barbarian forces.

143. Tāre Lhamo had three brothers who were incarnate lamas; a fourth died during childbirth.
144. A reconstruction into Sanskrit of Lha mo sgrol ma, the inversion of her own name Tāre Lhamo.
145. A reconstruction into Sanskrit of Blo gros grags pa. Ākāśagarbha is the Sanskrit for Namkhai Nyingpo, so there is an obvious parallel here to their lives in Tibet where he is the Namkhai Nyingpo incarnation of Zhuchen Monastery. This is even more apparent in the Tibetan where Nam-Nying (Nam snying) is used.
146. Lotus Radiance Palace (Pad ma 'od) is the palace of Padmasambhava in his pure land, Zangdok Palri.
147. This image recalls the animals of their respective birth years, hers the Tiger and his the Monkey Year. For this reason, in the correspondence overall, the tiger is usually gendered female (*stag mo*).
148. This may be a reference to her father, Apang Terchen Pawo Chöying Dorje, who figures prominently elsewhere in this letter.
149. These refer to various lists of Indian Buddhist masters.
150. This refers to one of the Buddha's past lives in the *jātaka* tales when the bodhisattva gave away his eyes, part of Tibetan folk performance tradition.
151. KTL 17: 112.4–118.1, 119.4–122.3.
152. The Tibetan is: *brtse*.
153. The Tibetan for these terms is respectively: *phyag rgya ma*, *bde ster ma*, *brtse mdza'*, and *yid kyi 'khrid shing ma*. This list of epithets is one of the few places in their correspondence using gendered terms for consort. More typically they refer to each other as "friend" or "companion" (*grogs*, *rogs*), which can connote an amorous liaison. But they typically eschew gender-specific endings in their correspondence (apart from this letter where he uses *snying grogs ma*) as one would in colloquial speech (either *grogs po* or *grogs mo*).
154. The Tibetan terms are respectively: *rab*, *thugs*, and *dman*.
155. Seven horses (*rta bdun*) is a standard kenning for the sun, based on the Indian notion that the sun is a chariot drawn in its orbit by seven horses.
156. NJP 19: 48.2–50.5.
157. The Tibetan is: *Rdzong me tog 'phreng ba*.
158. The three monastic seats in central Tibet are Sera, Drepung, and Ganden, given in this letter in abbreviated form (Ser 'bras dga').
159. This may be another past live identification for Tāre Lhamo in this period, along with Metok Lhadze and Ne'u Chung.
160. Recall that as a converted hero (*dpa' thul*), Yulha Thogyur goes into battle alongside Gesar against his own (corrupt) kingdom, Jang.
161. Ma likely refers to the area around Amnye Machen (also known as Magyal Pomra), as mentioned above. It is possible that the Yang (G.yang) and Ra (Rma) are tributaries of the Ma River or valleys farther afield.
162. KTL 18: 122.4–126.5.

163. This is transliterated: *tshe*.
164. The Tibetan is: *tshe ring lha mo*.
165. KTL 20: 128.3–129.4.
166. The Tibetan is: *ka dag zang ma thal*.
167. For a recent study of the "holy madman" (*smyon pa*) in Tibetan literature, see DiValerio 2015.
168. Here again, Namtrul Rinpoche uses Dzalandar to refer to the top of his head.
169. With Karma Lhadrön, Namtrul Rinpoche is no doubt addressing Tāre Lhamo. With Kundrol Rigpe Dorje, he may be including her attendent and scribe, Lama Thöpa. Below he playfully refers to himself as Karma Dorje and Rangjung Dorje.
170. NJP 52.3–54.4.
171. KTL 22: 136.4. Omitted section is KTL 22:135.3–136.5.
172. This is one of the few, if only, place(s) where Tāre Lhamo refers to herself as "consort" (*gzung ma*).
173. KTL 22: 131.5–135.2, 136.6.
174. The Tibetan is: *gnyis 'gros*.
175. Machen Pomra (Rma chen spom ra) is also rendered Magyal Pomra (Rma rgyal spom ra), the resident deity of the Amnye Machen range in northern Golok.
176. In the Gesar epic, according to Stein, Achen (A chen) is a region to the north of Ling. Possibly due to a caravan route through the region, the term highway or main road (*gzhung lam*) is used in this verse. See Stein 1959: 194–95 and 198–99.
177. Utsang (Dbus gtsang), refers to Central Tibet. Here it may be characterized as pure land due to its sanctity for Tibetans across the plateau. That said, it is not clear why this would be the destination for tantric adepts per se.
178. NJP 22: 54.5–56.6.
179. This term for "wondering" (*bsam*) appears at the end of each line, where verbs generally go in Tibetan, but I transpose it to the beginning of each line for emphasis.
180. KTL 24: 137.2–138.4.
181. The Tibetan term is: *rogs mthun*, alt: *rogs 'then*. Thank you to Nyingpo Tsering and Lama Jabb who explained the valences of this term to me.
182. KTL 25: 138.5–140.1.
183. Great Lion (Seng chen) is an epithet for King Gesar of Ling.
184. KTL 26: 140.1–6.
185. The Tibetan is: *dga' skyid gtam gi glu gzhas*. According to Pema Bum, the term *glu gzhas* is a type of love song (Pad ma 'bum 1997), yet the content and setting in this song is tantric.
186. The Tibetan is: *dus de ring bkra shis phun sum tshogs*.
187. The Tibetan is: *thabs shes rab mtshon pa'i rdzas chen*.
188. The yidam is one's tutelary deity in tantric practice.
189. Namtrul Rinpoche uses an epithet for the Tibetan people here, "black-headed"

(*mgo nag*), not to be confused with the "black hats" (*zhwa nag*) placed on class enemies during the Cultural Revolution. To avoid confusion for those unfamiliar with this epithet, I simply refer to Tibetans.

190. The thirty-two joys follows from the release of the thirty-two knots, per Lama Chönam.
191. NJP 25: 59.3–67.3.
192. In the appendices to Gayley 2016, I provide a tentative numbering of their letters, and there I list this as Tāre Lhamo's thirtieth letter. However, I am inclined now to think that what I listed as the two previous letters (KTL 28 and 29) are actually part of the same letter, which would make this her twenty-ninth (KTL 29). I leave the original numbering to reduce confusion for anyone cross-referencing these sources.
193. This is close to an epithet of Mahākāla, namely Swift-Acting Protector (Myur mdzad mgon po).
194. During field research, I was told that Tāre Lhamo has given Namtrul Rinpoche his new name, Namtrul Jigme Phuntsok. This is a close variant as *jigme* (*'jigs med*) and *jigdral* (*'jigs bral*) mean "fearless."
195. Another possible alternative for Yulha Thogyur.
196. This is an epithet for Padmasambhava.
197. KTL 30: 165.2–167.5.

Chapter 4: Travels and Teachings as a Couple

1. Personal communication by Namtrul Rinpoche in July 2006. A description of their collaboration in treasure revelation along similar lines can be found in *Jewel Lantern of Blessing* (A bu dkar lo 2001: 23.12–24.6).
2. As this and other revelations make clear, Tāre Lhamo was never merely a consort. Rather, she was a respected teacher and tertön in her own right, having revealed treasures prior to their union and being worthy of maṇḍala offerings, the ritual means to request a tantric teaching.
3. Its full name is Larung Buddhist Academy of the Five Sciences in Serta (Gser ljongs bla ma rung lnga rig chos sde chen po); it was officially certified as an institution in 1987.
4. They formed what David Germano has called a "vibrant, multipronged Ter [treasure] movement that has emerged as one of the most powerful and vital strategies for the renewal of traditional Tibetan culture among Nyingma traditions in Tibet." See Germano 1998: 90.
5. The Tibetan for "eminent couple" is: *skyabs rje yab yum*.
6. This is a euphemistic and formal way of indicating the purpose of their revelation and the sādhana that derived from it, namely to extend the lives of Buddhist masters remaining on the Tibetan plateau at that time.
7. Rāhula is referred to here by an epithet found in the treasures of Dudjom Lingpa, namely Drangsong Zachok Chenpo.
8. Given its placement in the text, the monkey year mentioned in the prophecy

inadvertently places their revelation at Nyenpo Yutse around the same time as their revelation at Drongri recounted above.

9. Guru Sangdrup (Gu ru'i gsang sgrub).
10. Myurlam Dechen Zhing (Myur lam bde chen zhing). Here the epithet, Unchanging Light ('Od mi 'gyur ba) is used. Given the context, it is most likely a variant of the epithet, Boundless Light (Snang ba mtha' yas) for Amitābha, although it can also be used as an epithet for Samantabhadra in Nyingma contexts.
11. Khandrö Sunlok (Mkha' 'gro'i sun bzlog). This ritual is performed for lamas who are extremely ill or on the brink of death.
12. The epithet given here, Boundless Life (Tshe mtha' yas), appears to be a variant on Measureless Life (Tshe dpag med), the standard translation of Amitāyus.
13. *Jangdul Pawö Gekyang* (*Jang 'dul dpa'i bo'i gad rgyang*). The hero who conquered Jang or the Prince of Jang, one of Namtrul Rinpoche's past lives, likely refers to Gesar of Ling.
14. Vajrakumāra or the Youthful Vajra (Rdo rje gzhon nu) is an epithet for Vajrakīla, a tutelary deity in the Nyingma schema of "eight command" (*bka' brgyad*) deities.
15. Thukchen Chakna Pekar (Thugs chen phyag na pad dkar).
16. According to the Tibetan lunar calendar, the tenth and twenty-fifth of the month are special days for ritual practice dedicated to the heruka and ḍākinī respectively.
17. Tulku Dampa (1928–1983) was the son of Lachen Tobgyal, and Tamdin Wangyal (b. 1952) was the son of Sonam Detsun; he passed away in the mid-2000s.
18. In March 2017, the 41st Sakya Trizin passed leadership of the Sakya lineage to his son, Ratna Vajra Rinpoche, who is now the 42nd Sakya Trizin. When using Sakya Trizin in this book, I refer exclusively to the 41st holder of that title.
19. Wangchen Nyima was Khandro Tāre Lhamo's elder brother and successor to his father's treasure corpus. Given that he did not survive the early decades of the Chinese occupation, Khenpo Jigme Phuntsok reinterprets the prophecy to refer to Namtrul Rinpoche.
20. Compiled by Jamgön Kongtrul in the nineteenth century, the *Rinchen Terdzö* or *Storehouse of Precious Treasures* (*Rin chen gter mdzod*) is an extensive anthology of treasure texts, mostly ritual in nature, by the great tertöns of previous centuries.
21. The terms "fearless" (*'jigs med*) and "good fortune" (*phun sum tshogs*), which I translate more robustly elsewhere as "plentiful good fortune," are elements of his name, Jigme and Phuntsok, respectively.
22. The five aspects of the degenerate age (*snyigs dus*) include (1) the decline in human values and conduct; (2) inwardly, the increase of afflictive emotions; (3) outwardly, the calamities of plague, famine, and war; (4) the shortening of life span; and (5) the decline in people's faith in Buddhism. See Dung dkar blo bzang 'phrin las (2002: 942–43).
23. Phurba Marnak Rakta (Phur ba dmar nag rak ta). There are several lamas with

the abbreviated title, Nyak La, before their name, but the most likely is the treasure revealer Lerab Lingpa, also known as Nyag La Sogyal, who is already mentioned in this episode as the original owner of the bell given to Namtrul Rinpoche. Vajrakīla rituals associated with "Marnak Rakta" can be found in vol. 13 of his collected treasures (*gter chos*) according to the outline provided by the Buddhist Digital Resource Center for W21810 (https://www.tbrc.org/#!rid=W21810).

24. The reference to "physical obstacles" (*sku gegs*) is obviously directed at Namtrul Rinpoche. Note that Tamgrin Wangyal is from the prestigious line of tertöns as the great-grandson of Dudjom Lingpa, hence his title of Rigse (*rigs sras*) or "scion of the family," and offer to propitiate the guardians of his ancestral line.
25. *Khandro Chökor* (*Mkha' 'gro chos 'khor*).
26. This is a modification of Ḍam bhu pa according to the transliteration from Sanskrit found in *Jewel Garland*. Ringu Tulku identifies Dombupa with Lawapa, one of the 84 mahāsiddhas.
27. Nam Nying is an abbreviation of Namkhai Nyingpo.
28. This is an abbreviation of Vajravārāhī, one of the forms of the female tantric deity, Vajrayoginī, with whom Tāre Lhamo is identified.
29. There is no attempt in the text to correlate this to any of Namtrul Rinpoche's names.
30. This is a variation on the title previously mentioned: *Thugs chen pad dkar 'phreng ba*. It is in parentheses as an interlinear note in the original text.
31. Pawo Chöying Dorje is Apang Terchen's primary name in religion with Orgyan Trinley Lingpa as his tertön name. The insertion of his name is an interlinear note.
32. The Tibetan, *lodrö* (*blo gros*), meaning "intelligent" translates the Sanskrit *mati*. Pema Drime Lodrö was Namtrul Rinpoche's Buddhist name prior to meeting Tāre Lhamo. As above, his name in parentheses represents an interlinear note in the original text.
33. This refers to the 41st Sakya Tridzin, the throne holder of the Sakya lineage based in Dehradun, India, who was recognized at an early age as the reincarnation of Apang Terchen.
34. Personal communication from Jamyang Nyima, the acting head of Tsimda Gompa in May 2006.
35. JLB 26.4–8. In addition to Nyenlung and Tsimda, these included: Zhuchen and Miri in Kandze; Drakor in Dzamthang; Ragtram, Taktse, Bumlung and Bumtsik in Serta; Tagthok Gongma in Padma; Gangpa in Darlag; and Öza in Serkhok.
36. Phurba Yangsang Tröpa (Phur ba yang gsang khros pa).
37. There were three reincarnations of the Third Dodrupchen: Yarlung Tenpai Nyima, Rigdzin Jalu Dorje (one of Tāre Lhamo's main teachers), and Thubten Trinley Palzangpo, who currently lives in Sikkim and regularly visits his home monastery.

38. On this figure, see Span Hanna, "Vast as the Sky: The Terma Tradition in Modern Tibet," 1994.
39. This could refer to the fasting practice (*smyung gnas*) of Gelongma Palmo.
40. Tashi Gomang is a monastery in Padma County with various sites associated with Padmasambhava.
41. I have adjusted a piece of hyperbole here, which refers to Larung Gar (here: *Bla rung chos sgar*) as a gathering place of "millions" (*bye ba*) of clerics and adepts. At its largest, before demolitions began in July 2016, it had grown to well over 10,000 monks and nuns.
42. Gu ru gter 'byung rgyal po.
43. Nangwa Thaye, which translates Amitābha, is an epithet sometimes given to the Paṇchen Lamas. The full name for the Tenth Paṇchen Lama is Blo bzang phrin las lhun grub chos kyi rgyal mtshan.
44. The reference to illness is most likely directed at Namtrul Rinpoche.
45. *Dagam Longgu* (*Zla gam klong dgu*).
46. This monastery is along the Do river between Dodrupchen Monastery and Dzamthang.
47. The Tenma (*brtan ma*) are female protector deities of Tibet, and the epithet Mayum (*ma yum*) refers to them as mothers.
48. Respectively, Manla (Sman bla) and Tendrel Lhamo (Rten 'brel lha mo).
49. Khandro Sangwa Yeshe (Mkha' 'gro gsang ba ye shes).
50. Personal communication from Namtrul Rinpoche in July 2006. This is also mentioned in *Jewel Lantern of Blessing* (A bu dkar lo 2001: 18.18–19).
51. The six Gesar sites in Golok include (1) Sengdruk Taktse in Darlak, (2) Mayul Gesar Rigne Netsok in Gabde, (3) Dimda Gon in Padma, (4) Padma Latse in Padma, (5) Lingri Pema Bumdzong in Machen, and (6) Hahrizha in Matö. The fifth is the temple which Tāre Lhamo and Namtrul Rinpoche constructed near Amnye Machen. Personal communication by Aku Norde in May 2006.
52. For more about the significance of Khenpo Jigme Phuntsok's pilgrimage to Wutai Shan, the sacred domain of the bodhisattva Mañjuśrī in Shanxi Province, see Germano 1998.
53. These sites lined their way home overland from Xining, the capital of Qinghai Province, with Lake Kokonor (Chinese: Qinghai Lake, Tibetan: Mtsho sngon po) to the west of Xining and Drakar Tredzong, the White Rock Monkey Fortress, which is a famous pilgrimage site in Xinghai County to the south. Lining the "white rock" outcropping are caves used as retreat hermitages by small clusters of Nyingma adepts, while the monastery in front of it is Geluk. The final destination mentioned is Amnye Machen, or more poetically here "the snow mountain Machen" (Rma chen gangs dkar), which rises high above Tawu, the capital of Golok, through which the couple would have to pass to return to Padma County and from there to Serta.
54. Shinho (Shin ho) may be a phoneticization of Xinghai County in Hainan Prefecture of Qinghai Province. When I traveled to Drakar Tredzong in 1997, the

county seat was several hours by car on a rough dirt road through a steep gorge and river basin. No doubt, a decade earlier, it was perilous to drive this route in the rain.

55. This site is to the east of the Amnye Machen Range, connected by road to Tawu. Here the couple constructed a Gesar temple that still housed their photograph on the wall when I visited in 2006.
56. This monastery lies along the main road south of the county seat of Gabde. Though the monastery was still relatively small in 2005 when I first visited, they have an outdoor teaching platform and field to host large assemblies for visiting teachers.
57. Dogongma is along the main road to Padma County from Tawu, where it crosses the Mar River.
58. These well-known texts are referred to by their abbreviations: *Spyod 'jug* for *The Way of the Bodhisattva* or *Bodhicaryāvatara* by the Indian master Śāntideva and *Rgyal sras lag len* for the *Thirty-Seven Practices of a Bodhisattva* (*Rgyal ba'i sras kyi lag len sum cu so bdun*) by the Kadam master Tokme Zangpo.
59. The was Dola Chökyi Nyima's son, named Sangye Pema Zhepa. See http://www.nyingma.com/artman/publish/dudjom_yangsis.shtml.
60. The two episodes, the horse race (*rta rgyal*) and golden fortress (*gser rdzong*) appear to be abbreviations of episodes in the Gesar epic, the full titles being *Rta rgyug rgyal 'jog* and *Me gling gser rdzong*. The first of these episodes is well known and recounts the horse race that Gesar wins, thereby gaining the throne of Ling and the hand of Lady Drukmo.
61. Tawu is a county that lies northwest of Dartsedo along the road to the prefecture seat at Gandze. This is not to be confused with another Tawu, the capital of Golok Prefecture. The other location is obscure, perhaps a small township in the region.
62. Kyilung Gompa is a Nyingma monastery in Kandze Prefecture, also a branch of Katok.
63. Wangda Gompa is a monastery farther along the same road as Tsimda Gompa. The Tibetan for the ritual they transmitted us: *Bde gshegs sgrub pa chen po bka' brgyad*.
64. The first child put forward as the Eleventh Paṇchen Lama was born on April 25, 1989.
65. These monasteries are located in Jigdril County of Golok.
66. These monasteries lie east of the county seat, Silethang, of Padma County toward Ngawa.
67. A lengthy vision during a Yeshe Tsogyal feast is omitted here: JG 71:3–77:17.
68. Dudul Phurba (Bdud 'dul phur ba).
69. Pad ma 'od 'bar.
70. There is an alternative account of this miracle attending their arrival at Abzö Gompa. According to one of the heads of the monastery, Jigme Wangdrak Dorje—who happens to be Tāre Lhamo's cousin and a reincarnation of her

father—their arrival at the monastery occasioned the blooming of flowers out of season. In addition, the seed syllable EVAṂ appeared on the grasslands, and today a stūpa commemorates the site. (Personal communication from Jigme Wangdrak Dorje in May 2006).

71. These sites are all in northern Amdo.
72. As this practice has gained in popularity, more care is being taken with the assessment of environmental impact, especially with respect to invasive species.
73. See my "Reimagining Buddhist Ethics on the Tibetan Plateau" (2013).
74. *The Concise History of Tsimda Gompa* (*Rtsis mda' dgon pa'i lo rgyus mdor bsdus*), an unpublished document shared with me by the current monastery head, Jamyang Nyima.
75. I discuss this in a section on "Masculinizing Thaumaturgy" in *Love Letters from Golok* (2016: 217–21).
76. Tulku Longyang is considered the Fifth Dodrupchen, the reincarnation of Tāre Lhamo's own teacher, Rigdzin Jalu Dorje.
77. *Zablam Chödruk* (*Zab lam chos drug*).
78. Rigpe Tsalwang (Rig pa'i rtsal dbang).
79. Trekchö Tsalwang (Khreg chod rtsal dbang).
80. Thögal Tsalwang (Thog rgal rtsal dbang).
81. This refers to Betsa Monastery in Padma County.
82. *Khandro Thing Öbarma* (*Mkha' 'gro mthing 'od 'bar ma*).
83. These are both located in Jigdral County of Golok.
84. *Rigdzin Tsadrup* (*rig 'dzin rtsa sgrub*).
85. I use "community" here for *dewa* (*sde ba*). This term refers to patrilineal clans, alongside the term *tsowa* (*tsho ba*), but also can be synonymous with a village or district.
86. The Tibetan for the terms "dharma connection" and "place connection" are respectively: *chos 'brel* and *gnas 'brel*. See Gayley 2016, chapter 5 for a discussion of these terms and the role they play in how *Jewel Garland* narrates the couple's activities in the 1980s and 1990s.
87. This is an honorific way to say that they set out on pilgrimage to visit Central Tibet.
88. The location of Jangyul is not entirely clear; some locate it in present-day Yunnan Province, which would have meant a detour on their way to Chengdu to fly to Lhasa. *Jewel Garland* seems to place it in Chamdo along their route overland from Golok.
89. This is also the name of a sacred Bön site in Central Tibet; see Samten Karmey, *The Treasury of Good Sayings*, p. 40.
90. Repainting sacred images in gold is considered to be an auspicious offering. The holiest images in Lhasa are the Jowo Śākyamuni in the Jokhang Temple and the Jowo Mikyö Dorje in the Ramoche temple. Legend describes these as gifts brought to Lhasa by the Chinese and Nepali wives of the seventh-century emperor, Songtsen Gampo.

91. Thigle Sangdzok (Thig le gsang rdzogs). The Great Orgyan (O rgyan chen po) refers to Padmasambhava.
92. Mkha' 'gro mthing 'od 'bar ma'i 'od gsal rang ngo sprod pa'i man ngag kun bzang thugs kyi thig le. Lonchenpa, known as the Great Omniscient One (Kun mkhyen chen po) had a hermitage in a cave at Gangri Thökar; for that reason, it remains a Nyingma pilgrimage site.
93. The *Longchen Nyingtik* (*Klong chen snying thig*) is a renowned treasure cycle that proliferated in Golok and surrounding areas through one of Jigme Lingpa's main disciples, the First Dodrupchen, Jigme Trinley Özer. The *Queen of Great Bliss* (*Yum ka bde chen rgyal mo*) is an important cycle dedicated to Yeshe Tsogyal within that (here given as *Klong snying yum dga'*). See Klein 1994.
94. This is likely Chapori (Lcags po ri), a sacred mountain just outside of Lhasa.
95. Kyabcig Mahāguru (Skyabs gcig ma hā gu ru). In this case, the two systems (*lugs gnyis*) refers to spiritual and worldly advice to the laity.
96. Draktsan may refer to the indigenous land deity, Bartsik Draktsan, associated with Samye, and Chimpu is the famous hermitage above the temple.
97. This is a site at the heart of Samye Chimpu.
98. Deshek Kagyekyi Druptab Dupa (Bde gshegs bka' brgyad brgyad kyi sgrub thabs bsdus pa).
99. This appears to conflate two important retreat sites of Jigme Lingpa—at Palri Monastery and at the Lower Nyang Cave at Chimpu, which he named the "flower cave" (*me tog phug*). See Gyatso 1998: 130–34.
100. This river crossing is made by many who go on pilgrimage from Lhasa to Samye and again when returning. More recently, a road and bridge have been constructed.
101. This is the name for Tradruk Monastery, southeast of Lhasa. Its well-known statue of Padmasambhava is more literally described as "just like me" (*nga 'dra ma*), a class of statues understood to resemble the great guru and sometimes claimed to have been made by him.
102. This is an epithet for Padmasambhava, also referred to in this passage as the Great Orgyan.
103. The Tenth Paṇchen Lama passed away in 1989.
104. The Paṇchen Lama's personal residence in Shigatse.
105. This site is near Riwoche in the Chamdo area. As mentioned previously, Jangyul is often associated with Yunnan Province to the east of Golok, while Chamdo is directly west on the overland route to Lhasa.
106. *Dzokchen Zablam Chödruk* (*Rdzogs pa chen po zab lam chos drug*). This is the longer title for a text of the same name, *Zablam Chödruk*, a treasure teaching by Apang Terchen, mentioned several times in the narrative above.
107. Gyabri is the informal name for the hillside behind Nyenlung Monastery.
108. This seems to be a precursor and antecedent to their annual dharma gatherings (*chos tshogs*), which began the following year in 1996. Over time, the annual dharma gathering at Nyenlung has grown to draw one or two thousand stu-

dents each year. Usually the *Six Dharmas of the Profound Path*, a Dzogchen teaching from Apang Terchen's treasure corpus, is only given to students who have completed their preliminary practices (*sngon 'gro*), perhaps accounting for the smaller number.

Chapter 5: Visions of Tāre Lhamo

1. Āyu appears to be the Sanskrit for Tshe, Namtrul Rinpoche's name in youth. This would suggest that Tāre Lhamo's vision here, on the eve of transmitting Apang Terchen's treasures widely, identifies Namtrul Rinpoche as her own father's reincarnation. This identification only becomes public later in their career.
2. These are abbreviated names of famed figures in the lore of the imperial period, Namkhai Nyingpo and Yeshe Tsogyal, to whom Namtrul Rinpoche and Tāre Lhamo trace their past lives, as well as Gyalwa Chokyang, another of Padmasambhava's disciples, and Lalung Paldor (Palkyi Dorje), the reputed assassin of Langdarma, the emperor who persecuted Buddhism in the ninth century.
3. *Nanggyu Desum* (*Nang rgyud sde gsum*).
4. The Guru here is no doubt short for Guru Rinpoche, or Padmasambhava, and Vima refers to Vimalamitra.
5. This likely refers to Padmasambhava's mantra, OṂ ĀḤ HŪṂ VAJRA GURU SIDDHI HŪṂ.
6. The Sampe Döndrup (Bsam pa'i don 'grub) is a prayer to Padmasambhava.

Chapter 6: Final Letter by Namtrul Rinpoche

1. The two systems (*lugs gnyis*) can refer to the religious and the secular, or alternatively the perspectives of the dharma and worldly concerns.
2. This is the name of their retreat hut at Nyenlung Monastery.
3. NJP 30: 181.1–188.4.

Sources in Translation

1. For similar reasons, I leave out an arcane visionary sequence midway through *Jewel Garland* (JG 71.3–77.17). With respect to prophetic passages from their correspondence that are included here, I indicate in the notes which are marked by *tertsek*, the orthographic mark that indicates their status as treasures.
2. Note that same spectrum of activities appear in a derivative and abbreviated account, titled *Jewel Lantern of Blessings* and published in 2001, yet its author Abu Karlo places them in the section on Tāre Lhamo's life. This confirms that the narration in *Jewel Garland* is indeed understood within their religious community to represent their joint activities, not those of Namtrul Rinpoche alone, although they are situated in his namthar.

3. This is the short biography of Sera Khandro, titled *Ku su lu'i nyams byung gi gnas tshul mdor bsdus rdo rje'i spun gyis dris lan mos pa'i lam bzang* (Se ra mkha' 'gro Bde ba'i rdo rje 1978, Vol. 4: 103–29). For translations, see Monson 2013 and Jacoby 2014b.
4. These are *Skyabs rje rin po che nam sprul 'jigs med phun tshogs kyis mkha' 'gro rin po che tā re de vī mchog la phul ba'i zhu 'phrin phyag yig rnams phyogs bsdus rdo rje'i phreng ba* and *Sngags skyes mkha' 'gro rin po che tā re de vīs nam sprul rin po che 'jigs med phun tshogs mchog la phul ba'i zhu 'phrin phyag yig rnams phyogs bsdus padma'i phreng ba*, published as a facsimile edition by Nyenlung Monastery, c. 2003.
5. Interview with Namtrul Rinpoche, August 2004.
6. The Tibetan for these epithets are: *skyabs rje yab yum* and *chos rje yab yum*. Sometimes I insert the "Eminent Couple" if there has been a long stretch in the narrative where the subject is presumed, as can frequently occur in Tibetan.
7. The Tibetan epithets are respectively: *rje nyid*, *chos rje*, *mkha' 'gro mchog*, and *mkha' 'gro rin po che*.

Bibliography

Tibetan Sources

A bu dkar lo. *Gter ston grub pa'i dbang phyug gzhi chen nam sprul dang mkha' 'gro tā re bde chen lha mo zung gi mdzad rnam nyer bsdus byin rlabs nor bu'i gron me.* Xining: Mtsho sngon nang bstan rtsom sgrig khang, 2001.

———. *Gter ston grub pa'i dbang phyug o rgyan sku gsum gling pa'i rnam thar mdo tsam brjod pa ma tshogs rig 'dzin bzhad pa'i rang gdangs.* Zhang kang then mā dpe skrun khang, 2003.

A bu dkar lo, Dung gces, and Gsang bdag tshe ring. *Mgo log sman rtsis rig pa'i lo rgyus ngo mtshar nor bu'i rlabs phreng.* Xining: Qinghai Minorities Publishing House, 2000.

A bu dkar lo and Pad ma 'od gsal mtha' yas. *Nian long shang shi fu mu ren bo qie lue zhuan* and *Light of Blessings: Brief Biographies of Namtrul Jigmed Phuntshog Rinpoche and Khadro Tare Lhamo Rinpoche.* Translations of *Gter ston grub pa'i dbang phyug gzhi chen nam sprul dang mkha' 'gro tā re bde chen lha mo zung gi mdzad rnam nyer bsdus byin rlabs nor bu'i sgron me.* Gser rta: Snyan lung dgon, n.d.

A phang gter chen O rgyan phrin las gling pa. *Rgyal dbang pad ma'i rgyal tshab o rgyan phrin las gling pa'i zab gter nor bu'i phreng ba.* Gser rta: Snyan lung dgon, n.d.

Bla rung ar ya tā re'i dpe tshogs rtsom sgrig khang (ed.). *'Phags bod kyi skyes chen ma dag gi rnam par thar ba pad ma dkar po'i phreng ba.* Lha sa: Bod ljongs bod yig dpe rnying dpe skrun khang, 2013.

Don grub rgyal. *Bod kyi mgur glu byung 'phel gyi lo rgyus dang khyad chos bsdus par ston pa rig pa'i khye'u rnam par rtsen pa'i skyed tshal.* Beijing: Mi rigs dpe skrun khang, 1997.

Don grub dbang rgyal and Nor sde. *Yul mgo log gi lo rgyus deb ther pad ma dkar po'i chun po* (abbreviated as *Mgo log lo rgyus deb ther*). Xining: Mtsho sngon mi rigs dpe skrun khang, 1992.

Dung dkar Blo bzang 'phrin las. *Dung dkar tshig mdzod chen mo.* Beijing: Krung go'i bod rig pa dpe skrun khang, 2002.

'Jam dbyangs nyi ma. *Rtsis mda' dgon pa'i lo rgyus mdor bsdus.* Unpublished facsimile in 10 pages; received from author, the acting head of Rtsis mda' dgon, in 2006.

'Jam mgon kong sprul Blo gros mtha' yas. *Zab mo'i gter dang gter ston grub thob ji ltar byon pa'i lo rgyus mdor bsdus bkod pa rin chen vaiḍūrya'i 'phreng ba (Gter ston brgya rtsa'i rnam thar).* In *Rin chen gter mdzod.* New Delhi: Shechen Publications, 2007–2008. Vol. 1: 341–765.

'Ju skal bzang (ed.). *Khra dge slong Tshul khrims dar rgyas kyi gsung rtsom gces bsgrigs.* Xining: Mtsho sngon mi rigs dpe skrun khang, 2000.

Krang dbyi sun. *Bod rgya tshig mdzod chen mo* (abbreviated TTC). Beijing: Mi rigs dpe skrun khang, 1985.

Krung go'i bod rig pa zhib 'jug lte gnas kyi chos lugs lo rgyus zhib 'jug so'o, Krung go bod brgyud nang bstan mtho rim slob gling, Zi khron zhing chen dkar mdzes khul chos lugs cud, and Dkar mdzes khul yig bsgyur cud. *Khams phyogs dkar mdzes khul gyi dgon sde so so'i lo rgyus gsal bar bshad pa thub bstan gsal ba'i me long.* Beijing: Krung go'i bod kyi shes rig dpe skrun khang, 1995.

Mkha' 'bum. "Bod kyi dmangs khrod glu gzhas skor gyi dpyad pa thar thor." *Mang tshogs sgyu rtsal* 88/1 (2005): 79–92.

Mkha' 'gro Tā re lha mo. *Sngags skyes mkha' 'gro rin po che tā re de vīs nam sprul rin po che 'jigs med phun tshogs mchog la phul ba'i zhu 'phrin phyag yid rnams phyogs bsdus pad ma'i phreng ba.* Gser rta: Snyan lung dgon, c. 2003.

Mkha' 'gro Tā re lha mo and Nam sprul 'Jigs med phun tshogs. *Khyab bdag gter chen bla ma 'ja' lus pa dpal mnyam med nam mkha' gling pa rin po che dang mkha' 'gro rin po che tā re lha mo zung gi zab gter nam mkha' mdzod gyi chos sde.* Chengdu: Si khron mi rigs dpe skrun khang, 2013.

———. *O rgyan 'jigs med nam mkha' gling pa dang dāki tā re bde chen rgyal mo rnam gnyis kyi zab gter chos.* Facsimile edition in 12 volumes. Gser rta: Snyan lung dgon, n.d.

———. *Skyabs rje rin po che nam sprul 'jigs med phun tshogs kyis mkha' 'gro rin po che tā re de vī mchog la phul ba'i zhu 'phrin phyag yig phyogs bsdus rdo rje'i phreng ba.* Gser rta: Snyan lung dgon, c. 2003.

Nam sprul 'Jigs med phun tshogs. *Mkha' 'gro sku gshegs pa'i lo rgyus mdor bsdus.* Unpublished account of Tā re lha mo's last testament and death, received from author at Snyan lung dgon in 2004.

O rgyan 'phrin las bzang po. *Gnas mchog bkra shis sgo mang gi gnas yig phyogs bsdus rin chen 'phreng ba.* Pad ma County, Qinghai Province: Snga 'gyur rnying ma dpal yul Bkra shis sgo mang thub bstan chos 'khor gling, n.d.

Pad ma 'bum. "Tun hong yig rnying gi mgur la dpyod pa'i sngon 'gro." In *Tibetan Studies: Proceedings of the 7th Seminary of the International Association for Tibetan Studies, Graz 1995.* Edited by Helmut Krasser. Wien: Verlag der Österreichischen Akademie der Wissenschaften, 1997.

Pad ma 'od gsal mtha' yas. *Skyabs rje nam sprul rin po che 'jigs med phun tshogs dang mkha' 'gro tā re lha mo mchog gi rnam thar rig 'dzin mkha' 'gro dgyes pa'i mchod sprin.* Chengdu: Si khron mi rigs dpe skrun khang, 1997.

———. *prul ba'i gter ston chen po rig 'dzin nus ldan rdo rje'i rnam thar bsdus pa dngos grub snye ma.* In *Gter chen bdud 'joms yab sras kyi rnam thar.* Edited by

Pad ma theg mchog rgyal mtshan. Chengdu: Si khron mi rigs dpe skrun khang, 2000.

———. *Yab mes rigs 'dzin brgyud pa'i byung ba mdor bsdus tsam brjod pa*. In *Deb chung a ru ra'i dga' tshal*. Chengdu: Si khron mi rigs dpe skrun khang, 2003.

Pad ma tshe ring. *Mgo log rig gnas lo rgyus*. Volume 4. Tawu, Qinghai: Srid gros mgo log khul u slob sbyong lo rgyus dang tshan slob rig 'phrod u yon lhan khang, 2004.

Rig 'dzin dar rgyas. *A paṃ gter chen gyi sras mo mkha' 'gro tā re lha mo mchog gi rnam par thar ba mdo tsam brjod pa ngo mtshar lha yi rol mo*. In *Mkha' 'gro'i chos mdzod chen mo*. Published by Bla rung ā rya tā re'i dpe tshogs rtsom sgrig khang. Lhasa: Bod ljongs bod yig dpe rnying dpe skrun khang, 2017, vol. 16, 177–296.

Se ra mkha' 'gro Bde ba'i rdo rje. *Ku su lu'i nyams byung gi gnas tshul mdor bsdus rdo rje'i spun gyis dris lan mos pa'i lam bzang*. In *The Collected Revelations (gter chos) of Se ra mkha' 'gro Bde chen rdo rje*. Kalimpong, India: Dupjung Lama, 1978. Vol. 4: 103–29.

Skal bzang ye shes and Sri gcod rdo rje. *Rdo grub chen dgon gsang chen dngos grub dpal 'bar gling*. Pad ma: Rdo grub chen dgon, c. 2005.

Stag sham Nus ldan rdo rje. *Bod kyi jo mo ye shes mtsho rgyal gyi mdzad tshul rnam par thar pa gab pa mngon byung rgyud mngas dri za'i glu phreng*. Kalimpong: Bdud 'joms rin po che, 1972.

Tshe tan zhabs drung. *'Phrin yig spel tshul lhag bsam padmo 'dzum pa'i nyin byed*. In *Mkhas dbang tshe tan zhabs drung gi dpyad rtsom mkho bsdus*. Edited by 'Jigs med chos phags. Wood block version. Bya khyung dgon, 2007 (vol. 9): 187–216.

———. *Snyan ngag me long gi spyi don sdeb legs rig pa'i char go*. Lanzhou: Kan su'u mi rigs dpe skrun khang, 1981.

Tshul khrims blo gros. *Snyigs dus bstan pa'i gsal byed gcig bu chos rje dam pa yid bzhin nor bu 'jigs med phun tshogs 'byung gnas dpal bzang po'i rnam thar bsdus pa dad pa'i gsos sman*. In *Chos rje dam pa yid bzhin nor bu 'jigs med phun tshogs 'byung gnas dpal bzang po'i gsung 'bum*. Hong Kong: Xianggang xinzhi chubanshe, 2002, vol. 3: 364–418.

Sources in European Languages

Allione, Tsultrim. *Women of Wisdom*. Boston: Routledge & Kegan Paul, 1984.

Altman, Janet. *Epistolarity: Approaches to a Form*. Columbus, OH: Ohio State University Press, 1982.

Anton-Luca, Alexandru. "*Glu* and *La ye* in A mdo: An Introduction to Contemporary Tibetan Folk Songs." In *Amdo Tibetans in Transition: Society and Culture in the Post-Mao era*, edited by Toni Huber, 173–96. Leiden: Brill, 2002.

Bessenger, Suzanne. *Echoes of Enlightenment: The Life and Legacy of the Tibetan Saint Sönam Peldren*. London: Oxford University Press, 2016.

Biernacki, Loriliai. *Renowned Goddess of Desire: Women, Sex, and Speech in Tantra.* Oxford: Oxford University Press, 2007.

Bulliard, Jean-Francois, trans. *Hagiographies de Taré Lhamo et Namtrul Rinpoché.* Ygrand, France: Éditions Yogi Ling, 2005.

Cabezón, José, and Roger Jackson, eds. *Tibetan Literature: Studies in Genre.* Ithaca, NY: Snow Lion Publications, 1996.

Campbell, June. *Traveller in Space: In Search of Female Identity in Tibetan Buddhism.* New York: George Braziller, 1996.

Cherewatuk, Karen, and Ulrike Wiethaus, eds. *Dear Sister: Medieval Women and the Epistolary Genre.* Philadelphia: University of Pennsylvania Press, 1993.

Chönyi Drolma, trans. *The Life and Visions of Yeshé Tsogyal: The Autobiography of the Great Wisdom Queen.* Boulder, CO: Snow Lion, 2017.

Constable, Giles. *Letters and Letter-Collections.* Typologie des Sources du Moyen Âge Occidental, Fascicle 17. Turnhout, Belgique: Éditions Brepols, 1976.

Cornu, Philippe. *Tibetan Astrology.* Boston: Shambhala Publications, 2002.

Cox, Collette. "Mindfulness and Memory: The Scope of *Smṛti* from Early Buddhism to the Sarvāstivādin Abhidharma." In *In the Mirror of Memory: Reflections on Mindfulness and Remembrance in Indian and Tibetan Buddhism,* edited by Janet Gyatso, 67–108. Ithaca, NY: State University of New York, 1992.

Cuevas, Bryan. *The Hidden History of the Tibetan Book of the Dead.* Oxford: Oxford University Press, 2003.

Davidson, Ronald. *Indian Esoteric Buddhism.* New York: Columbia University Press, 2002.

Davidson, Ronald. *Tibetan Renaissance: Tantric Buddhism in the Rebirth of Tibetan Culture.* New York: Columbia University Press, 2005.

Diemberger, Hildegard. *When a Woman Becomes a Religious Dynasty: The Samding Dorje Phagmo of Tibet.* New York: Columbia University Press, 2007.

DiValerio, David. *The Holy Madmen of Tibet.* Oxford: Oxford University Press, 2015.

Doctor, Andreas. *Tibetan Treasure Literature: Revelation, Tradition, and Accomplishment in Visionary Buddhism.* Ithaca, NY: Snow Lion Publications, 2005.

Douglas, Kenneth and Gwendolyn Bays. *The Life and Liberation of Padmasambhava.* Emeryville, CA: Dharma Publishing, 1978.

Dowman, Keith. *Sky Dancer: The Secret Life & Songs of the Lady Yeshe Tsogyal.* Ithaca, NY: Snow Lion Publications, 1996.

Dowman, Keith. *The Divine Madman: The Sublime Life and Songs of Drukpa Kunley.* Kathmandu, Nepal: Pilgrims Publishing, 2000.

Dudjom Rinpoche Jikdrel Yeshe Dorje. *The Nyingma Schools of Tibetan Buddhism: Its Fundamentals & History.* Translated and edited by Gyurme Dorje and Matthew Kapstein. Boston: Wisdom Publications, 1991.

Duncan, Marion. *Love Songs and Proverbs of Tibet.* London: Mitre Press, 1961.

Edou, Jérôme. *Machig Labdrön and the Foundations of Chöd.* Ithaca, NY: Snow Lion Publications, 1995.

English, Elizabeth. *Vajrayoginī: Her Visualizations, Rituals, and Forms*. Boston: Wisdom Publications, 2002.

Farrow, G.W. and I. Menon. *The Concealed Essence of the Hevajra Tantra*. Delhi: Motilal Banarsidass Publishers, 2001.

Gayley, Holly. "The Ethics of Cultural Survival: A Buddhist Vision of Progress in Mkhan po 'Jig phun's *Heart Advice to Tibetans of the 21st Century*." In *Mapping the Modern in Tibet*, edited by Gray Tuttle, 435–502. PIATS 2006: Proceedings of the Eleventh Seminar of the International Association for Tibetan Studies. Königswinter 2006. Andiast, Switzerland: International Institute, 2011.

———. *Love Letters from Golok: A Tantric Couple in Modern Tibet*. New York: Columbia University Press, 2016.

———. "The Love Letters of a Buddhist Tantric Couple: Reflections on Poetic Style and Epistolary Intimacy." *History of Religions* 56.3 (2017): 311–51.

———. "Ontology of the Past and its Materialization in Tibetan Treasures." In The Invention of Sacred Tradition, edited by Olav Hammer, 213–239. Cambridge: Cambridge University Press, 2008.

———. "Reimagining Buddhist Ethics on the Tibetan Plateau," *Journal of Buddhist Ethics* 20 (2013): 247–86.

———. "Revisiting the Secret Consort (*gsang yum*) in Tibetan Buddhism." *Religions* 9/6 (2018). DOI: https://doi.org/10.3390/rel9060179.

Gellner, David. *Monk, Householder, and Tantric Priest: Newar Buddhism and its Hierarchy of Ritual*. Cambridge: Cambridge University Press, 1992.

Germano, David. "Re-membering the Dismembered Body of Tibet." In. *Buddhism in Contemporary Tibet: Religious Revival and Cultural Identity*. Edited by Melvyn Goldstein and Matthew Kapstein. Berkeley: University of California Press, 1998.

Giddens, Anthony. *The Transformation of Intimacy: Sexuality, Love, and Eroticism in Modern Societies*. Stanford: Stanford University Press, 1992.

Goldsmith, Elizabeth, ed. *Writing the Female Voice: Essays on Epistolary Literature. Boston: Northeastern University Press,* 1989.

Goldstein, Melvyn. *Dictionary of Modern Tibetan*. Kathmandu: Ratna Pustak Bhandar, 1983.

Goldstein, Melvyn, and Matthew Kapstein, eds. *Buddhism in Contemporary Tibet: Religious Revival and Cultural Identity*. Berkeley: University of California Press, 1998.

Gyatso, Janet. *Apparitions of the Self: The Secret Autobiographies of a Tibetan Visionary*. Princeton: Princeton University Press, 1998.

———. "Drawn from the Tibetan Treasury: The gTer ma Literature." In *Tibetan Literature: Studies in Genre*, edited by José Cabezón and Roger Jackson 147–69. Ithaca, NY: Snow Lion Publications, 1996.

———. "The Logic of Legitimation in the Tibetan Treasure Tradition." *History of Religions* 33/1 (1993): 97–134.

———. "A Partial Genealogy of the Lifestory of Ye shes mtsho rgyal," *Journal of the*

International Association of Tibetan Studies, no. 2 (August 2006): 1–27, http://www.thlib.org?tid=T2719.

———. "Signs, Memory and History: A Tantric Buddhist Theory of Scriptural Transmission." *Journal of the International Association of Buddhist Studies* 9/2 (1986): 7–35.

Gyatso, Janet, and Hanna Havnevik, eds. *Women in Tibet: Past and Present*. New York: Columbia University Press, 2006.

Hanna, Span. "Vast as the Sky: The Terma Tradition in Modern Tibet." In *Tantra and Popular Religion in Tibet*, edited by Geoffrey Samuel, Hamish Gregor, and Elisabeth Stutchbury, 1–13. New Delhi: International Academy of Indian Culture and Aditya Prakashan, 1994.

Harding, Sarah. *Machik's Complete Explanation: Clarifying the Meaning of Chöd*. Ithaca, NY: Snow Lion Publications, 2003b.

Hartley, Lauran and Patricia Schiaffini-Vedani (eds.). *Modern Tibetan Literature and Social Change*. Durham, NC: Duke University Press, 2008.

Herrmann-Pfandt, Adelheid. *Ḍākinīs: Zur Stellung und Symbolik des Weiblichen im tantrischen Buddhismus*. Bonn: Indica et Tibetica Verlag, 1990.

Hirshberg, Daniel. *Remembering the Lotus-Born: Padmasambhava in the History of Tibet's Golden Age*. Boston: Wisdom Publications, 2016.

Jackson, Roger. "'Poetry' in Tibet: *Glu*, *mGur*, *sNyan ngag* and 'Songs of Experience.'" In *Tibetan Literature: Studies in Genre*, edited by José Cabezón and Roger Jackson, 368–92. Ithaca, NY: Snow Lion Publications, 1996.

Jacoby, Sarah. "The Excellent Path of Devotion: An Annotated Translation of Sera Khandro's Short Autobiography." In *Himalayan Passages: Tibetan and Newar Studies in Honor of Hubert Decleer*, edited by Andrew Quintman and Ben Bogin, 163–202. Boston: Wisdom Publications, 2014b.

———. *Love and Liberation: Autobiographical Writings of the Tibetan Buddhist Visionary Sera Khandro*. Columbia University Press, 2014a.

———. "This Inferior Female Body:' Reflections on Life as a Treasure Revealer Through the Autobiographical Eyes of Se ra mkha' 'gro (Bde ba'i rdo rje, 1892–1940)." *Journal of the International Association of Buddhist Studies*. 32/2 (2010): 115–50.

Kapstein, Matthew. "The Indian Literary Identity in Tibet." In *Literary Cultures in History: Reconstructions from South Asia*, edited by Sheldon Pollock 747–802. Berkeley: University of California Press, 2003.

———. *The Tibetan Assimilation of Buddhism: Conversion, Contestation, and Memory*. Oxford: Oxford University Press, 2000.

Karma Lekshe Tsomo (ed.). *Eminent Buddhist Women*. Albany, NY: State University of New York Press, 2014.

Klein, Anne. *Meeting the Great Bliss Queen: Buddhists, Feminists, and the Art of the Self.* Boston: Beacon Press, 1994.

Kolas, Ashild and Monika Thowsen. *On the Margins of Tibet: Cultural Survival on the Sino-Tibetan Frontier*. Seattle: University of Washington, 2005.

Kunsang, Erik Pema. *The Lotus Born: The Life Story of Padmasambhava.* Boston: Shambhala Publications, 1999.

Kværne, Per. *An Anthology of Buddhist Tantric Songs: A Study of the Caryāgīti.* Bangkok: White Orchid Press, 1977.

Lopez, Donald. *Prisoners of Shangri-la: Tibetan Buddhism and the West.* Chicago: The University of Chicago Press, 1999.

Makley, Charlene. *The Violence of Liberation: Gender and Tibetan Buddhist Revival in Post-Mao China.* Berkeley: University of California Press, 2007.

Monson, Christina, trans. *The Excellent Path of Devotion: An Abridged Story of a Mendican'ts Experiences in Response to Questions by Vajra Kin.* Boulder, CO: Kama Terma Publications, 2013.

Osburg, John. *Anxious Wealth: Money and Morality among China's New Rich.* Stanford, CA: Stanford University Press, 2013.

Paul, Diana. *Women in Buddhism.* Berkeley: Asian Humanities Press, 1979

Padmakara Translation Group. *Lady of the Lotus-Born: The Life and Enlightenment of Yeshe Tsogyal.* Boston: Shambhala Publications, 2002.

———. *The Words of My Perfect Teacher.* San Francisco: HarperCollins, 1994.

Robinson, James. *Buddha's Lions: The Lives of the Eighty-Four Siddhas.* Berkeley: Dharma Publishing, 1979.

Rossi, Donatella. "Mkha' 'gro dbang mo'i rnam thar, The Biography of the Gter ston ma Bde chen chos kyi dbang mo (1868–1927?)." *Revue d'Etudes Tibétaines* 15 (2008): 371–78.

———. "Some Notes on the Tibetan Amdo Love Songs." In *Tibetan Studies: Proceedings of the 5th Seminar of the International Association for Tibetan Studies, Narita, 1989,* edited by Shōren Ihara and Zuihō Yamaguchi, 705–9. Tokyo: Naritasan Shinshoji, 1992.

Schaeffer, Kurtis. *Himalayan Hermitess: The Life of a Tibetan Buddhist Nun.* Oxford: Oxford University Press, 2004.

Schneider, Hannah. "Tibetan Epistolary Style." In *The Dalai Lamas: A Visual History,* edited by Martin Brauen, 258–61. Chicago: Serindia Publications, 2005.

Shaw, Miranda. *Passionate Enlightenment: Women in Tantric Buddhism.* Princeton: Princeton University Press, 1994.

Siegel, Lee. *Sacred and Profane Dimensions of Love in Indian Traditions as Exemplified by the* Gītagovinda *of Jayadeva.* Delhi: Oxford University Press, 1978.

Simmer-Brown, Judith. *Dakini's Warm Breath: The Feminine Principle in Tibetan Buddhism.* Boston: Shambhala Publications, 2001.

Smith, Gene. *Among Tibetan Texts: History & Literature of the Himalayan Plateau.* Boston: Wisdom Publications, 2001.

Stein, R.A. *L'épopée tibétaine de Gesar dans sa version lamaïque de Ling.* Paris: Presses Universitaires de France, 1956.

———. *Recherches sur l'épopée et le barde au Tibet.* Paris: Presses Universitaires de France, 1959.

———. *Rolf Stein's Tibet Antiqua with Additional Materials*. Translated by Arthur McKeown. Leiden: Brill, 2010.

———. *Tibetan Civilization*. Translated by J. E. Stapleton Driver. Stanford, CA: Stanford University Press, 1972.

Sujata, Victoria. *A Commentary on the Mgur 'Bum (Collected Songs of Spiritual Realization) of Skal ldan rgya mtsho, a Seventeenth Century Scholar and Siddha from Amdo*. Ph.D. Dissertation at Harvard University, 2003.

Taylor, McComas and Lama Choedak Yuthok (trans.). *The Clear Mirror: A Traditional Account of Tibet's Golden Age*. Ithaca: Snow Lion Publications, 1996.

Templeman, David. "Dohā, Vajragīti and Caryā Songs." In Geoffrey Samuel, Hamish Gregor, and Elisabeth Strutchbury (eds.) 1994.

Terrone, Antonio. "Cyberspace Revelations: Tibetan Treasures, Information Technology, and the Transnational Imagined Reader." In *Edition,* éditions*: l'écrit au Tibet,* évolution *et devenir.* Edited by Anne Chayet, Cristina Scherrer-Schaub, Françoise Robin and Jean-Luc Achard, 381–409. Munich: Indus Verlag, 2010.

———. "Householders and Monks: A Study of Treasure Revealers and their Role in Religious Revival in Eastern Tibet." In *Buddhism beyond the Monastery: Tantric Practices and their Performers in Tibet and the* Himalayas, edited by Sarah Jacoby and Antonio Terrone, 73–110. Leiden: Brill, 2008.

Thondup, Tulku. *Hidden Teachings of Tibet.* Boston: Wisdom Publications, 1997.

———. *Incarnation: The History and Mysticism of the Tulku Tradition of Tibet.* Boulder: Shambhala Publications, 2011.

———. *Masters of Meditation and Miracles: The Longchen Nyingthik Lineage of Tibetan Buddhism*. Boston: Shambhala Publications, 1996.

Thondup, Tulku, and Matthew Kapstein. "Tibetan Poetry." In *The New Princeton Encyclopedia of Poetry and Poetics,* edited by Alex Preminger and T.V.F. Brogar, 1290–91. Princeton: Princeton University Press, 1993.

Tsering Shakya. "The Development of Modern Tibetan Literature in the People's Republic of China in the 1980s." In *Modern Tibetan Literature and Social Change,* edited by Lauran Hartley and Patricia Schiaffini-Vedani, 61–85. Durham, NC: Duke University Press, 2008.

Tuttle, Gray, ed. *Mapping the Modern in Tibet.* PIATS 2006: Proceedings of the Eleventh Seminar of the International Association for Tibetan Studies. Königswinter 2006. Andiast, Switzerland: International Institute, 2011.

———. *Tibetan Buddhists in the Making of Modern China.* New York: Columbia University Press, 2005.

van der Kuijp, Leonard. "Tibetan Belles-Lettres: The Influence of Daṇḍin and Kṣemendra." In *Tibetan Literature: Studies in Genre,* edited by José Cabezón and Roger Jackson, 393–410. Ithaca, NY: Snow Lion Publications, 1996.

Vaudeville, Charlotte. "Evolution of Love-Symoblism in Bhagavatism." *Journal of the American Oriental Society* 82 (1962): 31–40.

Wayman, Alex. *The Buddhist Tantras: Light on Indo-Tibetan Esotericism.* Delhi: Motilal Banarsidass Publishers, 1996.

White, David Gordon. *Kiss of the Yogini.* Chicago: The University of Chicago Press, 2003.

Willis, Janice, ed. *Feminine Ground: Essays on Women in Tibet.* Ithaca, NY: Snow Lion Publications, 1989.

Willson, Martin. *In Praise of Tara: Songs to the Saviouress.* Boston: Wisdom Publications, 1986.

Yü, Dan Smyer. *The Spread of Tibetan Buddhism in China: Charisma, Money, Enlightenment.* New York: Routledge, 2014.